The Victorian Age of German Literature

The Victorian Age of German Literature

Eight Essays

Norbert Fuerst

THE PENNSYLVANIA STATE UNIVERSITY PRESS
University Park and London

1966

First published 1966 by The Pennsylvania State University Press

Printed in England

Preface

The term ' Victorianism ' needs all the indulgence of the reader. It is not much more than a chronological and ideological approximation. What little more it contains is a reminder that in the main the waves of nineteenth century German literature did not flow with the revolutionary current of French (and in part even Russian) literature; that its artistic tides and its moral ground swell were more with English and American literature. It is therefore no mere civility that the ' Atlantic ' reactions to German literature are sought out here and made the most of — so that the treatment sometimes vacillates between a too American and a too German point of view.

Indeed, the origin of these essays was a curiosity about the English and American reception of German literature. But this curiosity could not stop short of the figures that had *no* reception abroad. A bit of revaluation is perhaps in order. In some respects general literary history has to be in arrear of national literary histories. It still emphasizes the revolutionary, emancipatory trends of the nineteenth century, whereas the national literary memory, American, English, German, has adopted the more conservative voices of that century. Thus in German literature it is by no means settled that the great dissolvents, Heine, Marx, Nietzsche, are more important or even more interesting than the great synthesizers, Grillparzer, Stifter, Schopenhauer, Keller, Wagner.

There are periods of German literature in which there is much more to admire; there is probably none in which there is as much to like. The absence of excesses, the homogeneity of the artist with the citizen, the concern of the literary men with the average individual, the average consciousness, the average mentality make this literature the opposite of an *art pour l'art*. The wide spread of regional interests and regional preoccupations make it the most blushingly provincial among the periods of German literature. In perhaps no other period do we so easily get the sense of what was German, in the largest and least offensive sense: centrally European, provincially European.

In contrast to the studious attention paid to nineteenth century Atlantic criticism, there is here no discussion with twentieth century German critics. They are absent, however, only from the surface, only formally. It lies in the nature of the essay that the many voices to which the writer has listened beforehand turn into voices *within* him, and that the essay proceeds by constant self-refutation and self-correction. In this I see the function of the scholarly essay: after absorbing everything anybody has said, to stress the things nobody has seen enough. Probably a great delusion is involved; one always starts by hoping to correct prevailing errors, one always ends by vainly contradicting them. But in the general mood of vacillation, it was a comfort to return as often as possible to the Atlantic judges who pronounced on their German contemporaries with confident but cautious sympathy, because they had no qualms at seeing the obvious.

CONTENTS

PART I:
THE AGE OF GRILLPARZER (1820-1850)

PART II:
THE AGE OF KELLER (1850-1880)

Ch. I: Gottfried Keller

Ch. II: The Metaphysicals

Ch. III: The Critics

Ch. IV: The Age of Wagner?

Part One

THE AGE OF GRILLPARZER

I

Grillparzer

A Questionable Representative

'Grillparzer . . . a devil of a name, to be sure, for posterity; but they *must* learn to pronounce it,' Byron wrote in a diary after reading the Sappho drama (January 12, 1821). Well, posterity saw no need to learn the devil of a name; no great writer abroad has proclaimed Grillparzer's fame since Byron's day, and his own compatriots received no later play of his with the enthusiasm that had greeted his early *Sappho*. Not only his claim to greatness but everything about the man with the impossible name is questionable.

We even have to ask the question, who are 'his compatriots'? the Germans? the Austrians? the Viennese? In the beginning of the nineteenth century Vienna was still the political capital of the 'German Empire.' After 1814 Austria was only the leading state in the 'German Federation.' By and by the term 'the Germans' acquired a new meaning in the mind of an Austrian. It never ceased to mean 'all of us who speak German'; for a long time it kept the meaning, 'all the states in the German Federation'; but gradually it also meant 'the other Germans,' those outside of Austria. In the mouth of Grillparzer it has the three meanings in turn. When we speak of 'his countrymen,' we must sometimes stretch it to include all those who wrote and read German, sometimes narrow it to the great city that enclosed his life, Vienna.

The idea of nominating Grillparzer as representative of a whole epoch in German literature raises other doubts. He was considered the foremost writer of Austria — in a grudging way by some, in an apologetic way by others. 'If his peculiar richness were equalled by a commensurate power, no other German dramatist would match him' (Gundolf). 'Grillparzer was a very fine dramatist, and he just missed being a very great one' (Fred Nolte). But he was in no way the leader of contemporary literature, not in Austria, much less in all Germany. If he was a secret king of German literature, he was it so secretly that neither he nor anybody else was aware of his kingship.

Yet this man, without influence, with hardly a temporary radiation, with only a local reputation, is the representative man of his time, because he shows up its negative aspects. His eccentric basis, in the southeastern corner of the German lands, fits a centre-less period.

His eyes fixed on the poetic heights of the past —

> Ich möchte am liebsten stehen bleiben,
> Wo Schiller und Goethe stand

— he embodies the historic sense discovered by his generation, the very ' historism ' which became the dominant viewpoint of his century. The huge anticlimax which makes up his life and work is typical of a period without power or vitality, where the best was doomed to failure and only the mediocre was destined to success. His lack of radiation outside Germany has been the lot of the best German writers of the nineteenth century. He is representative in that combination of traditional form with modern content which made his contemporaries relish his form beyond desert and caused our century to identify, beyond reason, his content with later Viennese psychoanalysis.

Perhaps he is simply representative of the bad luck of that literary epoch. Franz Grillparzer was born in Vienna in 1791, lost his father before he had established himself professionally, his mother (through suicide) before he had disestablished himself emotionally. Insanity hovered over his family. Music daily distracted this contemporary of Beethoven and Schubert from the pursuit of literature. ' He reads Sophocles in the original and Calderon and Byron likewise,' said the Viennese of the young man; but the knowledge of seven languages only taught him to find the good things inimitable. His love affairs ended in disillusionment, and he was never married. The best luck he had, that he was called to literature by the official voice of the theatre, the director of the Burgtheater, turned into the grief of his life; his sensitivity became deeply dependent on the voice of the public. As he was more severely self-critical than any other great poet, praise did him little good, but a poor success always alienated him from the beloved work. Because the enthusiasm of his Viennese public had a few times been lukewarm, he remained convinced that he was only half a poet.

> Halb gab ich mich hin den Musen,
> Und sie erhörten mich halb.

That ' surrendering only half ' was not untrue; no one worked with less assiduity. He produced a dozen dramas, it took him little more than a month to write one, but in between were years of doubt and hesitation.

Grillparzer had a sense of public affairs and a comprehensive view of public conditions. In ' private ' life he was an official of the Austrian state, protected and a little spoiled from the earliest days of his literary fame, but also taken not quite seriously as an official, and not promoted. It was felt that he did not think as an Austrian official should, at a time when the state felt safe only in an ultra-conservative attitude. After the subversions of the French Revolution and the Napoleonic occupations, the rulers of Austria, Emperor Franz and his minister Metternich, believed they owed Europe only two things, peace at any cost and the avoidance of revolution at any price. A single poem of ' the official ' Grillparzer was uncomplimentary to the Church of Rome; the Emperor never forgave him. But the two were not so different in their views of the national prospect. ' My realm resembles a rotted house; if you want to tear down a part only, you don't know how much of the rest will crumble,' said the Emperor to the Russian ambassador in 1829. In Grillparzer's diary, 1830, one gets an even clearer view: ' The national aversions of the different provinces . . . like wrongly teamed horses they will scatter, as soon as the progressing *Zeitgeist* rends the constraining yoke. When a fresh dawn breaks for the other countries, this land alone will not remain.'

This pessimistic observer had written the drama which remains the finest glorification of the Habsburg monarchy, *King Ottocar* (1825). Grillparzer based the detail of the action on thirteenth-century chronicles, but before his mind's eye loomed the contemporary figure of Napoleon. He unrolled a panorama of high politics, but he succeeded even better in certain flashes of private life. In a mighty exposition we approach, through concentric circles, the king of Bohemia, on the point of divorcing Margaret of Austria. The rough and lucky king is lifted by waves of success, as victories, acclamations, and deputations of newly subjected lands accumulate. In the midst of all this pageant stands, as silent reproach, the mournful former queen, and then the new bride, Kunigund of Hungary. The divorcee is chivalrously assisted by the insignificant knight Rudolf of Habsburg. The young princess is eagerly eyed by the brilliant knight Zawisch. When a delegation arrives offering to Ottocar the nomination for the office of Emperor, there ends a first act which has few equals for richness of scenic action. Grillparzer's stern rival, Hebbel, was not exaggerating when he deemed that ' Shakespeare would have lifted his hat to this first act.'

In act II Zawisch makes bold and ingenious advances to the new queen, before the very eyes of the king, who is concerned about his disgruntled Austrians. When the king seems at the peak of self-confidence, a new delegation from the Imperial Diet brings the news that the election has fallen on the Count of Habsburg. The political action and the amorous intrigue are again intertwined so astonishingly, that we regret Grillparzer did not keep up this delightful counterpoint in the next acts.

Unfortunately, act III rather belongs to Emperor Rudolf. There is too warm a light on these Habsburg scenes. The poet's heart is in them, and his patriotism makes them hard to resist; just as his eroticism makes the Kunigund scenes hard to forget. These two non-central lustres, of Habsburg and of Kunigund, encroach upon that of Ottocar; our interest will not return to him.

The King wars with the Emperor for his Austrian possessions, and the Emperor wins, by mere virtue. But when Ottocar has been persuaded to swear allegiance, the treachery of his Bohemians changes the scene of conciliation into one of humiliation. With relentless insistence, for the length of a whole act, the King impresses this disgrace upon himself and upon us. But he marches once more against the Emperor in the final act, where the dismal atmosphere of battle and defeat is wonderfully caught in every scene, until the sun of Habsburg rises victoriously, over Vienna, whereas the light of the first acts had shone on Prague.

This historical drama is brimful of original and strong effects, from the most elementary to the most delicate. Moreover, it promised the very fare which a state that had become self-conscious might prescribe to its demurring citizens. Yet this best of German patriotic plays got the worst official reception. It disappeared in the archives of the Vienna Censors, because it could not please the powerful Czech element in the Austrian nobility. An almost paralysing caution was the automatic reaction of an Austrian censor, whenever literature touched upon political matters. Grillparzer tells that, years later, he met a Censor and asked him what had been so dangerous in his drama. And the man said benignly, ' Nothing at all — but one never knows! '

Accidentally the Empress asked for something unpublished to read and with some effort secured Grillparzer's manuscript. Then the Emperor saw to it that the Censors did not withstand much longer. The play was presented in 1825 with a success more spectacular than intense. It was repeated twenty-five times for a year. But the Censors had their revenge, they allowed only adverse criticism to be printed. And after a year the most Austrian of plays was allowed to drop from the repertory of the state theatre for a whole generation.

To the author this affair was bound to appear as a calamity. He was past thirty, and his big successes were behind him. He was used to analyse his own art shrewdly and coldly, although in the work itself he was dependent on uncontrollable inspirations. It was the tragic figure of Ottocar which had tempted him, but Habsburg cannot make the slightest appearance without being idealized generously and winningly. The central act turns into a personification of the ideal emperor, the holy representative of all that is good on this earth, indeed the holy lieutenant of God himself. It takes all of Grillparzer's art of original characterization, sensuous imagination, and surprising inventiveness to make so much godliness passable on the stage. One might also say, it took so much moral cargo to weight his fanciful art. We never lose the suspicion that the ponderous moral purposes of Grillparzer and his artistic delights keep a certain distance from one another, have their successive climaxes instead of simultaneous ones, and are only kept from falling apart by an artist who is at the same time a great critic. ' In the catholic, delicate appreciation of things poetic and artistic, Grillparzer is not impossibly the most patiently and sensitively cultivated mind in the whole range of European letters.' (F. Nolte)

He was too good an artist ever to regret the waywardness of his art, and he was too much of a *good* man ever to lessen his moral freight. He thought he had brought the two together; it irked him that by turns his artistic calibre and his civic intentions were minimized by the professional critics. But he had another, deeper wound. He had resolutely assumed the task of naturalizing the *poetic* drama that had recently flowered in central Germany in the most fertile *theatrical* ground that existed, his home city. He sometimes doubted the rank of his poetic gifts, not that of his theatrical endeavors. All his life he bore the disparagements of his literary critics with equanimity and almost with contempt; but he could barely survive the lukewarm reception of any of his plays. Because there, he felt, history went wrong. He was giving, not his best, but the absolute best, the best theatre that was to be had, not only in Vienna, but in all Germany. But people did not take to it. Yet they were connoisseurs of good theatre.

Vienna Theatre

Vienna had five prominent theatres, all founded or reorganized in the 1780's. Two ' court ' theatres, ' Am Kärntner Tor ' and ' In der Burg ', took care of opera in one, of refined drama in the other. The Kärntner Theater had been almost Italian, the Burgtheater more or less French. But the local lifeblood pulsated in the suburban theatres, one ' In der Leopoldstadt ' (founded 1781), another 'In der Josefstadt' (founded 1788), and a third ' An der Wien ' (built 1787). The latter was rebuilt by Schikaneder in 1799 into the most spacious theatre with the best-equipped stage in all Germany.

Long before Grillparzer felt the vocation of bringing German classicism down to Austrian spectacle, those three theatres accomplished the task of elevating the popular theatre to the rank of high art. It is a long story, studded with talent and fostered by the instinct of a big city, suffused in every scene with the music of Vienna; but its fulfilment came with Ferdinand Raimund.

Raimund was a year older than Grillparzer, and when the poet had his sensational successes in 1817 and 1818, Raimund made a name for himself as a comic actor in the Josefstadt and moved up to the Leopoldstadt. He had begun by craving the acclaim of a tragic actor and ended by craving the laurels of a tragic poet. He had no voice, a speech defect, and 'he never was directly comical . . . but he was a humorist of the best and most effective kind. Where *Gemüt* alone prevailed he was irresistible.' We have to listen to an eye-witness, in this case Ludwig A. Frankl, to recapture some of the fugitive impression.

He had ten years of the hardest apprenticeship, as an actor in the provinces, before coming back to Vienna. There he had uncontested triumphs only in the last years of his life, after successes in Munich, Hamburg and Berlin. Meanwhile he had done his life's work, melting all the elements of Vienna theatre into the one pot of the 'fairy farce,' a unique genre reaching from the sublime to the vulgar. From 1823 to 1834 he wrote the classic examples of this genre himself, only eight pieces in all; none of them published till after his suicide in 1836.

For centuries it had been the function of the 'Volksstück' to travesty and drag down the 'higher theatre,' it had lived on leavings. Raimund, from the unsatisfied cravings of his unhappy heart, instilled into the Volksstück again a longing for the heights. He made it live on pathos, beauty and goodness no less than on parody, laughter and merriment. He taught first a big city and then a whole nation to enjoy these side by side, to increase the pleasure of one through the other; and even, in the end, to prefer the former.

Some of Raimund's masterworks, like *Der Verschwender* and *Alpenkönig und Menschenfeind,* are still played. In the *Misanthrope* the scenes of the Elf-King take up little room, although they are delightfully spectacular. All effort is concentrated on the psychology of the misanthrope and the realism of his surroundings. In the first act, the misanthrope evacuates a poor family from its alpine hut, in order to wallow there in his lonely rage; in the second act, the Elf-King batters the misanthrope into a truce; and in the last act, the Elf-King plays the role of the misanthrope to such perfection that not even the real one can stand it any longer, and reason and kindness return to a harassed family. But after all the platitudes and subtleties of this play we still listen with wonder to Raimund's greatest eye-witness, Grillparzer:

'His admirers have not noticed that the very collision of half-realized poetry and half-literate vulgarity makes the charm of Raimund's productions. . . . Whatever praise has been bestowed on him is fully deserved when applied to *Alpenkönig und Menschenfeind*. . . . Even Molière could not have imagined a better plot. A Misanthrope cured by seeing his behaviour enacted before his own eyes: no comedy author has chosen a theme of more psychological truth or more capable of development. . . . There is circulating, pulsating blood in every part of the fully organic whole. . . . I wish all German poets would study this work of an author, whom they all infinitely surpass in learning. They would then see that the mission of art is not in the idea but in the coming-to-life of the idea.'

Even that is only half the truth, the literary half. The other side is outside literature, is pure theatre. Raimund had become an actor against the advice of everybody, against the imploring wishes of his family, against his own solemn promises, against the curses of his father. In spite of a never appeased conscience, he could not help being an actor. He was also an exacting and passionate director. *All* the figures in all his plays were acted as *he* modelled them.

We still have an exaggerated impression of the percentage of literature in this. In the case of Raimund as of other Volksschauspieler there was a peculiar intimacy with their public, all nuances of familiarity, and a mutual reaction which sometimes led to actual dialogues between stage and audience. Add to this an almost constant self-irony of the Volkstheater, a constant vaporisation of its own illusions, and you get the range from the naive exploitation of stage magic to sustained intellectual subtlety. And in spite of all that, the aura of an accomplished craft: the proudest actors of the Burgtheater were devotees of Raimund.

This preponderance of theatre in Viennese drama is, to a lesser degree, a mark also of Grillparzer's plays. One dare not say that they have more body than soul, but it is true that their soul is anxiously aware of their body, is almost resentful of it. It is curious that the great impressions of Raimund's youth came from the Burgtheater, but those of Grillparzer from the Leopoldstadt: each had the wrong legacy! But Raimund was more successful in introducing his share of Burgtheater into the suburbs than Grillparzer was in inoculating his fine plays with Volkstheater. And his amalgamations never satisfied him. 'I am enough of a German to feel angry when I have achieved a theatrical effect. Still I cannot do differently, an inner necessity holds my nature to these goals.' (Diary, 1828.) But the secret strife in his breast was punished in the open. The theatre public did not take to his plays, or only to a few of them. Just as it did not take to those of Raimund for long. What they both wrote was theatre with a bad conscience.

The main difference between Grillparzer and Raimund is this, that no reading of a Raimund play can give the impression of a performance, while even the best performance of a Grillparzer play does not live up to our impression at the reading. The reason, in the case of Grillparzer, is his suggestiveness. He does not, like the Volkstheater, require stage equipment and machinery. His stage is more the human body itself; and no other dramatist has made it such a flowering and wilting microcosm, has showered it with such breathing, panting life. But that is a drawback in many respects, for it is neither theatre nor literature but a luxuriant excrescence from both. It is a field of radiations, of appeals to our nerves, to which we respond neither with our literary taste nor with our sense of drama, but with a higher biological pitch.

The drama which best illustrates his strength and his weakness is *Hero and Leander*. He wrote it with diffidence and many delays. When it was finally performed, in 1831, an elite noticed that this was Grillparzer at his best, but the public remained so cold that the play was soon discontinued. After its revival in 1851 it became customary to call it the most Viennese of his plays.

It is the well-known story of Hero who grew up to be the priestess in Sestos on the Hellespont. The first act opens on the morning of her consecration and gives her occasion to assure her uncle, the priest, how superior she is to the need of companionship and marriage. The second act focusses on two onlookers at the ceremony, but Leander is characterized exclusively by the words of his friend, as a boy untouched by love. In the third act Hero spends her first night alone in her priestly tower, but Leander has swum from the opposite shore to see her, and he wins her love. In the fourth act the suspicions of the priest are aroused, he keeps Hero awake for the whole day, and he extinguishes the lamp in her tower in the night. In the fifth act the storm has washed Leander's body to the shore, and when the priest wants to separate her from the corpse, Hero dies.

What Grillparzer, the dramatist, has added to this simple legend is a great boldness in the main situations. The girl of the first act is all virginity. At their first meeting, the girl is all mind, the boy is all inarticulateness. In the central act, her development from complete self-reliance to complete surrender is made next to inevitable. In the fourth act she is as fixed in her new state as she was first in the opposite one. And in the end she makes a religion of her love.

What Grillparzer, the Viennese, has added is that he softened all this boldness and made it grace and charm. There is no conflict of ideas or duties, there is only a multiplicity of impulses, and the question is, to which is it most beautiful to give in. For Vienna is the city of compromises, and Grillparzer is often endangered by his keenness in seeing possibilities where the true tragedian insists on incompatibilities. The perfect nun, the born vestal, whom Grillparzer stipulates in the first act, is really incapable of the third act. The combination would be impossible — elsewhere, but not in the atmosphere of Vienna, where even ideals make concessions. What is true? what is false? Everybody is right, and only the narrow-minded demand absolutes. Thus the young nun knows no categorical imperative, and the priest knows no fanaticism. There are two sides to everything, and everybody knows it. Thus there is really no tragic conflict. One thing leads to another. Thus there is really no freedom of the will. In life and thought and feeling a well-nuanced convention prevails. People are unchaste with good taste (Grillparzer's sensuality is exquisite); pious with art (often for art's sake); and sacrilegious with piety (only the ' love-death ' scales the temple).

With a ' German ' dramatist the hero's eloquence is all drive and self-explanation; with these Viennese it is all reacting and watching reactions. Their eloquence is oblique, it is lavished on the non-essentials, on the by-play, while the essential has a wonderful way of being communicated in expressive silences. Hence the richness in concrete hints, some inescapable, some evanescent, all so unsystematic that one won't belabor them as symbols. But each act has at least one prominent example: the dove; the drink from Hero's pitcher; the play with her lamp, her veil; the rise to the inner temple. Then there is so much play-acting in every play, and so much mutual tolerance for this delicate duplicity, that it sometimes surprises the feigner herself (the incomparable ' Komm morgen denn! '). Every agent seems to be composed of sympathy and empathy. This endangers the drama; but it is difficult to imagine finer commentary.

One could not be blamed for helping himself to a convenient word: music. This art in which the commentary is better than the text, the understatement as audible as the statement, and the relations as important as the lines, isn't it music? To be sure, the language of *Hero* is also, in the loosest acceptance of the term, the most ' musical ' (of Grillparzer); but what we are chasing by the term is something different. The Viennese themselves used to speak of the ' musicality ' of their atmosphere, of their life. In most Grillparzer plays such transference is almost necessary in order to allude to the peculiar quality of speech and gesture. In the Hero-drama, the whole concert of convention, artificiality and ' Natürlichkeit ' offers nothing but harmony, if one makes off into musical ' laws.' No one has more succinctly sanctioned *and* criticized such generalisation (music = music of speech, of thought, of feeling) than Grillparzer in his ' Abschied von Wien ':

Weithin Musik, wie wie wenn im Baum
Der Vögel Chor erwachte;
Man spricht nicht, denkt wohl etwa kaum
Und fühlt das Halbgedachte.

This hovering between eloquence and silence, outspokenness and allusion, meaning and melody, body and soul, is only another aspect of the Viennese gift for compromise. For ages the city has been a provincial cosmopolis between river and woods, with the vineyards growing into the suburbs, and the dialect creeping into the most solemn occasions. As one consequence we have the most homey hellenism (until we come to Gide and Cocteau). Who else would have thought of the home life of Hero and her parents? Another consequence is the infatuation with nature. There is hardly a drama of Grillparzer where the changing 'Tageszeiten' do not play a major role. Currents of fresh air seem to course through his acts, more than we sense in any other drama of the nineteenth century. Among his dramas, *Hero* is the one of dawn, three situations (out of seven) take place in the morning and breathe morning air. And the place too, the shore of the Hellespont, does not remain a backdrop. The sea murmurs audibly in the first two acts, symphonically in the third, becomes visible in the fourth and fifth. It is ever-present in the final speeches. The poet has almost balanced cosmos and chaos, surging love and engulfing death, and he has almost justified the rolling title he gave to the play: *Des Meeres und der Liebe Wellen.*

To be sure, to call such a masterwork 'Viennese' has often been self-flattery of the natives. One does not have to consider it in that light; nothing is easier than to deride such vague statements. But the point is that they are born out of actual feeling, even collective feeling. That is why they are rather worth proving than contradicting. At worst this one characterizes only half of the work's effect, its undertones and accompaniment, the half which Grillparzer imputed to all Vienna:

> Man lebt in halber Poesie,
> Gefährlich für die ganze,
> Und ist ein Dichter, ob man nie
> An Vers gedacht und Stanze.

Austrian Dramatists

Grillparzer was too generous when he bestowed the title of poet on every Viennese. He was certainly not thinking of the author who was then dominating the Vienna Vorstadttheater, Johann Nestroy. Nestroy was so far from Grillparzer's mind that his name never occurs in the notes of one who noticed everything. But the greater the lapse of time becomes that separates us from them, the more possible it becomes to see these antipodes together.

In a way it was Nestroy who drove Grillparzer from the stage. The public to which Grillparzer dared offer his comedy *Thou Shalt Not Lie* in 1838 was spoiled by a decade of Nestroy farces. Raimund, watching the effect of Nestroy's *Lumpazivagabundus* had drawn the conclusion, 'So it's all over with me and my plays — all in vain!'

Grillparzer, watching the unsuccess of his own comedy, drew a similar conclusion and stayed away from the stage.

Nestroy does not exist apart from the stage, although the twentieth century has endeavored to make him a literary classic. His own time had more reliable standards. He was a great comic actor, more indubitably so than Raimund. And he actually had as much 'genius' as Grillparzer, as much intellect, verve and wealth — only in an inferior genre: twice inferior, first because it was *ancilla theatri,* subservient to the theatre, and second because it was the parasitic genre of parody.

In descendence, education, and social standing, Nestroy was a duplicate of Grillparzer; in his actor's career the tall man with the grand voice was the opposite of hard-luck Raimund. And he excelled both rivals in the dedication to his two careers: for many years he was the most popular actor of Vienna and performed almost every night (880 parts altogether). And at the same time he wrote three farces a year, over 80 in all. The text itself, witty as it is, presents to us only the skeleton of its original meaning, because that was a web of local and timely sousentendus, a perfected mutual watching and catching between actor and audience. The essence of these texts is not art, it is Vienna as it was, or as its lower life was, from 1830 to 1850.

Nevertheless, some plays have survived into the present, and some have been revived. Thornton Wilder's *Matchmaker* (or *Merchant of Yonkers,* 1938) owes much of its good fun to Nestroy's *Einen Jux will er sich machen* (1842), which in turn owes little to John Oxenford's *A Day Well Spent* (1835), because Nestroy was careless as to his subject-matter, but very original in his handling of it. The most durable of his plays has been *Lumpazivagabundus* (1833). It marks the defeat of the fairy farce. The fairy machinery is misused and minimized, the author's attention goes to 'The Three Bums' (subtitle). Three journeymen dream the number of the winning lottery ticket (act I). One spends his share on drink, one on luxury, one reasonably (act II). The third act fondles the jovial depravity of the two, but ends in perfunctory conversion. The detail is of a riotous imbecility plus irresistible drollery. There also was in Nestroy a demon of caricature, which mercilessly exposed the meanness and falseness of the very middle-class which patronized him. On the strength of this pervasive satire his able champions in the twentieth century (especially Karl Kraus) have tried to make him out to be the greatest Austrian writer. However, there was so much complacent meanness in Nestroy's muse as to make one reluctant to elevate his local into national supremacy.

One chief witness for K. Kraus is the Prague critic Bernhard Gutt. His reviews of some guest performances in 1844 show how well the Viennese actor was understood in the chief cities of the Austrian empire. Most of Gutt's praise goes to Nestroy's acting; that of the writing is full of qualifications:

'August 2. May the kind reader permit a review of Nestoy's visit. . . . In Mr. Nestroy's career I think I can distinguish three periods. The first was that of boundless vigor. . . . A moral and aesthetic foundation was mostly lacking; negation was predominant and the dialogue was a series of brilliant but cold sarcasms. . . . The crassest figure in this line was shoemaker Knieriem in Lumpazivagabundus. . . . Then bloody sarcasm abated into satire which, to be sure, still attacked everything regardless of dignity and worth. But the outlines of the characters became human, the energy turned inward, it no longer forced success by colossal quantity but won by wit. . . . Now Nestroy has found a positive foundation; for his action, instead of disintegrating acid, an ethical stimulus; for his characterization, instead of grimace, an aesthetic law. . . . In a word, the lifegiving principle of this third stage is humor.'

Unfortunately Nestroy did not develop as much as this excerpt from Gutt leads one to expect. There was to the end enough of the clown in him to use indiscriminately *all* the effects which had ever proved successful. There are a few later comedies in which the caricature was less charged and the characters had more human consistency. But besides them Nestroy kept playing the more resounding successes of his earlier plays. We cannot help supplementing the voice from Prague with the voice of a Swabian from Switzerland, Fr. Th. Vischer, the most respected critic of the time. He was too moralizing in everything he wrote, but he does an excellent job of painting Nestroy into the picture of Vienna, as he saw it in 1859.

'. . . The next impression of Vienna is: deafening. . . . If the observer stays on the surface, he meets the old chasing after pleasure, the 'blossoming sensuality,' the well-known character of Vienna. The dance, the theatre, music, singing, wine, love, the Prater, Schönbrunn, and other goals for walking and riding, talking, laughing and fun of any kind still seems the axis around which life revolves. Not to forget eating, or rather a childlike importance granted the joys of palate and stomach. The service of Venus is conspicuous enough in all big cities. In Vienna it always had a color of its own. . . . It was steeped in an element of naïveté which forestalled a stern moral judgment. . . . It was sin before the Tree of Knowledge. . . . Still at the time of Raimund the theatres of the suburbs gave a good picture of the innocent sins of this buffooning capital. Now one must go to these very theatres in order to see what has become of the old humor. . . . Nestroy is still here, and I first saw him in the French farce *Orpheus* in the Leopoldstadt theatre. The frivolity of the French is tolerable in the specific levity with which they are able to imbue the most questionable. But now this Nestroy! He commands a range of tones and gestures where, for the right feeling, disgust and nausea are beginning. . . . I also saw Nestroy in *Seventeen Girls in Uniform,* where he let loose the smuttiest garrison jokes on the Maid of Orleans. Here the most revulsive passages were applauded the most. . . . Of course it needed comic talent as great and original as that which has run to seed in Nestroy, to make a public insensitive to its gradual sinking into baseness and to teach it the insensible transition from a hearty laughter to a billygoat's bleating and braying.' (*Kritische Gänge.*)

The last mentioned role had been Nestroy's earliest success; here we find it at the end of his career. Gutt in Prague storms in almost identical terms against Nestroy's obscenities in the same farce; on the whole, their pronouncements are complementary. Literature had its strict divisions of high and low, and poetry was limited in that one sense: it could not be low. It is strange how charged with obscenity Nestroy's adlibbing and acting was, and yet how insignificant and bloodless his women figures. It is equally strange how Grillparzer's best creations are a galaxy of women characters, sensuous, palpitating, strong-willed and of superior mind, and yet how every ardent scene is sublimated beyond suggestiveness. It is as if Nestroy personified the lower half of the male imagination and Grillparzer the upper. Vienna might acclaim the former more, because it contained a hundred times more topical reality. But German literature as a whole could not but see a hundred times more promise of life in the vibrant phantoms of Grillparzer.

If German literature sided with Grillparzer's sense of morality, the German public did not reward his sense of the theatre. He was stubbornly convinced of being the truest successor of the classical dramatists, but Germany regarded him as a local Viennese talent and hesitated to export him to the theatres of the other German states. In Vienna itself, some of his plays were polite failures; and he almost eagerly seized one such *succès d'estime* as a pretext for withdrawing from the stage. He continued to write, but for his desk only; and even the urgings of an obliging theatre director could not draw forth the still-born plays. But they were destined to a posthumous rebirth, slow at first, until they emerged, in the twentieth century, as Grillparzer's most impressive works.

The last one that he wrote was *The Jewess of Toledo.* It affords a melancholy study of what German literature missed by looking the other way. It is a subject taken from Lope de Vega, but the old Grillparzer's imagination (he was sixty when he wrote it) was so rich that not one scene, not one character remind one of the source. However, his imagination was surprisingly cool. The subject of a royal adultery is treated with the spiritual interest of an anti-sensual father-confessor. But while the moralist in Grillparzer is of the strictest observation, the observer in him is of the most modern description, and the father-confessor hides under his cassock the heart of a former knight.

With swift characterization the three Jews are fairly thrown at us, the grasping Isaac, the quiet Esther, the reckless Rahel; with pompous characterization, the king. An ideal prince, he knows what flattery is, and tries to deserve it. We have scarcely become cloyed with so much perfection, when we notice the queen. To the warm eloquence of her husband she only has to oppose her few words of evasion, and we have recognized the frigid woman. Scarcely has this penetrated, when we become aware of a war crisis and the concurrent anti-Jewish sentiment. This is the moment when the three Jews flee in panic to the king. The cool queen has recoiled from Rahel, and the impetuous girl displays her tempestuous emotions before the fascinated monarch. Gallantly he sends his lieutenant to hide the Jewish family from any insult of the populace.

Act Two. The lieutenant has a reputation with women, thus the king himself comes to see that no harm comes to them. But the frivolous Rahel is already playing a comedy which lures him outside the boundary of decorum. When the queen also comes to look after matters, the king is embarrassed and hides. The queen feels more embarrassed, and leaves. The king puts up a brave resistance to Rahel, his every word breathes virtue — but her every word breathes triumph.

It is unnecessary to follow the action further. Grillparzer hardly does himself. He is pastmaster at leaving out the obvious. One might even claim that he left out all the scenes of drama and preferred to compose a verbal music for numerous *entr'actes,* in which he plays up all the transitions which other dramatists would leave untried. With subtlety he has devoted the first two acts to the counterpoint of these three lines: (1) the king's chorale of lucid virtue, (2) the girl's nearly thoughtless scherzo, and (3) the queen's *ostinato* of pauses, which sound like refusals to play her part, whereas she really could not devise a better means of bringing the two other voices together.

When the third act begins, the liaison has crossed its high noon and is doomed. There is nothing conventional about the situation, at least every word which the lovers say about each other is unconventional. It is as far from passion as from satiety; it knows neither regret nor illusion. There is a vast landscape between those four poles, and in that landscape the characters move with dreadful ease; because all Grillparzer characters are at home in it. He is the dramatist of the *intermittences du coeur,* of the inconsistencies of passion. He has caught, in nearly every one of his dramas, the declines of a feeling, the falling-out-of-love. He is the painter of divorces or near-divorces. His characters, all of them, do not have just one crack, their whole surface is full of cracks. Their hidden recesses reveal a secret at every new look. We suspect them as we suspect our friends.

In the last acts we are absorbed by a cruel sensation: we see these people age so fast. They become wiser in such a quick and hurtful way! And we resent it that the poet wants us, his onlookers, to grow older and wiser so quickly. We resist this disillusioned impartiality which makes the king defend the Jewess as the only absolute he had found in life: 'Sie aber war die Wahrheit . . . war sie allein mir Wesen und Gestalt' — and almost in the same scene reject her, or the memory of her mean nature: 'Ich sage dir: sie war nicht schön.'

This disillusioned impartiality is played out to the full. In beautiful speeches the king appears to have set everything right again in the end, to have set his heart and his home in order. Everybody has left, when on the deserted stage a counter-cadenza is intoned, the voice of the other Jewess, the one left over. It suspends the Christian justification in a final retracting, disclaiming, human quaver.

This drama with its crafty alternation of mass scenes and duets, with its exploitation of colorful background and history, with its spectacular action of seduction, rebellion and reconciliation, is yet utterly depressing. There is a delicacy, almost a thinness, to the voice of Grillparzer, which always prevents it from reaching massive effects. No matter how generously he multiplies his effects, they never seem to cumulate, they always form transparent patterns. His fullest orchestra still makes the effect of chamber music.

Tragedy is a hymn to life; it is at the opposite pole from elegy. There is an elementary elation in the tragedies of other great dramatists. There is only exquisite resignation at the end of Grillparzer's. The fault is not only in his too intelligent, too knowing texture, it is in his very outlook on life. All his subtlety belongs to the analysis of anti-climax. Anti-climax practically starts with his first acts. It 'mounts,' no matter how uniquely disguised, through all his climaxes, all of which prove illusory. And at the end stands sobered, saddened, wide-eyed, and wizened disillusion.

Grillparzer's Austria

Grillparzer withdrew from the stage when he knew he had lost his public. The Vienna of Schubert became that of Johann Strauss: or rather, it became the Vienna of Strauss as it had never been that of Schubert. Grillparzer had been, during some years, much more popular than Schubert in his lifetime. But he was stubbornly disloyal to his successes. It was impossible for him to exploit any of his several hits, he had to try a new kind of drama each time; and the public did not favor his efforts at offering something more mature and more complex.

His last, most private dramas concern themselves most with public affairs, history and the state. He could not help watching with the interest of a child of the family the dilemmas of that state whose official he was. As private as his locked-up dramas were his poems and epigrams, and in most of them the discontented citizen criticizes with such asperity, with so much unrelieved sourness, that it has been said, not without justice, ' He was a petty official and a petty bourgeois not only in his position but in his nature. His mind conversed as an equal with heroes, kings and sages; but he did not dominate the petty; he stood beside it an embittered man.' (Gundolf.)

However, even in his helpless mutterings he is representative of the intellectuals in that reactionary period of Austria. In his constant detractions there is so much perspicacity that even his political opponents have, to this day, credited him with being a political mind of the first order. If this sounds extravagant, we can hardly make it more acceptable by alleging that Grillparzer made several critics think of Metternich, the statesman who governed the destinies of Austria, if not of Europe, in the age of Grillparzer.

Metternich was no despot. He felt his hands tied not only by the dynasty but also by his principles. He used as much diplomacy in internal affairs as in foreign. Like Grillparzer he thought of himself as a man without a party. ' I am irreconcilably hostile to Liberalism, but I flatter myself that I am liberal in the best sense of the word.' (To Varnhagen, 1834.) One is reminded of the epigram in which Grillparzer looked back (in 1850) on his inopportune party leanings, how he was considered a liberal in the conservative era and a reactionary in the revolutionary period :

Als liberal einst der Verfolgung Ziel,
Nennt mich der Freiheitstaumel nun servil;
Nicht hier noch dort in den Extremen zünftig,
Ich glaube bald, ich bin vernünftig.

From his avoidance of extremes he concludes that he possesses a good deal of sense. The man whom he considered to be at the opposite pole claimed the same thing. We may compare the two at least in one instance.

In 1845 a large committee of Viennese writers made a petition against censorship. Its most illustrious victim, Grillparzer, was most reluctant but signed to please the two instigators. The two cautiously had their names erased, so that Grillparzer's headed the long list. What his real thoughts about censorship were may be gathered from the following.

' Authors are individuals gifted with a talent; as such they participate in the rights of the other citizens neither more nor less. . . . Thoughts are free; but spoken and written words are subject to the moral law, and they bring to their authors advantage or disadvantage.'

'Actions are restricted everywhere. Society, the common welfare depends on such salutary restrictions. . . . If certain actions are prohibited, why not opinions which lead to them? Should really everybody have the right to say his opinion? Even if it is harmful, enticing to evil, corrupting the morals, ridiculing the good, assailing salutary restrictions? "True words are things," says Byron, and I believe he is right.'

'The norms which apply to authors are the same which proceed from the moral law, from the rules of wisdom and of life, and which apply to all expressions of the mind. To speak, to write, to print inappropriately has bad consequences, but these are a matter of course, and therefore unavoidable."

'Preventive force, preventive censorship of actions would be carried as far as making impossible the forbidden — if it were only possible in the case of actions. But in the case of written and printed works it is possible. Would it not be fortunate for humanity and literature, if by a good censorship every bad, every pernicious work could be destroyed before being spread?'

'The Press concerns the intellectual possessions of the people, the highest interests of science, and the sacred claims of truth. I consider this statement . . . as the true basis for the solutions we seek. . . . But which claims for protection are more urgent, those of society or those of the authors? The decision cannot be doubtful. As the whole is worth more than a part, the welfare of the state precedes the interest of the authors.'

'Should therefore a censorship exist? Yes, if there could be a good one. But since a good censorship is not possible, and a bad one more harmful than none: therefore none at all — but only for *that* reason.'

We have taken the liberty of quoting side by side the opinions of Metternich *and* Grillparzer, in order to show how hard it is to distinguish them. Paragraphs one, three and five are from Metternich's answer to the petition (quoted in *Grillparzer Jahrbuch* 21, 131). Paragraphs two, four and six are from a draft of Grillparzer's of 1844. (Even the Byron quote could be that of the statesman, who knew more Byron by heart than the poet.)

The single issues of that era are so outdated that we can hardly appreciate their wisdom or foolishness. What we can appreciate is that in the largest issue, the preservation of Austria, the poet rivalled the arch-preserver Metternich, but he did so in his own field, the drama. The most ambitious work that he left 'in his desk drawers' is *Family*

Strife in Habsburg, and it is as full of the anxieties of the time as it is — or has come to appear to us by now — timeless in its political intuition.

Determinedly Grillparzer singled out the figure who can claim to be the biggest failure in the whole history of Habsburg, Rudolf II., the man who could not prevent the Thirty Years' War. Around him move, not as accompanying instruments, but as counterpointed voices, not only his two brothers but also three archdukes of the younger generation. With so many voices, and with choruses of courtiers, soldiers, citizens, the poet orchestrates this *Dies Irae* of the Austrian Empire.

The complicated polyphony is unified by the one voice which dominates this drama as no other drama of Grillparzer is dominated, the voice of the grotesque old man who vainly tries to stem the tides. Often the old emperor sounds just like the old poet; but the petty rancour of so many epigrams is here sublimated into dignity and sweetened into paternal sorrow. Only in one instance did the poetic pamphletist Grillparzer match the dramatist. When in act II the soldiers claim,

> Im Lager hier sind alle Tapfren Brüder,

they claim that their different nationalities and especially different religions make no difference to their loyalty. When Grillparzer sent his notorious poem to Radetzki's army in 1848,

> . . . In deinem Lager ist Oesterreich,

he meant that the different nationalities and especially different parties do not matter in an army, and should not matter in a state, when the unity of a state is at stake. His shout was heard all over Austria and became the rallying cry of the conservative elements.

It is impossible for an outsider to feel the anxieties of a far-sighted loyalist in the supra-national Austrian empire of the nineteenth century. It is easy to guess them by recalling what happened to Austria in the twentieth century. And the old emperor sees in any action the overture to complete disintegration :

> . . . Soll nicht der Grundbau jener weisen Fügung,
> Die Gott gesetzt und die man nennt den Staat,
> Im wilden Taumel auseinandergehn. (act III)

The dense web of historical accuracy, timely allusion, and dim prophecy make this the most imaginative political drama in German literature. And since the powerful character of the old emperor is so craftily compounded of nothing but weaknesses, it almost does not matter whether Grillparzer is right or wrong. His errors become as touching as his insights in the magnificent speeches of the tottering emperor, each speech laboriously disengaging itself from an accentuated silence, each flapping off into another visionary silence.

The third act centers on the historical signing of the religious Charta to the Bohemians. But the unavailing old man correctly foresees that nothing will stop the chain of explosions which others have laid. He realizes better than anybody why he is a misfit in politics: because it is the ungrateful art in which human values are reversed, in which success gives value to a will, instead of the other way around: 'Der reinste Wille wertlos, wenn erfolglos.' Strangely, this dead center of the drama is the most moving part in it. There is something above the requirements of the art, and that is the artist's conviction. Grillparzer's most mature convictions come through here, overpoweringly, and we surrender to the weight of their sincerity. The bitter old emperor, in so many things his intellectual brother, leaves as his final advice to his successors this, the respect of not only their own convictions but also those of others:

> Was dir als Höchstes gilt: die Ueberzeugung,
> Acht sie in andern auch, sie ist von Gott.

In no other drama does the name 'God' reappear so obsessively, and always linked with the concept of 'order.' Indeed, if the failing emperor is the dead center of this drama, his own agitated mind gravitates about a sacred 'Ordnung' as its own still center. That word too reappears obsessively. It is amazing that the author dared poetize this unpoetical subject 'order,' and that he succeeded. In the turmoil of the historical tragedy it is present without any influence, it reigns without any consequence, as a utopia, as an impossible dream which gives value to an impotent life. Grillparzer's time considered poetry not as an expression of life, but as the other side, a complement to life. Over the political reality of this drama 'Ordnung' revolves as its poetry.

Only from the last act the word is absent; it has lost its efficacy, just as the dying emperor has lost his power. He is absent from this last act — as, we might say, Metternich was absent from the 1848 revolution. That Grillparzer was continuously thinking of contemporary events while writing the drama is beyond doubt. Often the allusions are introduced by tour-de-force, as when the emperor hears that his subjects shoot at one another, he shouts, stamping his feet,

> Man soll nicht schiessen! — Soll nicht, sag ich euch!
> — Da stehts vor mir, der Mord, der Bürgerkrieg. . . .

In Grillparzer's 'Reminiscences of 1848' the memory is equally indignant: 'They were shooting at the people, they were. Whoever ordered it, brought the monarchy to the brink of ruin. From then on there was no halt, especially as Prince Metternich was deposed, who with all his faults was the only one with the intelligence and the energy to put an end and an aim to the rolling-off of the events.' Thus the great antagonist Metternich, so severely censured in Grillparzer's writings, comes into his own, the moment he is missed. The opinions of Austria's two great men must have grown more alike with the years, just as their faces grew more alike. It has often been remarked how the last photos of the two resemble each other. Only, the eternally old Grillparzer had looked for a long time as abdicated as the suddenly aging chancellor finally did.

Like a good statesman, Grillparzer looked not only at the values but also at the propitious time. His last remark in the ' Reminiscences of 1848 ' is that no moment seemed to him less propitious for ' liberty ' then 1848. ' Freedom demands above all two things: sound judgment and self-control — and just these two were lacking in Germany.' That is why the patriot felt more and more isolated among his contemporaries and rejected by his time. He took his utopian refuge in history and in eternity:

> Will meine Zeit mich bestreiten,
> Ich lass es ruhig geschehn.
> Ich komme aus anderen Zeiten
> Und hoffe in andre zu gehn.
>
> (1860)

II

Young Germany

The Juvenile Delinquents

The French Revolution in July, 1830, threw all German governments into a fit and all German patriots into a fit of enthusiasm. The hope of the patriots was for more liberalism and more constitutionalism. The hope of the governments lay in ultra-conservative Austria, which held the presidency in the federation of the three dozen German states. These three dozen states were politically asleep, 'snoring,' as Heine put it in one of his gentler moods:

Und als ich über die Alpen zog
Da hört ich Deutschland schnarchen,
Es schlief da unten in sanfter Hut
Von sechsunddreissig Monarchen.

But the snoring was distributed as unequally as the territories of the thirty-six monarchs. There were three general areas. Vast and multinational Austria had the best reputation for sound sleep. In Prussia the Government was more awake than the subjects; it guarded them from all political dreaming, encouraged them to be progressive in other ways. The remaining third of Germany, the southwest, was geographically the most divided and politically the most restless. There, thirty-four princes jealously preserved their petty principalities; there hundreds of demagogues dreamed of past French revolutions and future German ones.

The power that tried its best to counterbalance the fitful slumber of the uneven thirty-six was the German press. It had developed into a real power only in the southwest. Its grand old man, its white knight was the Baron Cotta in Stuttgart. Cotta distributed his industry over the newspapers *Allgemeine Zeitung* in Augsburg, *Morgenblatt* and *Literaturblatt* in Stuttgart. He wanted his papers to express all the discordant voices of the present. He could maintain his papers only on the no man's and everyman's land between the powers of the past and the forces of the future. It was indispensable that he should secure the respect of the powerful, and he fully succeeded. It was almost as indispensable to secure the best talent among the young journalists, and in this he did not always succeed.

What the press had to contend with was the supervision by the Federal Council in Frankfurt, the so-called Diet. This Diet manifested an interest in literature and newspapers which was so flattering that it became quite embarrassing. The extent of this interest can be explained by the high literacy of those directing the Austrian affairs, especially the voluble Metternich himself. Indeed, every unpopular action of the Diet in Frankfurt was credited to the distant but efficient wire-puller in Vienna. He was copiously informed by a secret service scattered over the dozen literary centres of the German lands. That was exclusively a letter-writing institution, veritable rivers of reports gushing from those centers, flowing through the diplomatic channels, to their confluence in Vienna. The full-time or part-time agents of this secret service were mostly writers themselves, and their party leanings were in all the shades from ultra-conservative to very liberal. The ignorant public called them spies. Their official name was 'Confidants,' and the whole system remained remarkably confidential, in most of its aspects, as late as 1890-1910, when the important books on Young Germany were written. Not until 1912 K. Glossy published *Literarische Geheimberichte aus dem Vormärz,* which afford a depressing panorama of varied and intimate supervision.

It is against this backdrop of public and secret institutions — the very conspicuous Diet in Frankfurt as the federal legislative body, the supposedly omniscient and all-powerful Metternich in Vienna, and the really omnipresent and invisible system of Confidants at all publishing centers — that we must view the struggles of the press toward liberty of expression. Few of Baron Cotta's adjutants understood as well as he that victories have to bought by sacrifices, and that in politics the lasting improvements have all begun with compromises.

The most promising of the young talents which he attracted to his newspapers were Börne, Menzel, and Heine. If politics can be comical, here we find ourselves in a world of low comedy. It is difficult to find the right tone for discussing it; perhaps it is best to speak in no tone at all and let only the facts speak.

After Ludwig Börne had made a name for himself in journals of his own (in Frankfurt), he offered his services to Cotta, who promptly put him on his payroll, but sent a warning in his first letter (November 2, 1819): 'Now it would be very important that the essays and communications be written with all possible caution. One may say anything — as long as the proper moderation is applied.' Börne justified one hope of Cotta; he developed a mastery of veiled satire. But he was a lazy and desultory worker, he did not deliver what he was paid for. And when the time came to publish his *Collected Writings,* which might have reimbursed Cotta, Börne found a different publisher, Campe in Hamburg.

He promised his new publisher eight little volumes; but he found it difficult to fill the eighth one. All the time he was writing long letters from Paris to a dear friend in Frankfurt. Now it was this Mrs. Wohl who had the saving idea. 'If you only knew how fine your letters are! Every single one, if printed, would stir up a general interest!' (November 12, 1830). She persuaded him to let her edit his letters, he should only keep on writing them. This is the origin of Börne's best-known work, the *Briefe aus Paris* (1832-34). They breathe a new spirit. Börne, with many liberals, thought that the Paris revolution of 1830 was the turn of the tide in Europe, the beginning of a liberal era. Therefore he was much more outspoken now in his criticism of German conditions. The *Letters* were thought so dangerous that they were banned in one German state after another. But the volumes continued to appear under disguised names and made Börne the most popular author of liberalism. Not a little of this reputation was due to his stature as a political martyr. That was partly legend, a sentimental need of his German admirers who did not care to know that Börne enjoyed a modest pension from the city of Frankfurt and a sufficient fortune inherited from his father, a banker; and that he left France whenever he pleased and lived in Paris because he liked it. However, the man could not have been so universally respected without good reason. Besides, he was a perfect representative of the young political literature: satirical, witty, incapable of actual literary 'works,' satisfied with miscellaneous 'writings.'

When Börne observed the quick advancement of French writers like Thiers and Mignet, he remarked, 'It is just as if Heine had become a state-secretary, or Menzel, or I.' (November 3, 1830.) This Wolfgang Menzel deserved to be mentioned in one breath with the two other stars of liberal journalism, although he had a very different background. His ideals owed little to the French revolutions and much to the 'Deutsche Burschenschaft,' the national federation of student fraternities, which had the honor of the longest persecution by the governments. As soon as that started, Menzel emigrated to Switzerland. 'Whatever I might have attempted in Prussia' (he says in his *Memoirs*), 'the political servility there . . . would have spoiled any activity. If I had stayed, ten to one I would have had to emigrate later.' He never went back to his homeland Prussia, but six years later he began to work for Cotta in Stuttgart.

As Cotta found in him a more reliable helper than in either Börne or Heine, ne promptly left to him the direction of the *Literaturblatt*. His more historical writings were several times banned by order of the Diet. But as a literary critic he was almost uncontested. He wrote the first German literary history that was coordinated by one viewpoint, unfortunately that of national progress. It was the most frequently translated history of German literature for a long time. In contrast to the retiring Börne and to Heine, who had the talent of making enemies, Menzel seemed to know everybody and to have innumerable friends. He was always fair to Börne and was quick to greet the *Letters* publicly: ' His noble anger inspires high respect in any patriot. . . . But the detail of Börne's satire is only too well justified.'

Of Heinrich Heine, on the other hand, Menzel spoke at best with condescension, since he had known him in the Burschenschaft at Bonn, where Heine had cut a sorry figure, whereas Menzel had been the leader. Meanwhile Heine had become the prominent essayist (*Reisebilder,* 1826), as well as the prominent poet (*Buch der Lieder,* 1827). In 1828 he edited for Cotta the *Politische Annalen* in Munich. Now he became very chummy with his fellow editor: ' O Menzel, our own contributions excepted, how boring is the content of the Annals! ' When the 1830 Revolution came, Heine kept frantically looking for a position in Germany. He claimed he ' hurried to Paris ' like Börne, it took him half a year longer to get there. But he was quicker than Börne in furnishing Cotta's newspapers with his impressions. His articles on ' Conditions in France ' appeared till September 1832. In 1833 he published them as a book, provided with a vitriolic preface. ' This preface will perhaps forever prevent my return to Germany, but perhaps it will save me from swinging from a lantern at the next rebellion. It disarms villains like Börne and his sort.' Heine had come to find his fellow democrats worse poison than the German Diet.

He never realized how unreliable he appeared to others; but he fully realized his own importance and told it to any correspondent without the slightest byplay. ' Literature, that's ourselves and our enemies ' (to Immermann, December 19, 1832). He would have defined poltics the same way: it's just those for Heinrich Heine and against him. With another friend, Heinrich Laube, we come to the younger generation of ' Young Germany.'

Although ' Young Germany ' was the entire new movement of the thirties, we can single out only two exponents, Laube from Silesia and Karl Gutzkow from Berlin. Laube was a hearty Burschenschaft student like Menzel, but he found his ideal in Heine and was one of the few who adhered to him to the end. Gutzkow was a scholar, critic, and misanthrope like Börne, but at first he associated himself with the large-hearted Menzel.

The young men opened a rapid fire of small and larger arms, and their innumerable articles and yearly volumes of books stirred the quick approval of their three patron saints and the slow suspicion of the guardians of law and order. Laube made himself more obnoxious by loud partisanship for the insurgent Poles. Gutzkow offended more by attacks on Protestant orthodoxy. Their books began to be banned in several states — which only stimulated the book agents of the other little states. The Young Germans founded publishing houses, threatened to have new and big journals all to themselves.

If we look for the drop that made the cup overflow, we probably find it in the 'Saint-Simonian religion.' This newest import from France, with its 'emancipation of the flesh,' was too much for the more virtuous wing of the Young German party, led by Menzel. Jealous of his pupil Gutzkow, who was quickly outgrowing him, Menzel raised a cry of indignation at the immorality of the new school (*Literaturblatt*, September 11, 1835). And whereas before one or other German state had banned one or the other Young German book, at the cry of immorality the Federal Diet unanimously banned *all* Young German books, this 'wicked, anti-Christian, blasphemous literature, which deliberately tramples everything moral, chaste and decent' (December 10, 1835). The edict was not a screen for political persecution, as has so often been claimed: the political minds of the movement, Cotta, Menzel, and above all Börne, were notoriously ignored. Gutzkow, Laube, and two close collaborators were singled out; but the name of their professor in profanity had nearly been omitted, when Metternich reminded the Diet to put first things first. Then they placed Heine's name on top of the four.

They became very uneasy about their extremism. None of them wanted to have much to do with the others. Gutzkow challenged a few of them to duels. Menzel answered: Nonsense! these quarrels are just literary. Heine proved his importance by writing to the exalted Diet itself: 'My writings have not sprung from irreligious and immoral whims, but from a truly religious and moral synthesis.' At the same time he wrote to Campe, the publisher of the new school: 'Confident of not having written anything against the governments for four years, of having notoriously seceded from Jacobinism, in short with a good loyal and royal conscience, I will not be so cowardly as to disown the young men who are politically innocent.' (January 15, 1836).

Heine was only following advice which he himself had given Laube on November 3, 1835: 'Make a distinction between political and religious questions. In political questions you may make as many concessions as you wish, for political forms and governments are only means. . . . A later thing is the question, through what means the idea of life can be realized, through monarchy or republic or aristocracy, or even through totalitarianism (for which I have no great aversion).' Heine's advice contained more than clever tactics. It was simply truth that Young Germany was politically harmless. Also only Laube actually suffered hardship; only Gutzkow was put on trial. He defended himself well, and was sentenced to four weeks in prison (during which he wrote another book).

One man, perhaps, judged the Young German comedy more

detachedly than Heine. Grillparzer's judgment, in his diary, was prompt and comprehensive. ' One has felt obliged to exterminate the nuisance of the ' Young Literature ' by an express ban of the incriminated writings. Any such ban is objectionable, and in the human and literary respect it is a mistake and harmful. . . . Of course this young literature is nonsense and even madness. But by what should the old madness be fought if not by a new one? . . . The new mediocrity is always better than the old. . . . Besides, this young school has at least one good quality which is lacking in Germany at present: an uncouth honesty. . . . It says what it means, whereas mostly in Germany they mean nothing by what they say. . . . If we only let nature undisturbedly exert itself in its contrasts, the evils would soon find their cure in one another. From nonsense to nonsense civilization proceeds, and in the perpetual zigzag it perpetually progresses a little.'

The Dramas of Büchner

When the thunder of the Federal Diet called attention to the writings of Young Germany, Laube was twenty-nine years old, Gutzkow twenty-four. An even younger man, of twenty-two, would have deserved the sensational attention; but it did not come to Georg Büchner before the twentieth century. His was a much more political mind. He had tried to incite the peasant population of his native Hessen to actual revolution. He had the clairvoyance to realize that the era of liberal-political reforms was drawing to a close, and that radical social upheaval was waiting its turn. ' The opposition between poor and rich is the only revolutionary element in the world. Hunger alone can be the goddess of freedom. Feed the peasants, and revolution will die of a stroke.' (To Gutzkow, probably in 1835.)

However this young man, who was able to anticipate the fanatical logic of socialism, was not narrow enough to be a fanatic. Out of his disappointment with the impossibility of social action in his time grew a most disillusioned political drama, *Danton's Death*. While the Hessian conspiracy was being unearthed by the police, the student, rightly suspected, kept away from the university. He spent half a year in his home town (Darmstadt) and there, in the house of his parents, he suddenly laid aside his medical studies and, without any previous literary attempts, wrote ' in five weeks ' the oddest masterpiece among German dramas.

He offered the hasty product immediately to Gutzkow — hoping for some money to finance his flight into France. Gutzkow promptly recommended it to his publisher, but Büchner had as promptly fled to Strasburg. The drama was soon published, but Gutzkow remained almost its sole champion during the next few years. Gutzkow also said some of the undeniable truths about the precocious masterpiece.

His (or rather the publisher's) first condition had been that half the brothel witticisms which adorned every page be cut out. In the necrologue (which came due only two years later) Gutzkow said handsomely: 'Grudging the censor the satisfaction of cutting, I assumed that office myself and pruned the luxuriant democracy of the work with the shears of pre-censorship. But the refuse of the book, which had to be sacrificed to our conventions, was the best, most individual and most original part of the whole.' This is exaggeration, but the medic-student jokes do color the speeches of almost all the men in the play, high and low. They are the chief means of debunking all those revolutionary heroes. They were also the first thing which the author defended, in a letter to his family: 'I could not make paragons of Danton and the bandits of revolution! If I wanted to show their licence, I had to let them be libertines.' And he did so with gusto; it cost his imagination no effort to catch those heroes with their pants down.

The drama has, quantitatively, a quite different interest. Historical truth is carried so far that many passages (one-sixth of the text, according to Vietor) are literally transcribed from a then popular German history of the revolutionary epoch or directly translated from Thiers. Again it was Gutzkow who clearly formulated the danger in this, when he wrote to the author (June 10, 1836): 'Your *Danton* was no hit; perhaps you don't know the reason? Because you did *not* cheat history . . . and people forgot that there was more issuing from you than from history; so they judged it a dramatized chapter of Thiers.' This may indeed have been the main reason for the neglect of Büchner's *Danton* in the nineteenth century. People found the historians much more interesting than the dramatist. They knew the stories of the revolution too well not to recognize the genuine sayings. There was such a hard core of historical identity, that the arabesques which Büchner had woven around it looked insignificant. The great Revolution was, for a century, the object of either admiration (by all the Young Germans for instance) or of abhorrence (by all the reactionaries). There were many Germans who were split between the *two* sentiments; but there were few who could sympathize with Büchner's intimate indifference, a callousness grown out of familiarity, an unsentimentality which was only a passion grown over-ripe.

Büchner describes the last two weeks of Danton, the climax of the Terror, associated with the end of the man who had invented the Terror. By the instinct of genius he hit the tone in which it is possible to relate such extreme human experience: an ostensibly unpathetic, unrhetorical tone, insisting on nothing, alluding to everything. Instead of heightening the exciting events by an artful arrangement, Büchner neutralizes them by an alternation of serious and comic scenes. He distributes our sympathies instead of focussing them. He works as hard at the bloody logic of Robespierre and St. Just as at the sated scepticism of Danton and Desmoulins. He refuses to take advantage of the acquired momentum. Thus the entire drama is anticlimactic. Gutzkow justly said in his first review, ' in Büchner's drama there is more life than action.' It is indeed full of life, because Büchner was young enough to believe in realism without reservations. It is indeed poor in action, and when its time finally came on the German stage (after 1913), the great directors *added* things which were not essential to Büchner's work : Reinhardt added the political paroxysm of the crowd scenes, Falckenberg the expressionistic anti-realism, Gründgens ecstatic allegory (I. Strudthoff). After 1933 a reaction set in towards a more sober presentation of the many-facetted, counterpoised composition.

In the two years between the writings of *Danton* and his own death, Büchner wrote several other works, all with the encouragement of the enterprising Gutzkow. One of them cannot be passed over, his other tragedy, *Woyzeck*. Gutzkow was not able to decipher it, Büchner's brother was not able to decipher it; it was published forty years later, unsatisfactorily; and the manuscript has turned illegible. Büchner wrote the scenes down as they occurred to him, not in the sequence they were definitely to have. If *Danton's* structure is decidedly loose, the structure of *Woyzeck* is simply floating. We may imagine any arrangement we like.

This masterpiece of indetermination contains the finest Büchner. It has the saddest subject : the effort of a demented proletarian to keep things from getting worse, his mind from slipping, and himself from killing his sweetheart. But even that little is saying too much, there is no effort in all this, it just happens. Gustily the scenes drift by, with the lightness of clouds. There is no effort of the author either. With a very light hand he sets a stroke of color here, another stroke there, until the impression emanates, and we complete it in our minds.

It is as if we were not reading a book in a reasonable way, but as if we let the wind leaf through it, and we were reading wherever it opens. Indeed this is the way Woyzeck's sweetheart reads in the Bible : she leafs through it so that distant chapters move close to each other and make one indistinguishable sense. We cannot even distinguish whether there is a condemnation of the middle-class, although the doctor is satirized more certainly than other persons. Büchner was just getting his Doctor of Medicine. That is just like all the rest; the joke is on all human beings, woe is on some more than on others. And this is the only thing of which we feel sure : we are in the presence of a comprehensive compassion, which is still less vast than it is fine and light; not massive but quick, less resounding than responsive. It is veiled in poetry and witticism, both of so little density that it almost depends on our mood whether we admit their presence. There is probably no tragedy, for there is no will. If we try the word fatalism, we shrink from all the definiteness which it has acquired from other obviously more fitting applications. If we are ready to settle for nihilism, we shy at the weight of conviction which it carries. For where has there been a fatalism so suspicious, or a nihilism so poetic?

No doubt, Büchner's main value is the novelty of his approach: his freedom from former aesthetic habits, his non-attachment to any former ideal, any former conviction. That is why his art seemed so weightless that it made almost no impression in his time and was appreciated only when the 'unweighted' itself had become an ideal, that is through and after Impressionism. It is a question, however, whether this would have been Büchner's self-interpretation. It is more likely that he felt a dynamics there which we are unable to sense: a positive rejection of tradition, a shaking of fetters, a breaking of habits, a secession from idealism. At any rate, he was most unreservedly praised by those who saw in him the comrade-in-arms in the anti-bourgeois revolt of the masses, the herald of socialism, the precursor of communism. Should not his own time have seen in him those flares of the future? No, he was indistinguishable to it, because he wore its own colors, the colors of a dying Weltanschauung, of the endform of idealism, of a transition which amounted to a mere loss. To those who have occupied themselves with him intensively, he seems to hover almost indifferently between the positive and the negative interpretation, in a fine though unstable equilibrium.

The Persecuted

From Büchner's solo we must turn again to the brassier choir, whose din filled the literary news of the time. Then it all seemed full of promise and progress; but at this distance it makes the impression of a fatuous political farce. Once again we let its actors and their actions speak for themselves.

At the time when the precocious genius of Büchner failed to arouse any attention with his *Danton,* and when the other Young Germans aroused too much for their peace, the titular head of the school published his enlarged *Romantische Schule*. Heine began the newly added pages with an advertisement that was as benevolent as it was acute: 'The writers of the present Young Germany do not want to make a difference between living and writing; they separate by no means politics from science, art and religion; they are at the same time artists, tribunes and apostles. . . . A new faith animates them, the faith in progress. . . . I have mentioned the name of Heinrich Laube, for how could I speak of Young Germany without thinking of the big fiery heart which shines forth among them most splendidly. . . . In Karl Gutzkow too I must acknowledge the finest qualities of creative force and critical sense, his writings too gladden me by the right grasp of our time and its needs.'

To be sure, this was written before the storm had broken. Afterwards, Heine was the first to disclaim political tendencies. But his next move was to make the most of the publicity. He harped on the phrase, 'One has condemned five authors to a literary death.' The condemnation by censorship was executed in the following way. Some (southern) states did not accept the federal ban at all. Prussia (the instigator) took it most seriously — for three months. Then it modified the 'perpetual' ban into the authors' submission to Prussian censorship. Thus the Young German works were hardly worse off than others. Indeed, four volumes by Gutzkow bear as publication date the very next year, 1836. Laube was less prolific (only three volumes) because his sentence had not been passed. Finally he was condemned to one year of imprisonment for his literary sins plus six years for his Burschenschaft activity. As that too patriotic activity lay far behind, a year meant a month in the then current practice; the six years shrank to six months. The lesser but fresher sin, however, had to be expiated more fully. How was the total penalty paid? Prince Pückler-Muskau, a fellow-liberal, was allowed to invite the newly-wed Laubes to his castle in the famous park of Muskau, and there they spent the eighteen months (!), he editing, writing and studying.

Even less productive was Heine (himself tempestuously newly-wed, in a sense) who in 1836 published a poem now and then in *Mitternachtszeitung* and 'Florentinische Nächte' in *Morgenblatt*. But it was only the year 1837 which saw the publication of four new volumes by Heine. While the younger authors tried to understand (literary criticism was their main interest now), Heine tried to misunderstand. He knew very well that what hampered him in reality was an *old* ban, existing since 1832, of his more subversive writings, but he pretended publicly that he was the special target of the new ban of 1835. In a missive to the *Allgemeine Zeitung* of Augsburg (April 26, 1836) he claims: 'They issue the strictest bans of my future writings. Thus I lose my fortune, which consists in the exploitation of my works.' In the same article, he admits that Prussia has just re-released his writings, provided they are censored. But he cannot submit to censorship. 'One would think that I sacrifice my political opinion in order to calm the Berlin censorship . . . and that I sold myself to the Prussian interests for my own money.'

Heine was so touchy because he had a great secret to hide. He had just sold himself (that was the way his enemies put it, when it was discovered twelve years later) to the French interests. He had applied — well before the federal ban of 1835 — to the French government for a stipend, and he was just beginning to draw it. But his public indignation was not quite artificial; there really was a difference. When he sounded less cynical as to the French government thereafter, at least he was getting 4,800 francs per year. If he became more polite towards the Prussian government, he would only get back the sale of his own books, ' his own money.'

Heine was desperate. One ' Confidant ' got the impression that ' he would buy his return on any terms.' In June 1836 we have (a trace only of) that incredible letter to Metternich where ' he implores Prince Metternich to be generous, as it behooves the victor . . . he implores him to receive him and pull him out of his misery.' But Metternich was of the opinion that ' Heine's dangerousness stands in no relation to the monetary sacrifice that would have to be made to win and to keep him.' In 1838 (February 12) Heine wrote to Varnhagen to reconcile him with the Prussian government. ' I am no enthusiast for German constitutionalism. Only not to lose my popularity with the liberal mass I have not heartily pronounced against the constitutional monkey business. . . . I will take my news of Prussia only from newspapers which have passed the Prussian censorship. . . . In the selection of my correspondents I will never risk the displeasure of the government.'

But it was not the edict of the Diet which threatened a literary kill of Heine. Rather it was Campe, who was the publisher of the left-wing liberals just as Cotta was that of their right wing. But Campe had a weakness for seeing his own authors belittling each other, ' to keep the trees from growing to the sky.' He enjoyed telling them they sold poorly and paying them poorly. All of Heine's bragging that he was the best horse in Campe's stable did not get him an extra allowance of fodder. Now Heine was, for unexplained causes, in debt for 20,000 francs. So he sold the rights to all his works for eleven years to Campe for the same sum of 20,000 francs. On the side of Campe, that came close to extortion. We realize how little the sum was when we compare it to the 10,000 francs which Heine needed yearly as a minimum, and of which he got half from the French government and half from his millionaire uncle.

His works degenerated into a series of personal feuds. The first was the pamphlet against Menzel, ' The Informer.' Everybody knew that Menzel's attack had been in the form of public articles in the *Literaturzeitung,* but Heine's jokes are good enough to associate the name of Menzel with the idea of an ' informer ' for good. Börne had again anticipated Heine and issued his own *Menzel the Frenchman-Eater* earlier, although it was much weightier. Just as ' Börne's *Letters from Paris* were far more epoch-making than Heine's *Französiche*

Zustände' (E. M. Butler), so Börne's book against Menzel was the more impressive, indeed it became Börne's political testament. When he died, he left many mourners, all over Germany — the first to write a book of homage was a Confidant of Metternich's institution (E. Beurmann) — and left only one notable enemy, Heine. Börne had been the first to suspect Heine's unreliability, also the first to satirize Heine's enraptured self-dramatization. After several minor polemics, Heine turned his wit on the dead Börne (*Ludwig Börne,* 1840), and this time a major caricature resulted, by a genius of caricature. Heine could not help putting as much of himself into the book as of Börne. Much of Börne's wit is there, generously; and all of Heine's wit, maliciously. Also much of Heine's bad taste: not able to find enough good jokes by and on Börne, he invented a battery of bad ones against a fine woman, who had been the angel of Börne's life. Heine never understood why this incisive and engrossing book was found detestable by all contemporaries. All the liberals fell out with him, and most of the Young Germans. With Gutzkow there was open warfare, and almost with Campe himself, the publisher of them all. Heine even had to fight a duel with the husband of the libelled lady. Too much public attention finally forced the reluctant fighters to it, after a year's delay. Börne had been dead for four years, and the wrath of the contemporaries subsided. But they would not have found believable that a century and a half later Börne would be alive mainly because Heine wrote a wickedly spirited book about him.

We have listened to confusing stories of the Young German contestants themselves. It may not be amiss to hear a word from one casual observer. In the last year of Börne's life, Grillparzer happened to travel to Paris, and of course he paid the two famous Germans there several visits. His diary records the impressions. ' I am glad that Börne has enough to live on, or he would be badly off with all these censor's bans. . . . Two German exiles joined us. . . . I wondered why such an intelligent man keeps rolling in movements which have lost their last chance and thus their object. . . . I bet they are honest men, whether inspired or deluded. . . . Börne apparently did not like the political talk, either because he does not quite trust me, or because he does not take me seriously, since I made my moderate views plain at the outset.' (April 20, 1836) ' Finally found out Heine's address. When I rang, a handsome fat young man in house coat opened. . . . Mad household: he lives with one or two grisettes, of which he pointed out one (not very pretty) as his ' petite.' And he is indeed a picture of life and vitality with his broad neck. He made a very agreeable impression. . . . We soon talked literature, found we had much the same sympathies and antipathies. I had the rare pleasure of finding common sense in a German author. . . . He does not want to have anything to do with ultraliberalism and speaks with contempt of the German refugees. Is on bad terms with Börne.' (April 27, 1836)

Although there is another, more extensive, entry on Börne, it remains clear that Heine made the livelier impression. Therefore it comes as a little surprise that fifteen years later, in the retrospect of his *Autobiography,* the proportion should be so clearly reversed. 'With Börne something like a friendship developed.' And he imputes to Börne almost the stoicism which he himself showed in political things: 'He probably thought the Germans so thick skinned that he had to beat them with sticks to make any impression at all. He believed he could never disturb the peace of Germany, if he indulged humoristically in his hatred of tyrants.' In his recollection of Heine, he puts his finger on the impermanence: 'He said much that was flattering to me (which he probably didn't remember an hour later); but for that hour we conversed with great gusto. I have hardly ever heard a German author talk with more sense.' Then he goes on to tell that he disliked only Heine's behaviour to others, his using them and mocking them at the same time. 'And that is why our acquaintance was not continued' — a sentence characteristic of Grillparzer, but applicable to many just men, in their relation to Heine.

The Novels of Sealsfield

When Grillparzer remembers Börne and Heine in the *Autobiography* he is still surprised that they thought more of German literature than he did. He tells what is wrong with it: 'It lacks vitality and character. When I read a book, I want to meet a personality. . . . But they rob their subject of its original pith and abstract it into opinions.' Grillparzer regrets the lack or the loss of substance.

In no other genre is this lack as noticeable as in the German novel of the nineteenth century. Foreign literatures were hospitable until the middle of the century, and many German novels were translated. None of them kept alive, none joined the ranks of world literature. Even in Germany, the popular demand favored foreign novelists, as Börne stated summarily (in a review of Cooper's novels): 'Novels are written by the English, and read by the Germans.' It was just in the field of the novel that the Young Germans had their most crashing fiasco, because their bid had been such a big one.

From 1833 to 1837 there appeared, in Zürich, nine novels by an unknown, who simply identified himself, after the first novel, as the author of 'Der Legitime und die Republikaner.' In that novel the 'legitimate' had meant the aboriginal American Indian, the 'republicans' had meant the American settlers. From the second novel the readers mostly identified the author as 'the Transatlantic Unknown.' All novels treated American themes, from fashionable life in New

York to the recent Mexican revolution. The German novel seemed to have found a new substance.

As the journalists of Young Germany oriented their ideas towards revolutionary France, so the unknown novelist preached American democracy. This was not mere imaginary exoticism for Germany, it was a concrete outlet. America as an eventual escape was tried by thousands, as a possible last resort it was in the minds of millions. There was virgin soil, there were for a long time expanding frontiers, and there was a young democratic state. It had occupied the imagination of fiction readers since the twenties, when Cooper's novels had become more popular in Germany than in his homeland. But here was more than Cooper, thought the readers of the Transatlantic Unknown. (This opinion was so official that the article on Cooper in Brockhaus' *Conversations-Lexikon,* 1843, adds the supererogatory remark: 'While Cooper has merits as a painter of American conditions, here too he is far surpassed by the lifelike pictures of the author of "Transatlantic Sketches".') Cooper seemed tame both in his themes and in his presentation. The Unknown always found a new border, where he could let American civilization advance, in the swamps of Louisiana, in the Spanish Southwest, in the assimilation of immigrant elements, in the commerce and exchange with Europe, in the financial capitals of Europe itself. And although the assertion of freedom was in every chapter, there was no propaganda, there was indiscriminate objectivity, which liked to paint the bad with the good, as long as both were full of life. The public was even taken in by the hybrid form, 'the Great Unknown's pretense of writing in an adopted [German] idiom: The bold experiment of transposing the foreign scene by means of an artificial language, outwardly German and inwardly English, stands justified, for it is generally acknowledged that in Sealsfield's fiction the America of his period is faithfully transcribed, the *genius loci* of its principal theaters — the western frontier, the slaveholding South, the East with its rough-and-tumble politics and its sophisticated and pretentious high life — adroitly seized.' (Otto Heller)

What made the new novels such a high bid for the great novel was the unique form which seemed to put the stamp of genuineness on the new substance. Besides the fantastic international jargon, there was the greatest freedom of organization. There was no convention of the novel, everything was sketch, experiment, impression. There was no line of development, everything was blotches of color. There were no proportions of the parts, no coordination of effects, everything was distorted and exaggerated at the whim of the bungling author. If this was realism — as the amazed contemporaries called it — it was a fantastic realism, consisting of fantastic descriptions, fantastic dialogues, and fantastic grimaces. The faces and bodies of these people are in continual convulsions. The physiological and physiognomic attention of the author is so insatiable that he endows his victims with the endless capability and the eternal condemnation of physical self-expression — unless he needs them as the contrasting pillars of equally grotesque imperturbability. Everything works by reiteration and cumulation. But the strange thing is that, in spite of such primitive quantitative means, he achieves — in every volume — areas of sheer intensity, where his theme and his technique, his obsessions and his very shortcomings coalesce into a crude and boisterous fulfilment. Things like the behaviour of 'Nathan, the First Squatter in Texas,' or the description of 'The Jacinto Prairie.' have rightly remained famous to this day. A collector as exacting as Hofmannsthal asserts: 'I could not omit him, he narrates in a way that no one forgets who has once listened to him.'

How much the more were the Young Germans stunned by this Unknown, who had blundered into succeeding with everything they had ever tried: write the great new novel, preach the great new liberties, be permitted to be read everywhere, and be popular to boot. They were trying so hard to catch the public eye; but he was sensational by anonymity. Laube made a good guess (1835) when he surmised that the 'New Unknown' (Scott was the old Unknown) was perhaps only a Swiss returned from the United States. Gutzkow felt sure it was the other way around. Only an American could credit high finance with such powers as Sealsfield did. The publishers claimed that his first novel was translated from the American. Oddly enough, it was the truth. Of *Tokeah, or The White Rose* the (Philadelphia) *National Gazette* had said at its appearance (1829): 'The novel we have named is purely American, and we venture to say that in the delineation of Indian character . . . it has been seldom equalled.' The publishers however were far from knowing the whole truth. They did not know that before *Tokeah* its author had published three other books in English, and of the first two, about the United States, the *North American Review* had written: 'We have not seen a more correct view of 'the western people,' and also of Mississippi and Louisiana, than is here presented.' At that time American and English reviews thought the questionable English was intentional, to suit the author's *pretence* of being visitor. 'That a German ever wrote such English as this we neither believe nor believe possible.' Likewise the English claimed him for his sensational book *Austria as It Is*. *Meyer's British Chronicle* insisted: 'The author's manner of reasoning is too much of John Bull's to admit the slightest doubt of his birthright. . . . John Bull's fatherhood is testified by every sentiment and every line.' The *Monthly Review* too found weighty proofs of his Britishness, considering that he was able 'not only to think, but to write, like a John

Bull. We do not mean as to his style, which frequently betrays an alien hand; but as to the freedom and the unprejudiced intelligence with which he delivers his remarks on every subject.' Sealsfield remained all his life unidentified with the author of these once-notorious books. And when he had the weakness to admit that he had also been the editor of a French journal, not even his biographers believed him. He was proven correct only in our time (K. J. Arndt). Some parts of his mysterious biography have not been sufficiently elucidated even today.

For a short time the American public actually seemed to put their stamp of approval on Sealsfield's works. It was after a mouthpiece of the Young Germans had hailed him as 'The Greatest American Author' that condensations and book-length translations came out in England and America. Several dozens have been identified for the years 1842-52. *The Cabin Book* or *Sketches of Life in Texas* was an especial favorite and was reissued till 1871. At the height of his popularity, in 1847, no less than Longfellow attests to have been inspired for part of *Evangeline* by 'our favorite Sealsfield.' But it happened soon after that, 'in the era of "elegant" writing that followed . . . the glaring impurities of his prose . . . could not but make it abhorrent to the cultivated reader. . . . The Great Unknown of the thirties and forties became for many decades simply an unknown.' (O. Heller)

If Sealsfield has been forgotten in America and has had only sporadic revivals in Germany, he owes it to the very qualities which made him the top novelist of the Young German era: the lack of self-limitation, the chameleon-like adaptability. Grillparzer said he wanted to meet a personality (' will mit jemand zu tun haben ') when he read a book. Nobody ever had to do with Sealsfield himself. He had made masquerade and mystification his very character. Only posthumously (he died in 1864) did he reveal that he was an Austrian monk who escaped from monastery and Austria in 1823, at the age of thirty. After a century of research his activities have been pieced together. During his first three years' stay in the United States he established contact with the publisher Cotta, who also published his first book, *Die Vereinigten Staaten* (1827). But in 1826, back in Europe, his first documented contact was with Prince Metternich, to whom he offered himself as a secret agent, 'because people would not mistrust him, as an American.' It was Metternich who did not trust him, and Sealsfield prepared his slashing attack on *Austria as It Is* (London, 1828). On his return to the United States he considered himself a correspondent of Cotta at first, but next tried novel writing in English. Then he was a journalist for the Bonapartes. In their service (probably) he went to England, then to Switzerland, where the German reworking of his

English *Tokeah* in 1833 finally started the gush of his successful novels. Notwithstanding, back in the United States in 1837, he could not resist offering his secret services to the Secretary of War. Retreating to Switzerland, he wrote his best books, now published under the name of Sealsfield, from 1839 to 43. Why nothing new was published after that has not been fully explained. Perhaps the public at large could not warm up to the author — just as no person ever seems to have been close to the man. None of the women to whom he proposed trusted him enough to marry him. Even when he was well-to-do, he surrounded himself with a palpable web of pretences. His books do not suspend our disbelief, as novels must. He never learned that reality is exclusive : it does not admit of two things in the same place. In Sealsfield's novels we often have the impression that reality keeps changing its mind, it keeps pretending it is still possibility.

His exasperatingly uneven works are worst when they occupy themselves with human truth. They are best when they concentrate on the inhuman, ' the poetry of wilderness ' which his contemporaries praised. There is not enough substance in them to amount to true novels. The best of them make us regret that the author did not conceive them as novelettes. It was the very opposite when he conceived them as ' sketches.' He never learned that the *promises* which any form holds, even the free form of narrative, are *binding*. In his autobiographical sketch (1854, for the next edition of the *Konversations-Lexikon*) he considered all his major works as one ' plan . . . to picture the public life of America in sketches which, although loosely connected, would form one whole.' The plan was of the most promising, and even in the execution there are traces of genius. Sealsfield's knack of finding everywhere sharply contrasted *national* characters which he lets collide or co-operate makes him the (later disowned) father of the international novel. It was also the happiest of inspirations to settle on America as his great theme. The greatest novels have discovered new worlds, not only technically, by a new treatment, but also substantially, by a new subject-matter. That is why the Young Germans were so nearly right when they expected the great novel from the unknown who had discovered the most timely subject-matter, the New World itself. ' He stands out . . . among protagonists of realistic narration . . . by the permeation of all his work with a profound and loving understanding of the New World which makes him in truth a poet and apostle of American Democracy.' (O. Heller)

Grillparzer would have been skeptical of the literary merit of that point, because he was convinced that any occupation with politics, good or bad, could only be detrimental to literature. Indeed, it was as political exponents that the Young Germans were soon forgotten, Börne and Menzel the soonest. The rest of German literature, however, did not forsake politics, at least not for a while. If the thirties had been the decade of political journalism, the forties were the decade of 'political lyrics,' and the most popular writers of the time gained their popularity in that genre. We shall not follow the popular taste of the time but heed the grumbling of incorrigible Grillparzer, who hated German political conditions no more than he did German political lyrics. He prayed that God have pity and grant the Germans political liberty, if only to free them of political literature :

> O Gott ! lass dich herbei
> und mach die Deutschen frei,
> dass endlich das Geschrei
> darnach zu Ende sei.
>
> (1847)

III

Old Germany

The Patriarch of Swiss Fiction

In 1841 there appeared in Zürich an unpretentious novel, *Uli der Knecht,* written by a pastor from Berne under the name of Gotthelf. The work got quickly known beyond the borders of Switzerland. When ten years later Taillandier, the chronicler of German literature in the *Revue des Deux Mondes* introduced Gotthelf to his French readers in a long article, he greeted him with this explicit salute: ' In the midst of the moral anarchy of Europe . . . it is a stroke of good fortune for the critic to be able to point to a symptom of resistance.' The discerning French critic pointed in his very first line to the driving force behind all of Gotthelf's fiction: it was the first voice in the rising resistance movement. Resistance against what? The encroachments of ' moral anarchy.' In the thirties the field had belonged, to all appearances, to the propagandists of ' modern ' amorality. The opposing front formed slowly and rather inconspicuously in the forties. Tailandier's next page has this surprising sentence on Gotthelf and Germany: ' He sent back to that country, instead of its glum sad gifts, some of the inspirations of the Germany of old.'

In purpose or pretention Gotthelf's fiction is at the antipodes of his ' great unknown ' contemporary. While Sealsfield's novels were the substitute for participation in international politics, the village pastor's books were moral treatises aimed at his most immediate and local surroundings. They were meant as farmers' literature, even as ' Dienstbotenliteratur,' servants' literature. Gotthelf wanted to give something to read to those who did not read. That is why he combined a stupendous variety of methods with a subject-matter of the farm-servants' concern. It is claimed that he achieved his purpose, that *Uli* was read ' in every farmhouse ' in Switzerland. We only know that a different audience, those who are worn out by much reading, revive when they chance upon his books.

Uli the Farmhand starts out as a series of sermons which a good farmer gives to his reluctant and distrustful farmhand. The circumstances which induce master and servant to their uneven exchanges are observed with a loving accuracy, which should have given away the novelist's secret from the start: here was a writer who, no matter how sincerely he believed in his lessons, liked the stories in which he clothed them even more. The wild young hero has little to recommend him but his physique; but to his master as well as to his author this seems enough justification to waste on him a patient effort of good offices. The doings in the fields, in the stables, and especially in the kitchens are of the most trivial kind. But soon we notice that they are caught with such a curious eye and infallible ear that we abandon ourselves to them as if they were full of suspense. Indeed, the author invents so many retardations and reverses to the moral regeneration of the young rascal, and motivates that regeneration so plainly by economic emancipation, that we do not know, whether we are more edified, more convinced, or more amused. The story delights in showing, doggedly, that the good is always one's own good, that a wholesome determination always attracts good luck and good friends, and that the will to be a good man, immediately, creates a mental climate fit to live in and, ultimately, creates all the chances for success.

And so the story of Uli becomes the most plodding, most cumbersome success story ever told. We get less and less interested in the success and more and more delighted with its intermediary stages. After the first hundred pages we have been made to feel that the central group of characters are simply in a state of grace, physical, mental and spiritual; and that it is fitting, it is just, it is salutary for us to walk with them through the coarse and sly adventures of their everyday.

The novels of Gotthelf have a heaven stretching over them openly and almost palpably. The patriarchal manners, lived so patently in the face of the Lord, have given many a reader the sensation of living in the Bible. Yet that heaven is so very Protestant, so plainly in accord with every rational behavior, even with every principle of economy, that one cannot but call it a down-to-earth heaven, which recommends itself more by its tenacious roots in the ground than by its lofty elevation. As it is difficult to illustrate something as far-stretched as this heaven, we take recourse to the first epiphany of the real angel of the Uli volumes. We are a good third of the way in *Uli*. After ten years of well-guided foolishness and good will, Uli has got himself 'a good name,' and he becomes foreman at a big but god-forsaken farm. It is in the first dismal hour there that he has his first glimpse of Vreneli. Lots of females have appeared in the story before; none got more than a passing look from the author. Hence our surprise at the following close-up. 'Outside he found a bright and pretty girl, nutbrown her hair and eyes, red and white her cheeks, lips right for kissing, dazzling her teeth; tall, firm, but slender, with serious mien, hiding a good sport but also a good nature. All about her was the well-known indescribable something which, where it shows, vouches for inward and outward cleanliness, for a soul which hates the unclean, whose body therefore never seems unclean in the messiest work. Vreneli was a poor relation in the house. . . .' One might think that this is the beginning of a love story. But no, the author's instinct is too sound for that. The all-too human Uli looks first in every other direction before he looks upward. And the reader too takes a long time before he comes round to Vreneli, before he becomes aware both how far from a model and how intact she is. For this good angel of Uli is herself an illegitimate child, and the author never lets us forget it, even while the features of this illegitimate angel attain their finest proportions.

One cannot help feeling that Gotthelf's eyes have a naturally horizontal sweep. In the human-earthly domain he is so complete that one might say, the heavenly is only present in the light that always was on land and people. This is what the best of even his early readers noticed to their surprise. The would-be edifier revealed himself as a writer who was exciting because he was himself excited, fascinated by the doings of men and women. He wrote about the farmer's life which he had had in his blood for generations, and which he knew by a lifetime of experience (he was forty when he began writing), but at which he looked with the insatiable admiration of genius. The heavenly *paradiso* was the level which the author had set his mind to most deliberately. The earthly *purgatorio* is the level which has arrested his readers for a hundred years. Yet it may be that literary history will give him the palm for his thorough covering of the subhuman *inferno*. It is nothing perverse to admire the impartial attention which Gotthelf has for the wide area of meanness and treachery. His attitude there, in contrast to his over-explicit ' moral theology,' must be deduced from the happenings in the stories. It shows several facets. First of all, he is not obsessed by ' sin.' He does not suspect human nature. Sex, for instance, is ' selbstverständlich,' so much so, that it does not form part of the *inferno,* it dwells safely on the human level. His favorite iniquity is nothing better than a mean selfish dishonesty; only the combination of unscrupulousness and incurableness lifts it to the rank of infamy. Second, Gotthelf does not find the realm of subhuman wickedness grand or satanic. Dickens and especially Dostoevsky have found it much more dazzling, and yet theirs looks shadowy or pathological or simply novelistic beside his world of robust villains. Third, while he admires his villains not in the least, he seems to describe them with more loving care, with a more steady attention, with a more complacent identification than any other great novelist. He shows that the underworld is the vulgar, the common, the most populous world, and it fills the whole background behind his heroes. He believes in the etymology of ' mean, common, vulgar '; he believes that they inherit the earth. But he lets his good men (and especially women) walk among them like Noahs or Lots, minus their solemnity. For if his heroes have an obligatory virtue, it is that of seeing folly where they find it, of not being fooled for long, of liking to have the first chuckle and of always having the last laugh.

Gotthelf treats all scoundrels with contempt, but with that of familiarity. Whenever a scoundrel speaks, he speaks in Swiss dialect. The most selfish thoughts are always uttered in the voice of the people. The moralizing or religious meditations are in pure, at times a little stilted, High German. And on the middle, human plain there is versatility and ease; the persons like to intersperse their unrefined High German with juicy bits of dialect. The good man is the man in the middle, the one who partakes of the highest as well as of the lowest; Gotthelf always makes him the man of choices, of self-determination, of free will. And again Gotthelf's own literary habitat was that middle level of a homely German, from which he could range freely, up into the mannerism of the pulpit and down into the manners of the people. But the reader remembers how one-sidedly he responds to the scale: he yawns when Gotthelf minces, he beams when Gotthelf slums. Linguistically, Gotthelf's genius is most at home in the nether regions, the peasant in him towers over the pastor, and the painter of meanness overshadows the preacher of probity.

He called himself Jeremias Gotthelf (with the primitive name-symbolism so appropriate in all his stories) after Jeremiah ' the doleful denouncer of the times,' who turns so easily into the poet of the Psalms exclaiming, ' God, help; for the godly man ceaseth; for the faithful fail from among the children of men ' (Psalm 12, 1). The moral aspirations of the pastor of a village near Berne would today interest only some specialist, if the books had not developed the disquieting habit of growing, under the eyes of the unexpectant reader, into the most substantial novels of their time. It is wise to listen not only to his generous modern exponents but also to the verdict of a century. That verdict has been singularly consistent since the *Westminster Review's* first article on Gotthelf's works in 1847 : ' They possess, indeed, almost too few of the conventional attractions of fiction; they are now and then a little tedious, and sometimes approach rather nearer to the disgusting than is strictly admissible in an aesthetic production.' Two out of three times the critic was right. Gotthelf did despise even the most slow-grown conventions of fiction to his detriment; Gotthelf did not mind, or was not aware of, being more than a little tedious. But disgusting, even in spots, he can have appeared only to a Victorian reader. The critic is equally right when he continues by applying the acid test of fiction : is the author capable of interesting us in his realities? He answers with the response of all Gotthelf readers. ' . . . Yet we feel ourselves following their adventures — no, the daily course of their plodding lives — with anxious interest.' Indeed, his friends were not the only ones to dare think, ' You are our Boz ' (1842). The

British Quarterly Review of 1863 made the same comparison: 'Dickens might envy the power. . . .'

Gotthelf is a river of fiction: he has its inexhaustible supply of substance, its rhythmical propulsion, its eternal current. But it is neither calculated nor predictable. Now narrow then wide, now precipitate then sluggish, it eddies, it meanders, it forms useless bayous, even unpleasant swamps. But again and again its own course gathers momentum, its own impetus presses onward; and then we assent to it as to a phenomenon of nature. That happens when his steady moral inspiration and his intermittent narrative inspiration flow together. Then his river of wisdom is identical with the river of fiction. In the Victorian decades, the wisdom could not but be uppermost. John Ruskin often thought of Gotthelf, when his mind looked for an example of 'good influence.' The fullest assent is in *Fors Clavigera* (III, letter 30): 'I think him the wisest man, take him for all in all, with whose writings I am acquainted.' In Letter 34 Ruskin elaborates on the specific mixture which makes the 'wholesomness' of Gotthelf: His works 'generally show the most wholesome balance of the sentimental and rational faculty I have ever met with in literature.' And then Ruskin draws a not unwelcome triangle between three older English writers in order to place Gotthelf morally: 'The part of Gotthelf which is in sympathy with Pope and Fielding enables him to touch, to just the nearest point, the lower grotesqueness of peasant nature, while his own conception of ideal virtue is as pure as Wordsworth's.' Ruskin, who had been much in Switzerland, does not fail to claim for Gotthelf his due as a folklorist. In *Modern Painters* (ch. 11) he makes the then inevitable comparison with Scott: his writings 'contain a record of Swiss character not less valuable in its fine truth than that which Scott has left of the Scottish.' In the Preface to the *Uli* translation of 1886 Ruskin wrote an intimation of Gotthelf as the Balzac of Switzerland.

Gotthelf never wanted to amuse or entertain by his descriptions. From first to last he was an activist and engagé, he wanted to influence, to advise, to help. Hence the state of literary innocence, an almost extra-literary state, in which most of his books remain, and into which they transplant us, if we are lucky. To enter into them is a privilege insofar as they are not meant for us, as they are very much a closed circle. Their subject-matter is also their object: in describing Berne country life they want to teach Berne country life. Their heroes are also their readers: the peasants and farmhands who look into the books are supposed to see nothing but their own reflections looking out at them. In an entirely unfigurative sense the reader is to find himself there, not his general humanity, but his particular problems, habits and needs. And in no other novelist's lifework do the underprivileged occupy so much space. Several volumes are given over to their life. However, they rarely remind us of the sentiment, 'Blessed are the poor.'

His heroes act from a triple motivation: from instinct, from reasoning, and from religion, and there is no conflict. Actually, the experience which they have of the surrounding scoundrels drives them to be 'better'—for the scoundrels leave them no other way out. Hence Gotthelf's almost unchristian sympathy, not with the weak, but with those who prove by character or magnanimity or longanimity and, mostly, by success, that they are the weak in appearance only. Often he shows an undisguised preference for the well-grown individual, for the privileged children of God, those who are at the same time healthy and handsome and wealthy: they are his chosen people. What saves him from a moral cliché is that he never trusts his characters, not even 'the best' ones. To the last page of every novel he casts doubting eyes on them, discovers new weaknesses, new temptations. The Christian in him loves the state of grace; the novelist knows that his characters can breathe only as long as they are in an atmosphere of danger. Perhaps even this is not the artist's tact but his taste, since he shares it with his worst characters. No one of them trusts anybody, or rather they trust everybody to do the worst, so they unflinchingly do it to others. At any rate, Gotthelf has a masterly hand in the vastly humourous villain scenes and often displays a frightening gusto in them. So much so that one is inclined to think that Carlyle saw deeper than Ruskin, when the latter disputed him (letter of Dec. 1871), 'Tell me . . . why you call Bitzius "cruel"?'

The present-day English expert on Gotthelf, H. M. Waidson, introduces the shorter tales with these words: 'After the great novels the realistic tales, particularly those with a peasant background, are Gotthelf's most important contribution to literature.' Indeed the novelette of *The Black Spider* is as much the representative Gotthelf story for the twentieth century as *Uli* was for the nineteenth. One dares not call one of the dozen novels a masterwork, even though one remembers the strongest impressions from half of them. However, among the shorter tales there is an even dozen of which each has that proportion between interest and length, that unity of conception and execution, which remind one that the Germans were always better off in the novelle than in the novel. Gotthelf was well aware of his powers, he cultivated them to an extent in the novelettes. But in his major efforts, the novels, they were subservient to his 'higher' calling. His biographers tell us that he never subscribed to a preference for his shorter works. In the long ones, which he felt to be his main duty, he was novelist and pastor and pamphleteer in turn, and in his latest novels as much as in his first.

The mixture of Swiss German and High German makes Gotthelf practically a bilingual author, understood only in a small region. Only a southwestern German can comfortably guess most of his meaning, only a Swiss can be sure of it all. Gotthelf himself realized that and wrote a great part of his later fiction in dialect-free German, and some of his books simply had a second, High-German edition. The twentieth century revival of Gotthelf has considered that a linguistic crime; and as a result he is again, for the reading public, a Swiss provincialism. The nineteenth century policy was the wiser one. All of Gotthelf should exist in German translation, before it can take its place in world literature. And its place is, if not in the forefront of that literature, if not in its top ranks, at least in its deep center. For it is blessed with unliterary qualities. There is in his fiction such a comprehensive and massive, elemental and overwhelming, genuine and original picture of human life that, looking up from one of his books at the shelves of great nineteenth century fiction, one is tempted to mutter: ' Et tout le reste est littérature ! '

Gotthelf and Mörike

It is easy to wax eloquent about Gotthelf; it is almost impossible to say anything about Mörike. Yet the two challenge a comparison, and one is almost entitled to demand of them a reciprocal elucidation. They were two Protestant pastors, contemporaneous, rooted in the same large dialect (Alemanic), separated only by the Swiss-German boundary, by the Lake of Constance, so to speak. No, they were separated by everything that can separate two men close in time and space, by everything that made them what they are, the one the broadest novelist of Victorian Germany, the other its finest lyricist.

Eduard Mörike grew up and lived in the small towns and villages of Württemberg. He seems to have been recognized as the personification of a poet, before and above the recognition of his poetry. A remarkable circle of friends, most of them from his youth, testified to the great charm of his personality. He was easily charmed himself, by people, by landscapes, by the intimacies of a quiet pervasive culture that was scattered over the Württemberg countryside. But the charm rarely led to anything else but a poem. It was absorbed into that poem to such a degree that hardly a ray here and there was left for Mörike's life. Hence a lightless, unsteady and unsuccessful life, not filled with any praiseworthy activity, but full of pottering and dawdling. Hence from early to late a poverty which was so multiform and ever-present that Mörike allowed it not a breath of presence in his works. The economic condition as the modern version of ' condition humaine ' is absolutely banned from that paradise. Mörike managed to treat it with sovereign neglect even in his professional life, in which every dictate of the needs for income, security, stability was calmly ignored.

Mörike had as hard a time as his confrater across Lake Constance in finding a pastorate, both were thirty before they were settled in an office. Then Gotthelf was not filled by his office: Mörike never filled his. Gotthelf enlarged his care of souls by his writings; Mörike escaped or evaded his pastoral duties by means of his poetry. But we must face the fact that however we strain our contrasts, they turn out appropriate enough on the Gotthelf side, they invariably appear as overstatements on the side of Mörike.

That much is true, whereas Gotthelf stumbled into a literary career by 'accident,' Mörike had never been anything but a poet; that at an age when Gotthelf began novel-writing, Mörike had written nearly all his perfect lyrics; and that when Gotthelf loaded on his broadening shoulders the expanding duties of pastor, pamphleteer, school-politician, and author-for-the-people, Mörike retired from his ill-administered pastorate into an insignificant pension (before he was forty). Does it add anything to the character to say that this man, who was pathologically dependent on mother and sisters, this retired pastor and ex-fiancé of pastors' daughters, married a Catholic girl? Does one add that a regain in health and energy made him a sort of literature professor at a Stuttgart girls' school? Does one add that his dignified old age was not wise enough to preserve his peaceful marriage, that the parents separated when the daughters were grown up? The precarious muse had not been able to steady the precarious man. His fame was phenomenal only among the great minds of the time; it was very slow in reaching a wider public. But there is perhaps no German poet of the nineteenth century of whom so many lines have kept echoing in the minds of one special audience, the German poets of the twentieth century.

Both Gotthelf and Mörike were pastors, but their faith was poles apart. Gotthelf made his the cornerstone of his Weltanschauung and the inspiration of his art. Almost accidentally he discovered that the struggle for the *good* life was also the most *life* for the purposes of simple fiction. All his excursions into literature were undertaken from the stronghold of his religious and moral conviction. They were sallies which developed into mighty safaris, because to that man everything turned out big. Mörike trifled with everything, many fields of art, many shades of religion, but he never subjected one of them to the other. That makes him so perfectly just to things and moods which do not stay the same. They require a light touch, and Mörike has the lightest we know, he never insists. He is the opposite of Gotthelf, who has the merciless grip of a giant. But one knows what to expect of him, whereas Mörike never commits himself. He was the friend of the leading sceptics of his time, like D. S. Strauss, the debunker of the gospels.

But if there was any gospel truth for him it was the very legend lore of the New Testament, the thing the Bible critics abandoned first. With the tolerant frenzy of a poet he believed in all the mythologies of which he had heard, as well as in those which he added of his own invention. Gotthelf's muse is as proud an *ancilla theologiae* as any medieval poet's; Mörike's is a fairy princess who follows her every whim but follows nobody else.

Mörike's world is full of idylls (in verse) and fairytales (in prose). That puts its content almost outside any modern interest. Only by accident does the modern traveler stay overnight in those quaint towns off the highways. These genre-paintings are still more off the road than Gotthelf's monumental canvasses. But between these genre-paintings there are miniatures where the modern reader forgets any relation to the little world of Eduard Mörike, to his puppet-size space and his short-sighted time, and gazes aghast into what Rilke called ' Weltinnenraum,' where things become so intimate that they reveal a sudden universality. A dozen poems of his have for this reason become classical in German. As Mörike has no method either of form or of thought, it remains unpredictable what he will do to the reader — even in passages through which the reader has passed before. The gifts of his muse are gratuitous still.

Kein Schlaf noch kühlt das Auge mir,
Dort gehet schon der Tag herfür
An meinem Kammerfenster.

Es wühlet mein verstörter Sinn
Noch zwischen Zweifeln her und hin
Und schaffet Nachtgespenster.

— Aengste, quäle
Dich nicht länger, meine Seele!
Freu dich! schon sind da und dorten
Morgenglocken wach geworden.

The formal characteristics are so slight that one hardly notices how appropriate they are to the movement and the countermovement, the first in rising iambic (for the restlessness), the second in falling trochees (for the reassurance). The sextet is almost too placidly self-contained to mirror the anguish of a sleepless night. The double couplet is powerfully set off by the apparent half-line, in truth fermata-line, where in the two words ' ängste, quäle,' the content of the preceding and the sentiment of the following audibly fight it out. The first half of the sextet is all objective picture: ' I did not find sleep, and day is breaking.' The second half is all subjective turmoil, with a delicate crescendo from ' rumple — deranged sense — doubts — to and fro ' to the telling rhyme 'nightghosts.' Then the weighted, negative imperatives which arrest the worrying. Two lines which yet hover on the anxious ä-sounds of 'Gespenster.' Then, for the positive imperative 'be glad!' no other reason is given but another objective image: some morning bells have begun to ring. Two lines which rest on the deep vowels a and o. The rhymes form almost a descending ladder: in the first half of the poem, the highest vowel i; in the third quarter, the next highest, e; at the end, the lowest vowel, o. From fretting insecurity to consolation.

Herr! schicke, was du willt,
Ein Liebes oder Leides;
Ich bin vergnügt, dass beides
Aus deinen Händen quillt.

Wollest mit Freuden
Und wollest mit Leiden
Mich nicht überschütten!
Doch in der Mitten
Liegt holdes Bescheiden.

This is maddening, because it is the crassest mediocrity expressed in double perfection. For they are really two epigrams, each exquisitely complete, independent, of different movement (a quatrain of three-foot iambics; a quintet of two-foot dactyls, with some upbeats). Yet when he joined them, they marvelously increased each other (and were formally held together by the two assonances i and ei in all the rhymes). In the humdrum prayer 'Lord, send what thou wilt,' the antiquated or dialect form 'willt' is downright cosy. The philistine word 'vergnügt' derives from the neighboring 'Leides' (a hurt) a dark coloring, which forces us back into etymology, and we must discover its cousinship with 'begnügen' (resign oneself). And the verb 'quillt' contains a spring of living water.

As if quickened by grace, the following prayer almost dances before the Lord. Familiarly it stays His hands: not too much of either, please! And the request is reasonable too, because to 'over-whelm' would be unkind in either case. Finally the peak of mediocrity. Again a dialect form, 'Mitten,' to exclude formality. Then the tongue-in-cheek 'holdes Bescheiden,' where the one word makes the other suspect, just as before 'Leid' made 'vergnügt' suspect. 'Sich bescheiden' is again 'resign oneself.' But how can it be 'lovely'? 'Hold' hovers between moral and aesthetic doting; and that is why he used the precious word here. In Mörike's world, beauty is only in measure and moderation. Only the mean is golden. The narrowness of this worldview is mitigated by a drop of regret, by the realization that this kind of beauty is made of renunciations. Consisting of moderate sufferings and moderate happiness it can be a moderate beauty only. The result would be pitiful, were it not of the most genuine reality. Not only is Mörike's biography filled with the avoidance of extremes, of anything grand, of anything passionate. It is the secret of his art too, which so deeply satisfies because it is everywhere equidistant from all extremes and poles. It is an equator art, the glorification of the commonest. Its aims were so low that achievement was always within reach. But this quietest, surest art, this glorification of the equator of existence, is naturally without the effects that impress the common reader. It has always been an art for connoisseurs only. And yet it expressed, like nothing else, a central ideal of the middle-class, the beauty, wisdom and achievement in resignation, a high measure of self-realization within resignation.

Much of the contrast between the two southwestern authors has more to do with the two genres which they represent, the roughshod novel and the delicate lyric. It is the character of the genres as much as the personality of the artists which makes a healthy robustness the preponderant quality of Gotthelf and precarious finesse the evasive appeal of Mörike. By the right sense of narrative dynamics Gotthelf is led to a lusty exaggeration of situations and characters. By a need to balance within the narrowest frame Mörike is compelled to weigh so gently, to counterpoint so harmoniously and to compensate so quickly as often to forego any emotional impact. Not out of coy 'modesty' but out of the imperative need for the lyrical eqilibrium did he utter — and fulfil in every poem — the prayer for moderation, 'Doch in der Mitten/Liegt holdes Bescheiden.' Yet in his miniature frames the world is less provincial and less specialized than Gotthelf's, whose proper study is mankind and man, only. Nature, for instance, the beloved landscapes of Württemberg, but also the handicrafts, beautiful things made, or venerable things left, the world of thought and tradition from antiquity down, the arts of music and painting, these are viewed with much more sympathy, are given voice with much more authenticity in the lyrical than in the epic world. Must it be that way? Or do we touch here an unnecessary limitation of Gotthelf? There is, however, one prerogative of the lyric: the moods that are not, except in the lyrical mode; the dialogues of the soul with itself, without a subject-matter; the hovering which needs no certitude, the suspense of the mind without an object; the aesthetic act in its purity. This is outside the ken of Gotthelf, and it is a realm in which, some think, nobody in the nineteenth century was as naturally and naively at home as Mörike.

The Master of Austrian Fiction

In contrast to 'world literature' of mid-nineteenth century, German literature bores us by the absence of violence, crime, passion, sin. The impression is only superficial; but the great writers tried hard to create it. The one dramatist among them realized that he could not work except with the materials of sin; Grillparzer stated it paradoxically: 'The basic errors of human nature are the truths of poetry.' (*Autobiography,* 1853) In an imaginary 'Conversation in Elysium'

(1841) between the two most emancipated minds of the eighteenth century, he makes the freest thinker, Frederick the Great, say to Lessing: ' Sin was and is with us, and in life man must get along with it as he can; for an author, however, it must be not only a misfortune but a crime.' As if he caught the astonished look of Lessing, he adds with the irony of enlightenment: ' Since nobody hears us here, we may exaggerate a little.'

We do not know what Grillparzer thought of those contemporaries who shared his opinion. He became well acquainted with his countryman, Adalbert Stifter, but admiration was there from Stifter's side only. Stifter did full justice to the moralist in Grillparzer, and at the end of his early work, *Vienna and the Viennese,* he can introduce Grillparzer, without having to name him, by the mere characterization of his achievements: ' A thousand hearts he has enraptured, a thousand souls elevated, and into thousands he instilled fine and gentle virtue by his words.' ' Fine and gentle virtue ' is a poor translation of ' die schöne sanfte Sitte seiner Worte.' Such simple words for fundamental concepts make one aware of the barrier not only of languages but also of ages. German Victorianism developed an idiom for its cherished ideals which is untranslatable. ' Sitte ' has neither the personalness of ' virtue ' nor the abstractness of ' morality.' It is collective like custom and dynamic like culture. What interests us here is that Stifter saw in the admired older writer the qualities to which he himself aspired most: one third art and two thirds moral culture, that is what he wanted to instil into his own works much more deliberately than Grillparzer ever did. And if a twentieth century reader saw, without a name, the characterization, ' Herzen entzücken — Seelen erheben — schöne sanfte Sitte einflössen,' he would sooner think of Stifter than of Grillparzer.

Stifter's tales were much loved in his own time. They have been loved more, and for different reasons, in the twentieth century. They are so simple of surface and so intricate of texture that we are sure of blundering whenever we generalize about them. They are so different from any other narrative writing that we cannot give enough detail to set them off. Let us look at one of the tales published as *Studien,* ' Der Waldsteig ' (Forest Path, 1850). It has the average length of a Stifter ' study,' about fifty pages. On the first page we are told the end of the story, also that it is a rather simple-minded story, also that it is told for the profit of fools, also that it is the story of a big fool, son of fools. Then we are treated to five pages of inheritance and education, to ten pages of desultory occupations and imaginary diseases. Then the sick rich Tiburius sends himself to a mountain resort and prescribes to himself the daily exercise of a walk. And once by accident he, ' who had never seen a forest from inside,' gets lost on a forest path. If we have read that far, we are lost with him, for here Stifter begins to paint forest scenes, drily, exactly, searchingly, as the eye of slightly curious slightly furious Tiburius takes them in. And we, the detached readers, see how the charm works, how he is released from years of false confinement into an open-air idyll, and genuine anxiety, and sweat, and a day's march. It takes him a week to recover from the exertion; but when he investigates how he got lost, he finds out. ' He did not know that the same thing happens to anybody who enters forests. Each time they are clearer, more comprehensible, until they turn into a beauty and joy for the visitor.'

This is what happens to Herr Tiburius. He becomes, timidly, gayer, stronger and healthier. As the last of his desultory occupations had been painting, he begins to sketch the objects from his favorite forest path. We realize that his little art had been the first step to his salvation; regeneration had started in his eyes. We also realize that Stifter was a considerable painter: he sees the objects as objects, interesting for themselves, by their infinite shapes and colors, and then by their infinite correspondences with our moods. But the correspondences establish themselves, independent from the story or parallel to the story. They have a ' thereness ' almost as in good paintings, not as in other good literature. They speak their own language, not that of the persons of the story. The persons listen to their language with hardly more privilege than we, the readers.

We are past the middle of the story when Tiburius meets a young girl on his forest path, a strawberry vendor, with whom he strikes up a conversation and then a friendship. As soon as they begin to speak we have a new surprise. People do not talk that way. None of the conventional paths of conversation are followed. In the brief or leisurely cadences of these speeches there is the same mysterious beckoning as in Stifter's ' descriptions ' of nature. Nature and people are equally simple-plus-strange. Tiburius accompanies the young girl to her father's house. She teaches him how to walk the woods, how to find the late strawberries. There is so much unspoken intimacy in their doings, and none at all in their words, that one has another pang of recognition: Stifter is the master of the suppressed, unexpressed; he manages the reader's collaboration more than any other prose-writer. The pleasure of the two people in each other is not told in a word.

Early next summer Tiburius is back; and after many a visit to his favorite path, many a day of walking and sketching, he meets Maria. After many meetings he ventures to show her his sketch book. ' She was in very great delight, that with nothing but plain black strokes one could imitate the things of the forest, so faithful, lovely and true, as if they stood there.' After many more days he gets to the question, why she was never afraid of him. ' Because you are good and because you are different from the others.' Even in this lightest of his stories, being good and being different are two standards which are very high. To be interested at all, Stifter wants heroes who have the qualities of goodness and differentness to the degree of greatness.

Whether his talent or his character, his artistic taste or his ethical demand found this requirement, he hit in it the central problem of Victorian fiction: how to make goodness interesting. All nineteenth century fiction, from Stendhal to Henry James, agreed that only the extraordinary character would do, at least for the extended novel; that the commonplace rules the real world but won't do as the nucleus of a fictional world. The Victorian core of the century, from Dickens to Dostoevsky, added to the rule of the 'interesting' hero the more precarious rule of the 'good' hero. The German novel in its most satisfying specimens — Immermann's *Epigonen,* Gotthelf's *Uli,* Freytag's *Soll und Haben,* Stifter's *Nachsommer,* Keller's *Grüner Heinrich* — owes much of its over-sober staidness to the all-too obstinate pursuit of the 'good' hero. But Stifter was the most determined in excluding even from his shorter fiction a subject which was not in itself both rare and 'good.' The masters of the short story chose otherwise; Balzac and Maupassant for instance found common people quite good enough, as long as they got into unusual circumstances. But Stifter elected the opposite: extraordinary characters in ordinary situations.

This recipe should by rights have led to nothing but failures. That Stifter turns it into repeated successes is due to a strange painterly-poetical technique. We can get glimpses of it in the rest of 'Forest Path.' Nothing happens that one does not foresee, and everything was foretold anyway. But Stifter isolates his people, their behaviour, their fates so thoroughly that one becomes all attention. His precise and almost laconic words add stroke by stroke of a panoramic impression that is extremely time-conscious and time-consuming. Since he wrote in the middle of the nineteenth century we should be content to say that his 'description' is dictated by his roaming painter's eye. But it would be more accurate to compare his vision to a movie camera. It loves to follow a moving object, and if the object does not move, it loves to move itself: to or from the object or past it. Frequently both the observer and the observed are on the way. Stifter's eyes, and his feet, and all his heroes, love to go awandering, and his books are full of plain or ingenious reasons for it. His oil paintings or pencil drawings are all devoted to landscapes. But in his stories he is above all the painter of time, of the sameness in time or the changes in time, of the times of day, the seasons of the year, and the long spans of a human life. No other writer of the short fiction, the Novelle, has so often encompassed an entire life in that frame. Yet Stifter is relentlessly unhurried. Sometimes his movement is so inexorably slow that we think he wants to take as long as the described passing of time.

The Germans have a well-worn definition according to which the main difference between talent and genius is that talent *can* do several things, but genius *must* do one thing. Stifter would be no talent, he is not good at many things. He has little humor, he is poor in abstract thought, he is inferior in reasoning, he is mediocre in expository prose. But let his sacred subject seize him (a visible and audible situation in atmosphere) and he will respond with a prose so saturated with its objects that it becomes the most concrete we know.

The story 'Kalkstein' (Limestone) (in the volumes *Bunte Steine,* Minerals, of 1853) is representative of his developed technique. As the first sentence tells us, it is a story 'in which nothing unusual happens, yet which I have not been able to forget.' He puts the story in a 'terrible region' consisting of many small hills of naked gray limestone. In the beginning the hero says of 'this disgusting region': 'It is as God has made it . . . and sometimes it is more beautiful than any other in the world.' This remark sounds weakminded and is meant to sound so. But when, toward the end, the hero repeats it — 'People say the region is ugly; but that is not true, you just have to look at it closely' — he has convinced us that here lies a secret of the story and even of Stifter's art.

Again he has a trained observer, one who knows how to use his eyes, this time a geological surveyor. This surveyor meets the parson of that poor region. Every bit of information about the parson has to be taken in by direct observation, by seeing him and his poor habitat, by hearing the simpleton talk. The whole story is a waiving of the difference between big and small; or a counterbalancing of generosity of heart and paltriness of opportunities. The childlike man proves something of a good shepherd, more of a lone wolf; and most of all a man of 'deep and enduring and delicate feeling.' The only riches of the parson, his impeccable linen, is revealed to have been treasured 'aus einem tiefen, dauernden und zarten Gefühle' — because he was once almost in love with a washerwoman. The abject parsimony of his living is revealed to have been for the purpose of a schoolhouse which would safeguard the children from periodic danger. His heroic savings for the purpose are childishly inadequate. But when his death reveals the extent of his saintly ineptitude, all the rich of the neighbourhood subscribe to his testament.

As in a poem, we see only in the end how well the story was 'made': why in the first scene the shabby parson disappeared, as if into a halo, into the afternoon sun; why the surveyor, when thinking of the wretched clothing, had to keep his eyes fixed on the landscape; why the figure was edged so sharply; why the first half of the story climaxed in a magnificent thunderstorm (the unforeseen magnanimity of the hero). Only in the end do we understand the other obvious leitmotifs. All the symbolism is delightfully evident and yet kept suspended, undefined and operative for the entire fifty pages. There is an immediate communication between our senses of eye and ear and our feeling. And all abstract thought, even all intelligence, is effectively shortcircuited.

It cannot be Stifter's hypnotic technique which has made him, in the twentieth century, the most beloved master from the nineteenth. It must have to do with his subject-matter. He represents the most methodical transposition into art of the city-dweller's nostalgia for the country. He is, more than any other writer, the monumental adieu of the nineteenth century to nature, rural life, the woodlands.

An early notice on the two volumes of *Minerals,* in the *Westminster Review* of April 1853, already hinted at the complex, nature plus simple society plus childhood, which those stories evoked. 'The processes and appearances of external nature occupy so prominent a place in these tales, that they might almost be described as "landscapes with figures".' The reviewer competently foresees that 'Rock Crystal' is 'likely to be a favorite,' and singles out 'Kalkstein.' 'Limestone . . . and the figure of the lonely priest in the quiet heroism of his voluntary poverty, is deeply though quietly impressive.'

Still more insistent on Stifter's custody of the 'primitive landscape' is — in the London *Athenæum* of August 26, 1848 — a review of the first four volumes of *Studies,* which is surprisingly well informed. We find the reviewer in the first column giving an account of Stifter's geography. 'In all the other sketches we find the painter — for such he may justly be termed — ever wandering in Austria. . . . The Boehmerwald is still in parts a solitude. . . . Half foresters, half peasants. . . . Here, then, may still be found in undisturbed power the awfulness as well as the beauty of forest and mountain scenery; the deep impressiveness of which is to the German what the ocean influences are to the English poet.' Evidently the last sentence hit at that commodity of which Stifter has, for the twentieth century German, almost a monopoly. But the English reviewer does not miss the intersection of time and space marked by Stifter: 'It is one of the few districts now remaining in the heart of modern Europe where Nature may still be found . . . where a lover of her looks and voices may still for a time forget the restless work of human energies and human wants, that has nearly effaced her original features from the Europe of our day.' Stifter himself would scarcely have found fault with this echo from abroad.

Brought up in the Bohemian Forest, he was educated in a monastery near the foothills of the Alps. Those were his first twenty years. From twenty to forty, he lived in Vienna, as something of an eternal student and a highly considered private tutor (his last pupil was the son of Metternich himself). It was here, after fifteen years of metropolitan life, that he finally began that series of country tales which in their anxious undertones betray that he was looking at a vanishing Arcadia. After the 1848 revolution he believed that even he should be an official servant of the tottering civilization. He became a school inspector in Linz. Thus the works of his last twenty years were also written in a city.

But he was the most assiduous of home-comers. He returned to his corner of southern Bohemia in all periods of his life with striking frequency, and in some periods for extended stays. That is why he writes comparatively little of the work in the fields and woods, and so much of the wanderings of people who are free to wander. Gotthelf's farmers have hardly a glance for nature. Stifter's wanderers almost pray to her, even if they do not express it by anything but the almost desperately steady gaze in which they hold her. There are few town scenes in his extensive work. There are, in timeless permanence, the Alps and their foothills, the Danube and the Moldau, the fields of Austria and the Bohemian Forest. His actual paintings portray these landscapes. Most of his stories are elaborate wanderings or reminiscences of life as far from collective settlements as possible.

The nineteenth century is full of 'village tales,' in all European literatures. Stifter has nothing to do with them. He is not sentimentally attached to one way of social life. He wants man to be alone. In the monumental figures of his wanderers and outsiders he has unconsciously perpetuated man's fear of being less and less left alone. We must say, unconsciously, because he has not theorized about the subject but simply accumulated his figures of kind and wise lone wolves. And in the half-articulateness of these figures there is half the earnest yearning of a man who looks back on paradise lost, and half the sophisticated composure of a man who just looks forward to a vacation.

There is little prettiness in his landscapes. They are not flower gardens; he has an affinity for the wild, the desolate, the dreary landscape. His love of nature is not sentimental, because it does not pick out and favor. It is elemental, because his eye rests with impartial insistence on all its essential constituents. Therefore his people blend almost structurally with the landscape. Some are like flora, to be sure; but others are like fauna; and not a few remind us most of all of minerals, the elemental realm of mountain, rock, stone, sand.

The early reactions suggested some comparisons which might deserve to be pursued. It was not inappropriate that the *British Quarterly Review* (1854) compared Stifter with an American, and the *Westminster Review* (1853) thought of an English poet. 'Stifter's writings bear resemblance to Hawthorne's *House of the Seven Gables,* though without its gloom, more than to any other book we know. It is the same mosaic work of small facts, not the severe analysis of thought and emotion common to much of our modern fiction; there is, indeed, little of reflection, everything is stated baldly or poetically as the case may be.' The *Westminster* was content to notice that Stifter's 'confession of poetical faith appears to bear a strong resemblance to that of Wordsworth.'

It is not our purpose to look at Stifter's novels also. The hypnotic spell which the best of the stories cast over us could not well be prolonged for 1,000 pages. Hardly anybody, however, who has read the novels, has failed to recognize their nobility and massive power. In the year 1865, when *Witiko,* the second novel, was published, a notice of the first, *Nachsommer* (1857), appeared in the *Christian Examiner* of Boston. It is an appraisal which does Stifter much justice, even the insistence on the more poem-like than novel-like character of *Nachsommer.* 'It is a poetic creation, indeed a *Dichtung,* of a naive and original kind, but not a novel which pictures life as it ought to be or is. It is rather an ideal portrait, just far enough removed from reality to make it idyllic.' 'There is really no plot in the work. . . . And the marvel of the book is, that this description, drawn through three volumes of at least 500 pages each, instead of being tiresome, should grow more and more fascinating, so that we read slowly, anxious not to finish it.'

The kind of aesthetic = moral fanaticism, which we sense in Stifter's work, did not appeal to American readers in the nineteenth century, and further echoes are practically nonexistent. Stifter himself seems never to have abandoned the search for his nature = humanity equations. He made it the very subject for his late paintings and plans, those symbolic landscapes (all unfinished) the remnants of which, the very titles and subjects of which keep us musing on the mystery of his art: 'Serenity' (temple ruins); 'Movement' (rocks in river); 'Quiet' (Alpine lake); 'Solemnity' (Grossglockner Alps). Stifter's nostalgia is for the elemental and primordial. His mystery yearns for the original innocence of creation. His art yearns so effectively, that it accomplishes part of its desire, partakes of that morning of creation, and lets us partake. But there is something exclusive and exacting, something uncomfortable about that. That is why for almost a century readers and critics preferred to this exclusive poet of the Novelle more authentic Novellen written by (lyric) poets, by Eichendorff, Droste-Hülshoff, Mörike, and even Grillparzer.

The Four Evangelists

'In general one may well profess this: Only the combination of a character and a talent produces what one calls genius.' This profession of Grillparzer, in the Weimar episode of his Autobiography, is aimed against himself, because he was convinced that in his case 'an unmanly character has ruined a considerable talent.' It would not need this self-incriminating edge to recommend the statement. To a German it is almost a truism that genius = character + talent. One is surprised not to have met it a hundred times in the hundred years before Grillparzer wrote it down. However, like any solid truism, it deserts you when you want to prove something by it. You have no sooner tested it on Mörike, when you react with 'Mörike is a genius without character.' And you feel tempted to put Eichendorff, the other great lyricist of the time, in the same category. You would priggishly contrast the two lyrical talents with the two epical characters, Gotthelf and Stifter. But you need only compare all four with the Young Germans in order to realize your error. The source of the error was in the application which Grillparzer made of the claim, turning it against himself. The 'manly' or strong character is only one variety, and the variety does not matter. What matters, and what these four men possessed, Eichendorff and even Mörike not excepted, was moral character which had a particular affinity with their *art,* moral character which was much more pronounced in their works than in their lives. Literature cares little that its protagonists are model citizens; but it is greatly interested if they are great moralists.

This *artistic* affinity with morality, their need for seeing 'the good' and 'the beautiful' as kindred aspirations not of the human soul in general but of the 'poetic' soul as they knew it, makes their world a vacation land for the visiting soul. Things are kept different there. The visitor does not care that underneath lie the same conditions and the same conflicts which make up his yearlong life; he is satisfied that there he can change at least the pace of his life enough to have moments of stillness which allow him to wonder, perhaps even to ponder. If he lets himself be lured into the stillness, to the moment where it becomes meditation, he will hear the demand of just this art: 'Du musst dein Leben ändern,' you must change your life!

The impression that the air is higher and cleaner here comes largely from the obsession of these four men with what Goethe had formulated for them in the simplest way, 'Edel sei der Mensch.' Nobility of soul seemed as indispensable to them as good air; the need for it was such a matter of course that they were not even aware of their being rather uncharitable to the bulk of mankind. In their lives they were modest and largely helpful ministering attendants of the offices and the public. But their art could not make this democratic virtue do, it needed for its themes the rarer virtues of the noble soul. They composed their ideal of nobility out of their own intimate drives — hence the marked differences between the four ideals — but one strong component was that junction of Christianism and Humanism which they were almost capable of writing as the equation Christianism = Humanism.

They knew that they were fighting a rearguard action. The wind of the century blew in the other direction, and all the volatile spirits were flying with it. The four felt the wind about their ears, but they had too much weight to be carried along; perhaps also too much obstinacy. For it is apparent that they slowed their pace as they grew older. In their youth they make the impression, all four of them, of walking in the direction of the current, their eyes turned toward a not unfriendly future. As they grow older we get rather the picture of a current which has condensed into rushing water, and of four giants who have slowed down their pace until they stand still, rocks in the middle of the stream. And if we look closer, we find that the faces of the boulders are turned toward the past.

Yet, while fighting for an apparently lost cause, they also knew that they were the real voices of mute multitudes: of those masses whose entire human culture was their Christian culture. They were artists first for themselves, as they stood for the unquelled cry of their individual aspirations. But they also wanted to be artists for society, standing for that vast complex of *Sitte,* collective moral culture, which they regarded as the most promising field in which to cultivate the rare flower of the noble soul. Even without that promise, they would have loved *Sitte* as lovers of folkways and traditions, as lovers of culture altogether, if culture goes deep down into the past, reaches high up into the moral life, and covers a wide and populous region of communicability.

Hesitantly, we introduce Eichendorff into this selective description. Eichendorff is so very German that perhaps he cannot be exported at all. No German can resist him, no foreign critic seems to have fallen for him. When his exquisite tale, *Memoirs of a Good-for-Nothing* (1827) was finally translated, the Boston *Atlantic Monthly* had on the last page of July 1861 a short review which at first sight looks like cruel misunderstanding. ' Eichendorff wrote plays and poems and novels to the tunes set by the masters of his school, but for himself practically he was a wise man, held comfortable offices all his life long, and in spite of vast literary yearning, sentiment, and misanthropy, was a Philister of the Philisters.' With the perspicacity of ill will the reviewer detected two things, which strike especially one who turns from Stifter to Eichendorff — who were almost fellow countrymen, the one from nothern Austria, the other from southern Silesia. Eichendorff did not invent a form of his own, he 'just' perfected those of the Romantic school, which means that some of their forms have only in him reached perfection. And Eichendorff was indeed not the man who experienced his stories and poems of mercurial wanderlust. He stayed very much at home and overcompensated a very sedate life by a very vagrant poetry. 'The tale which Mr. Leland translates so gracefully is an extravaganza. . . . But being translated into our pitiless English, its poverty of wit and feeling and imagination is apparent; and one is soon weary of its mere fantasticality.' This seems not worth quoting, but our intermittent dialogue with English criticism is worth something only if we take the opposing side seriously, even when it is 'absurdly' contrary. It is hard for a German to find a trace of insight in the quotation; but the man of good will finds, with a threefold sigh, three traces. (1) Eichendorff is lyrical to his fingernails; the inflections of his voice mean more than his best thoughts; poems, even his poems in prose, will always lead a precarious existence in translation. (2) Eichendorff's wit is as poor as his imagination and perhaps no poorer than his feeling; that is why his reader never distinguishes the one from the other; but the indissoluble fusion of the three in his best work is magic. (3) To most of Eichendorff's stories, and even to 450 of his 500 poems, the 'wearying of fantasticality' justly applies; indeed whenever it does not apply — it is a miracle, but in every sense.

Joseph von Eichendorff (1788-1857) practiced Romanticism longer than anybody else, because he did not use it up in a compromise with life. A Silesian baron, he lost his possessions in the general impoverishment of the landed aristocracy. His happiest years, of study and later of retirement, were spent in Vienna. His career placed him in administrative jobs in the Prussian north: in Berlin and Königsberg. He was fifty before a substantial collection of his poems appeared. Insensibly many of them became common property, so much so that it is rare for a German not to look at his favorite landscape through Eichendorff glasses. It is even difficult to gaze at a Stifter landscape without subconsciously humming an Eichendorff tune.

The two eastern authors compel a comparison even more than the western pair, Gotthelf and Mörike. They are, among our specialists, our greatest 'nature poets,' Stifter in prose, Eichendorff in verse. Their primary landscapes were two parallel mountain ranges (Böhmerwald and Riesengebirge), but how divergent the parallels! In Stifter we have the eternal nostalgia for a cosmic paradise; in Eichendorff the untiring homesickness for his childhood chateau. Stifter's landscapes stand in all the glaring detail of the *Tageszeiten;*

Eichendorff is exquisite when he speaks in the night. Stifter's almost scientific justice to the elements concretizes with every means at his disposal. Eichendorff dissolves every human, every landscape element into wind and whim. Any consistency in the subject-matter is alien to him. That is why, when we come from Stifter's density, we lose the bottom under our feet as we sink into Eichendorff's web of improvisations.

Eichendorff is so lyrical, so subjective, that everything whirls around him in a dance of symbols. Nothing stays the same; the symbols are not identical with themselves, they are only identical with him. That is why they are so crazily exchangeable (most frettingly in the stories and novels). In Stifter, the symbols define themselves cumbersomely and change like the lingering seasons. In Eichendorff they are changed like the garments of an actor, and one who has only a few. 'All poetry is symbolic,' Eichendorff says. But the quality of poetry depends on the substance of the symbols and their intense relation to something. Here we look into a whirl of symbolizations — of what? They flit about us like flocks of migratory birds, each alike and all going in the same direction. The probing critic can come to Stifter by patiently looking at his objects; he need not be in agreement with the author, he need not even care for him. The way to the other's work is through Eichendorff himself, a spontaneous sympathy is prerequisite. The two represent not the typical epic and lyric poets, not essential fiction and pure poetry, they are extreme and fringe cases. Stifter arrests us by the substantiality of his objects; Eichendorff overwhelms us with the tautology of the subject.

Subjectivity is tautological. Eichendorff cannot get away from his favorite subjects, and the more they are the same, the more they speak to us. A later poem of his shows one of his favorite subjects, salvation by forestry.

> Ach! wie ist es doch gekommen,
> Dass die ferne Waldespracht
> So mein ganzes Herz genommen,
> Mich um alle Ruh gebracht!

The poet simply shakes his head at his infatuation with forestry. The 'distant forest splendor' could refer to forests 'there in the distance,' it could also mean very 'far away.' The second quatrain apparently resolves the doubt, by substituting 'over there.'

> Wenn von drüben Lieder wehen,
> Waldhorn gar nicht enden will,
> Weiss ich nicht wie mir geschehen,
> Und im Herzen bet ich still.

Now we must realize that the situation is blatantly imaginary. Songs and horn solos do not come floating from 'distant' forests, even if it is a distance ' over there.' The poet only hears them so well, and so endlessly, because they are in his mind. They are only the symbolic chords which his heart plays and, as the last line says, prays. Now we know why Eichendorff needed so little wandering in his actual life. ' Berg ' or ' Wald ' had simply become the symbols for ' holy places.' We know why he needed so little actual music. The constant music which floats from all his forests is simply the eternal concord between the voices of nature and his response. Eichendorff's poem looks, with obsession, out of his urban servitude to the forests of the heart and the mountains of the soul. The word ' eternal ' in the last line of the poem,

> . . . Zög auf ewig wälderwärts,

is by no means equivocal, it is comprehensive; it means both ' for good ' and ' into eternity.'

We cannot exaggerate enough the contrast between the elemental Stifter and the sentimental Eichendorff, between the concentration of Stifter and the dissipation of Eichendorff, in order to realize: their manner has little to do with their merit. The percentage of Stifter's successes is incomparably higher; but where Eichendorff is best he is ineffable. He goes on rhyming the same rhymes and toying with the same images for ever. But when the angel goes by and troubles his water, a quatrain results in which not only all the happiness or all the sadness or all the piety of his thousand other quatrains seems distilled, but a hundred years of German poetry reverberate, a hundred years of German feeling recognize themselves so naturally, as if not the one man Eichendorff, but the spirit of the collective language had whispered its word.

The spirit of the language is forever a child; it only stammers. It does not find wisdom, but wisdom comes to it, by an act of grace. And thus meaning seems to come to an Eichendorff poem, after many preludes, gratuitously.

> Wie wird nun alles so stille wieder!
> So war mirs oft in der Kinderzeit.
> Die Bäche gehen rauschend nieder
> Durch die dämmernde Einsamkeit. . . .

Actually, he has neither brooks nor solitude, he sits in his room or in his office and rhymes. That is why he can imagine the most incongruous things. But sometimes the nonsense is changed by an angel into all the sense of the world. The heart pauses and remembers, especially childhood, especially a country childhood, and its brooks, and its solitude, and its twilights. And it was all an eternal presentiment. Now meaning comes to all these twilights: the title word ' Im Alter ' (Old Age) has fully provided it. And the meaning saturates line after line of the three quatrains, until it overtops the mountains.

Noch Abendröte an den Bergesspitzen

and overbrims into eternity,

Wie Morgenrot der Ewigkeit.

But how *Abendröte* is transsubstantiated into *Morgenrot,* that is so childishly beautiful that it hurts.

Sometimes however he does not strum his old chords. Then it is the new rhymes which come to him as by grace. And then it is as if his old meaning had been waiting, for a hundred poems, for just this tone to complete his fitful scale.

Es wandelt, was wir schauen,
Tag sinkt ins Abendrot,
Die Lust hat eignes Grauen,
Und alles hat den Tod.

What could be more trivial than that everything changes, before our very gaze. But that the gaze should look straight into the rhyme of 'shudder' is here made just as plain as that Abendrot means Tod. Each three-foot line has an over-simple pair of complements, but the four pairs form a double chain, and the two halves of the chain can be exchanged (as they actually are in the first line). As we gyrate from triviality to triviality we are possessed by them in ascending degree. When we have grasped 'Delight has its own shudder,' we cannot read 'And everything (its) death' as we had ever read it. It 'has' us with the unforeseen force of the uncannily simple finite verb. And when our ear has absorbed the four variations, each changes the meaning of the three others, and in exchange each receives the three others as overtones. And thus the ditty expands into the slowest strophe of infinite perspective.

Eichendorff, the oldest of our four Evangelists, is also the eternal youth among them, their Johannes, the profound mystic and lofty eagle. Gotthelf and Mörike were Protestants. Lucas the painter and Johannes the dreamer were Catholics. Eichendorff's Catholicism was the most narrow-minded of the four temperaments. Yet in his poems it is fused with such a limitless infatuation with nature that the blend is simple nature-piety, or simply universal piety. Here too, he soars erratically above the other three, but all four form a chamber concert of Christian voices such as German literature had not heard — with such a range of instruments — for centuries.

The personal acquaintance between the four was of the slightest, even between Eichendorff and Stifter, who met several times during 1846-7 in Vienna. In Eichendorff's history of literature (1857) Stifter's name appears in the end as warrant for the future. And Stifter's later works were, in a sense, written for his most loyal fan, Eichendorff's sister. That was the extent of the association. In contrast to the Young Germans, who were so chummy that they constantly got into each other's hair, their opponents relied on aloofness in literature and life.

No doubt, they withdrew into themselves in the face of an expanding world. These men used the railroads extensively, but shrank from mentioning them in literature. The middle of the century saw a scuffle of technical advance. A still small voice warned them, that way lay danger. But they did not raise their voice in warning, they had an indirect way of reacting: they spoke with tenderness of the things they had known all their life. They must have loved *their* way of life. In no other period of German literature do we find such a kind light, such a benignant sun irradiating things as they *are,* without the wish to change them, rather with the unspoken tremor: o that they would stay!

That is one of the effects of their work, an effect from which it is difficult to withdraw. They are evangelists not of a future paradise, but not of a past one either. The present, a conservative, preserving, storing present was their paradise. A century earlier, the spokesmen of the middle class had been believers in progress. After the turn of the century, the popular writers had been infatuated with the middle ages. The conscience of our four writers, the conscience of (their) middle class, seems to rest easily on the double proposal: the past is golden — the present is good. They abstain from speculations on the future. Their strength lies in that they know what they are speaking of: of their place in their time.

It may be a deception of art, it may be a trick of perspective, but it probably is just the conviction of these obstinate men, which makes us inclined to see their world as actually a good time to live in. Why should they have been so fond of their small reality, if reality had not indeed become better for the little people? The question is wrongly put in our context. Their actual conditions, social and political, should not interest us here. But it is curious that the beginnings of German realism found in the conditions of their time so much room for beauty, nobility and morality. It is true, our four early realists do not like to dwell on public conditions. They and their heroes like privacy. But that so much privacy was possible without misanthropy, so much individualism without rebellion, so much self-fulfilment without selfishness, that makes us wonder wistfully: Was that Biedermeier time really the good old time? We do not want an answer from social or political history. We barely accept a confirmation from other arts. On the paintings from the old C. D. Friedrich to the young Menzel, on the Richters and Spitzwegs and Waldmüllers, we see the same light that caresses *their* world, not imaginary worlds. And why should a time, that did not like what it had, excel in the conservation of art in countless new-founded museums, in the conservation of 'classical' music in new-founded public concerts? This new trend of hoarding and safekeeping could only grow in a time which had much that seemed worth keeping.

However, the message of our four masters of Old Germany is only half made of conservation. The other half is e-ducation, a leading-upward of whatever audience they could reach. All four worked more or less in education in their professional careers. In their writings no less they belong with the throng of preachers with which German literature is stuffed. What they preached, now heavily now subtly, was personal moral culture, 'das Edle,' and collective moral culture, 'die Sitte.' In either case a moral culture which had a halo of beauty; which was as much aesthetic as it was ethical; and to which their artistic inspiration responded as much as their sense of good and evil. But even in their most inspired hours they heard the clocks of their conscience ticking away: 'Schöne sanfte Sitte einflössen!' Even under their most aesthetic works they could put as motto: 'Edel sei der Mensch!' Stifter was able to write (in 1847): 'The only mortal sin of an artist is that against the original godlikeness [Gottähnlichkeit] of the human soul.' And all four could not forget that Goethe had given his poem, 'Edel sei der Mensch,' this title, 'Das Göttliche.'

IV

The Age of Heine?

The English Legend

For the foreign reader, the second quarter of nineteenth century German literature is not the age of Grillparzer but that of Heinrich Heine. He stood for the spirit of the time, of which he was more conscious than any contemporary. As a journalist-poet he had an almost commercial interest in that spirit. As a congenitally polemical nature he kept sifting and shifting enemies and allies. As the quickest intellect he constantly gave himself, and the world, accounts of the past, present and future of German civilization. And as a writer whom fate placed between Germany and France, he took it upon himself to interpret them to each other, and with such impact that he figures among the great Europeans.

A European, however, he was more for Germany — in letting in all the winds from abroad, holding open the doors for all the cross-currents of air — than for the other countries, where his reputation was stable while his action was shortlived. To this day the actual knowledge of Heine abroad has not gone much beyond his first book of verse, *Buch der Lieder,* and the first volume of his *Reisebilder.* In vain have the German critics maintained, for a hundred years, that his later poems are his greater ones. The world at large was satisfied with his early poetry, as if that contained something cloying which took away the appetite for more. The most popular poems have been those in which Heine imitated the Romanticists, whereas his importance in literary history lies in outdistancing Romantic poetry. He has been best liked where he was least himself, he has aroused least curiosity where he was most original.

Where he was most original, he was also less representative of 'the spirit of the time.' Because he was insufferably personal in all his affiliations and recantations, he will stick out from any timely trends less as an index than as a sore thumb. The movements within Liberalism with which he was affiliated — toward national unification, toward constitutionalism, toward democracy — sternly repudiated him when they found out that he had mockingly repudiated them. Only one movement, nascent Communism, was wise enough never to show publicly how indifferent they found each other privately. No matter how faithless he was to his friends, he was constant in his aversions, some of which can even be put into a word, like anti-royalism, anti-feudalism, anti-Catholicism, anti-Christianism, anti-Judaism too, and anti-moralism in general. This sounds as if he were one of a crowd. But here too he had no talent for partisanship. He fluctuated so constantly between these aversions that he came close to merely misusing them for inspirations. In Heine's case, as in Grillparzer's, we find that the great writer seems representative to us mainly because we do not care to know the lesser ones, the truly representative ones. We limit our picture of the time to that which he makes available. Even if he did not succeed in changing its face then, he has changed it for posterity.

The *Buch der Lieder* (1827), on which Heine's international fame rests, was not his first book of poems but the first collection of his poetical works, his apprenticeship up to the age of thirty. From the earliest parts of the collection, it is evident that this young man is not taking the clichés of Romanticism seriously. That is the source of his freedom, of his superior play with them, and of his abuse of them. To a generation which was under the sway of those clichés, Heine's misapplication must have been a liberation. It was, in poetics, a liberation without revolt, because with a grace so natural that one might call it animal, he hid the fine thrusts of his wit in an expanse of sentimentality, his sharp claws in a velvety paw. The essential thing is that wit became the main ingredient in the work of a major poet — whereas so far it had made minor poetry only. In the symphony of German poetry Heine simply is the scherzo; and since he has to furnish the entire movement almost by himself, we should not mind if he rather overspecializes.

He found the right tone for voicing his nihilism in the bleak voices of *The North Sea*. There theme (ironic skepticism), form (rhymeless free rhythms) and atmosphere (the jagged seascape) make for a stark unity. Still, the distance from Goethe's and Hölderlin's free rhythms is appalling. Free rhythm needs a poetic thought too powerful to be bound: Heine's is just loose. The result is that we miss the tension between flagrant poetic form and flagrant prosy statement which seasons the rhymed quatrains in the rest of *Buch der Lieder*.

The sea pieces lingered on into the next collection. We think of 'Es ragt ins Meer' because it calls up Tennyson's equally beloved 'Break, break.' Tennyson is more careful to prepare his effect, and he blandly voices his hesitation: 'And I wish that my tongue could utter. . . .' There is indeed something not quite articulated about the poem. Only the third quatrain arrives at the theme:

> And the stately ships go on
> To their haven under the hill;
> But O for the touch of a vanish'd hand,
> And the sound of a voice that is still!

The picture of the ships and the lament do not immediately go together; they were both so very real in the poet's mind that he left them 'there,' face to face, expecting that they would interpenetrate somehow. Heine is much more to the point. No lost friend is the unavowed center, he places himself in Byron-posture, he dramatizes even his sitting-rock into a menhir. But the picture complete with wind, waves and gulls, and the four verbs (whistle, shriek, wander, spume) which vocalize the three nouns could not be more pithy:

> Es ragt ins Meer der Runenstein,
> Da sitz ich mit meinen Träumen.
> Es pfeift der Wind, die Möven schrein,
> Die Wellen, die wandern und schäumen.

When the quatrain has taken its effect, we no longer find any Byron-pose, we find the one non-objective line, 'Da sitz ich mit meinen Träumen,' of the finest proportion to the other three and the necessary basis for the second quatrain:

> Ich habe geliebt manch schönes Kind
> Und manchen guten Gesellen.
> Wo sind sie hin? Es pfeift der Wind,
> Es schäumen und wandern die Wellen.

In craftsmanship, this is superior to the English poem. The content of the dreaming is stated unsentimentally ('many a pretty girl, many a fellow'); the point is muted in a nearly pointless question ('Where have they gone?'). And it gets the answer it deserves in the perfect tiny rondo — empty in its recurrence, delicious in its slight variation, bitter in its taste to the heart, mellifluous to the inner ear. In comparison, Tennyson's feeling is dangerously close to overflowing. It fills the monosyllables to make them easily equivalent to the three-syllable feet of the following line:

> Break, break, break,
> At the foot of thy crags O Sea!

But it does not save him from unnecessarily restating the well-stated theme. And he has a bad conscience about it, he does not look at what he is doing, for the last two lines are practically made of lapses:

> But the tender grace of a day that is dead
> Will never come back to me.

It does take Tennyson's poem to make us detect a trace of coarseness in Heine's 'many a pretty girl.' That is a mixture of bluster and flippancy. If he loved many, there are many left; where is the loss? Tennyson is delicately withholding the object of his regret, but we feel there is no philandering included. On the contrary, when we consider that the four quatrains contain the whole friendship and mourning of *In Memoriam,* we must admit that 'Break, break' surpasses 'Es ragt ins Meer' as much in genuine feeling as Heine surpasses Tennyson in dispassionate craftsmanship.

Heine cannot maintain an atmosphere; but he can catch it again and again, and always differently. That gives his longer poems and his collections so many fresh starts; but it also leaves many air pockets in them, into which our flight drops repeatedly. Yet for the large public, the unpoetic public, the appeal of *Buch der Lieder* was perhaps just the built-in air pockets. What better thing could happen to a generation overfed with poetry than to find that here were cookies suddenly complete with bromo? Those who could not stand the sugar found the antidote, the acid, the anti-poetic baked-in. This was the gradually perfected technique of Heine's poems. They succeeded in bringing the poetic, ' the pleasurable elevation of the soul,' to a smaller focus, thus making room, in the very same poems, for an equally concentrated counteragent. It was probably not his ideal to furnish every poem with its built-in parody. Something in his nature, and something in the nature of the large public, encouraged him to give in to this specific temptation of his talent. For much talent was required to feel the temptation at all, and only Heine was able to live up to it for such a long time. The encouragements from his public came only slowly; his readers also needed to be educated to the new tone. The *Buch der Lieder* was not immediately popular, at least not as much as is commonly assumed. It took ten years for a second edition to be needed (1837).

A good picture of Heine's stature, as it evolved in Victorian Europe, is to be gained from his English reception. For almost thirty years after the appearance of *Buch der Lieder,* the sentiment among the English was overawed by their main authority for things German, Carlyle. He simply considered Heine a blackguard. (' Brotherly sympathy with the *downward* side . . . . not even blackguard Heine has it.' *Reminiscences* II, 127) Perhaps he had inherited the sentiment from Goethe, who is said to have had for Heine only the epithet ' Gassenjunge.' (W. Wadepuhl, *Goethe-Jahrbuch* 1956) The controversy about him was largely negative. We find an independent reaction in the American who got to know German poetry best. Young Longfellow wrote in *Grahams Magazine* (1842): ' The style of Heine is remarkable for its vigor, wit and brilliancy; but it is wanting in taste and refinement. . . . He is always in extremes, either of praise or censure; setting at naught the decencies of life. . . . With all his various powers, he wants the one great power — the power of truth ! '

This is the keenest estimate in English for decades, and its negative tenor may well stand for most of the English and American sentiment up to the time when translations of the *Book of Songs* (by Wallis, 1856) and *Complete Poems* (by Bowring, 1858) appeared. But with 1856 we have reached a milestone in English Heine criticism,

George Eliot's essay, 'German Wit: Heinrich Heine,' on the first pages of the January issue of the *Westminster Review*. Not for nothing had George Eliot been the translator of the most radical works of German philosophy. She could take Heine's ideological boldness in her stride, and she was in the highest degree susceptible to the subtleties of his style. Years of painstaking work on insipid German prose made her recognize with rapture the great writer. 'In Heine's hands, German prose, usually so heavy, so clumsy, so dull, becomes, like clay in the hands of a chemist, compact, metallic, brilliant; it is German in an *allotropic* condition. No dreary labyrinthine sentences . . . but crystalline definiteness and clearness, fine and varied rhythm, and all that delicate precision, all those felicities of word and cadence, which belong to the highest order of prose.' Again and again, in discussing his different works, she finds the apt phrase for those qualities. The sentiment of a certain comradeship pervades this beautiful apology by a fellow artist. For an apology it is. In the beginning, George Eliot does not spare the severe words which she probably knew the English public still expected to hear on the subject. 'The audacity of occasional coarseness and personality is unparalleled in contemporary literature.' She even goes as far as advocating 'a friendly penknife to exercise a strict censorship.'

The much reprinted essay of George Eliot was not the last word of English Victorianism. That was to come in 1863, in the even better known essay 'Heinrich Heine' by Matthew Arnold, in the *Cornhill Magazine*. Arnold thinks above all of Heine as representative of the state of modern literature. 'He is significant because he was, if not pre-eminently a brave, yet a brilliant, a most effective soldier in the war of liberation of humanity.' In the discussion of individual works, Arnold, like George Eliot, still singles out the early ones. As she has a fine ear for Heine's stylistic qualities, so he has a quick eye for the political activity. 'His direct political action was null. . . . "It is all of no use," he cried on his death-bed, "the future belongs to our enemies, the Communists, and Louis Napoleon is their John the Baptist".' 'That for which France, far less meditative than Germany, is eminent, is the prompt, ardent, and practical application of an idea, when she seizes it. . . . It is because he operates a junction between the French spirit and German ideas, that he founds something new, opens a fresh period.' 'The magic of Heine's poetical form is incomparable; he chiefly uses a form of old German popular poetry, a ballad form, which has more rapidity and grace than any ballad form of ours; he employs this form with the most exquisite lightness and ease, and yet it has at the same time the inborn fulness, pathos, and old-world charm of all true forms of popular poetry. Thus in Heine's poetry, too, one perpetually blends the impression of French modernism and clearness with that of German sentiment and fulness.' As G. Eliot began, so M. Arnold ends, on a note of moral disapproval. 'He dies, and has left a blemished name; with his crying faults, his intemperate susceptibility, his unscrupulousness in passion, his inconceivable attacks on his enemies, his still more inconceivable attacks upon his friends, his want of generosity, his sensuality, his incessant mocking, how could it be otherwise? '

But the objections have become brief, the understanding is long, and the very wording of almost every paragraph of George Eliot and Matthew Arnold leaves us a clear and sympathetic picture of the Victorian phase of the English legend of Heine. Their views became common property. Even a man of his own mind like Whitman comes back continually to Eliot and Arnold when he thinks of Heine. More differentiated and pertinent is the view of W. D. Howells, as presented in the *Atlantic Monthly* of 1873: 'Heine can never be read aright save in the pale moonshine of the German tongue; dragged into the daylight of our speech . . . he becomes harsh, sharp, sometimes shabby, and you see how, occasionally, he forces his fantastic attitudes. Perhaps also he is best read by very young men not past the age of liking even the faults of genius; he wearies middle life a little, though he remains wonderful.'

Heine and Eichendorff

George Eliot and Matthew Arnold prove that enthusiasm for Heine does not have to be in inverse proportion to knowledge of his poetry. On the other hand, the idea is not absurd that in Germany there continued to be more critical voices because the Germans kept reading so much more of him. 'Old Germany' could not but be afraid of his teachings. If Heine's *Romantic School* (1836) was the manifesto of Young Germany, one might consider as the belated counter-offensive Eichendorff's book with the insistent title *The Ethical and Religious Significance of German Romanticism* (1847). At the end of this book Eichendorff introduces Heine, fails altogether to acknowledge the fellow-lyricist, and only points to the hostile ideology.

'Heine, after the ironic destruction of certain poetic illusions, caught the new religion in the air and set it down on its natural and massive legs. He declared Christianity unworkable, because its spiritualism would do away with sensuality, and on this score he and his associates understood no joke. The choice is easily made, they slaughter the spirit that it may cease molesting poor dear matter.'

In Eichendorff's critical writings there is, on the whole, more common sense than in Heine's, who tried to be especially fanciful when he had to write in prose. (As Eichendorff's poetry is irrational with more abandon than Heine's, who tries to be especially 'cool' when writing poetry.) But in the case of their mutual judgments, Heine has the edge. When Eichendorff expanded his . . . *Romanticism* into the *History of German Literature* (1857), he did find, in the end, a good one-line characterization of Heine. He describes the carnival of Saint-Simonism, and then: 'The maître de plaisir in this carnival is Heinrich Heine.' In view of the affinity of Heine for mummery, masquerade and theatricals (Barker Fairley), this one trait is more meaningful than the earlier paragraph; and Heine might have recognized himself. Still, Heine's cleverness is more remarkable when in the *Romantic School,* with a knowledge only of the earliest poems of Eichendorff, he compares them with Uhland's, which were universal dogma then. 'What an excellent poet is the Baron Eichendorff, there is no difference between his songs and the very best of Uhland's—unless it be in the greener forest freshness and the even more limpid truth of Eichendorff's poems.' With so scant material, with no critical predecessor, only a critical genius could have hit the mark so surely.

To compare the wild flower Romanticism of Eichendorff and the hothouse Romanticism of the younger poet, we have to look at some poems on similar subjects. One Heine poem that suggests itself is the famous Fir or Spruce of the 'Lyrisches Intermezzo.' Heine's trees are not metaphysical like Eichendorff's; their symbolism is made so selbstverständlich that it must penetrate the densest reader. The parallelism between spruce and palm is wonderfully incisive, even if it is a little bit drawn with a ruler. One may show it off in this way:

Ein (1) Fichtenbaum steht (2) einsam	Er träumt von einer (1) Palme,
Im (3) Norden auf kahler (4) Höh.	Die, fern im (3) Morgenland,
Ihn schläfert; mit weisser Decke	(2) Einsam unde schweigend trauert
Umhüllen ihm (5) Eis und Schnee.	Auf (5) brennender (4) Felsenwand.

Heine is as fanciful as Eichendorff could ever be. The fir in Scandinavia and the palm in the Middle East dreaming of one another is a charming conceit, the literal impossibility of which facilitates a quick transfer to the 'other meaning.' (Punctilious people might speak of a little allegory.) The impossible love situation is delicately kept in flux by the verbal progression, where much is achieved within a narrow economy: 'stands—dozes—envelop—dreams—is silent—is sad' (two German verbs sorely missed in English vocabulary). In the artfully magnified distance and impossibility-of-convergence achieved by the first lines of the two quatrains; in the stupendous amount of descriptive detail packed into the second halves (bleak height, white cover, ice and snow—parched rocky cliff); but especially in the knowing repetition of one word, at the end of one line, at the beginning of another, ' lonesome ' : in all that, it is a little masterpiece. But it is devoid of any truth, poetic or personal; for Heine's oriental palms (his Jewish cousins) were not responding to his dreams at all. Heine's poems are often triumphs over truth.

Even when Eichendorff introduces himself in the first person, he vanishes into the sentiment of the poem so that his identity is lost. This happens in ' Frühlingsgruss,' a poem exactly in the form of Heine's ' Fichtenbaum.'

Es steht ein Berg in Feuer,
In feurigem Morgenbrand,
Und auf des Berges Spitze
Ein Tannbaum überm Land.

Und auf dem höchsten Wipfel
Steh ich und schau vom Baum,
O Welt, du schöne Welt, du,
Man sieht dich vor Blüten kaum!

There is no parallelism here, no expert correspondence between words and values, no subtle or energetic suggestion of second meanings. Instead there is a rocketing of words out of words, which from the second line on makes this a passionate poem. Eichendorff places before us the mountain in fire, and fire, fiery, brand, is said three times, so that the picture is framed in the flaming sunrise. Then he leads us to the top of the mountain, tops the top with the fir tree, leads us up the tree, into its highest tip; and there he stands himself. A soul in bliss stammers, Oh how beautiful! The logical disconnections of lines 7 and 8 form the main impacts of this poem. It is almost based on a platitude. ' Not to see the forest for the trees ' becomes ' not to see the world for its blossoms.' But the poem has moved so fast, and the outbreak has come so suddenly, that no one thinks of the old saw. It is a discovery, a morn of creation.

Eichendorff was not a professional writer like Heine. The bulk of his poems is less than half that of Heine. But the variety is just as great on both sides. Or rather, the monotonies on either side balance. At his fringe, either author is in the center of the other's domain. Eichendorff has funny and perspicacious satires on the time; Heine has deep-felt glimpses into nature. The few poems which incite comparison by some surface oddity do not show these affinities, they rather show how diametrically opposite is the core of each.

The lovely conceit about the ' grammar in the face of the beloved,' from the beginning of the Lyrical Intermezzo may be vaguely compared with any of Eichendorff's readings in the face of nature. Heine's poem plunges with bravura into an especially shallow infinite of pathetic fallacy. The stars (whom no Romantic troubled so often as Heine) are looking at each other, lovesick :

Es stehen unbeweglich/Die Sterne in der Höh,

Viel tausend Jahr, und schauen/Sich an mit Liebesweh.

The second quatrain, aware of the enormity, brazenly claims this interpretation to be too difficult for the learned linguists:

Sie sprechen eine Sprache,/Die ist so reich, so schön;
Doch keiner der Philologen/Kann diese Sprache verstehn.

The third quatrain, with a delightful bravado, claims that only the unhappy lover understands that language of the unhappy stars correctly:

Ich aber hab sie gelernet/Und ich vergesse sie nicht,
Mir diente als Grammatik/Der Herzallerliebsten Gesicht.

The felicity of the trifle is not merely in the turning up of 'grammar,' but in the whole shift from heavy sentimentality to light witticism. Here, sorrow is overcome by the freedom of the mind. More exactly, a fancy of sentiment is modulated into a fancy of wit. Heine's poems make light, and liberate; Eichendorff's frequently move toward dark and doubt. That is why they hold us longer. There is an uncertainty, a wondering, a self-questioning about them that is the opposite of Heine's talent for making everything plain and brilliant.

When Eichendorff reads in the book of nature, he reads mysteries there. But far from the conventions of the pathetic fallacy, he does not pretend to have the interpretation. The subject of which he knows most is that of the night. Here is how he broaches it in the poem 'Der Abend.' The poem is all confusion, in both syntax and idea. In form it is a succession of cheap rhymes, the fine disposition of which obscures rather than creates a meaning.

Schweigt der Menschen laute Lust:
Rauscht die Erde wie in Träumen
Wunderbar mit allen Bäumen,
Was dem Herzen kaum bewusst,
Alte Zeiten, linde Trauer,
Und es schweifen leise Schauer
Wetterleuchtend durch die Brust.

Under the surface of the indifferent melody, a harmony establishes itself, without regard to syntax. An appeal to the instincts sets in, fostered by the very half-articulateness. When the 'loud pleasures' of the day are over, the dreams 'of the earth' become audible. 'Wunderbar' means here 'mysteriously.' But what can the earth voice, to us, except our own voices? And of those only the subconscious ones (kaum bewusst), the submerged ones (old memories), the undefined ones (mild melancholy). And the soul is assimilated into this evening landscape. In the last two lines it becomes itself a twilight landscape, over which the tremors of the enumerated half-perceptions play like distant sheet-lightning. Heine turns off the poetic impulse, as if he were afraid that it might work. Eichendorff labors through to it, often reaches it only in the end. Or the end only shows that he had it working all the time. Heine works from the essence of a poetic image toward the brilliant and superficial. Eichendorff works from the common face of things toward their dark core.

The different reaction which the two poets elicit is perhaps based on a very elementary difference. Heine is so unwilling to leave the realm of the impurely personal that he forces us back continually upon biographical considerations. Our other writers of that age are willing to disappear behind their works. They make it easy to treat their lives as negligible quantities and to keep their works before our eyes. Not so Heine. The fellow was so much bigger than his works that he remains visible behind their every corner, no matter how we look at them. He shares this bad habit, of an excess of the personal, with the other Young Germans. They are more interesting as persons than they are through their works. Literary history takes its revenge by paying attention to their personal opinions and personal relations, to such a degree that these people furnish the 'historical' background behind the aesthetic existence of their unpretentious opponents. If their diffidence had permitted, the 'Old Germans' might have shuffled a later *mot* thus: 'As to living, our Young Germans will take care of that for us.' But some beholder cannot suppress the sigh: how drab is biography compared with the contemplation of art!

Poet in Paris

In France, Heine was received as a poet famous in his home country; in Germany, Heine had the reputation of being highly considered in France. The assumptions reinforced each other, not by propaganda only. In Germany it was Heinrich Laube who spread Heine's French reputation. He had been dazzled by Heine's commerce with Balzac, Janin, Girardin, Custine, and especially George Sand, the French novelist at that time most highly considered in Germany. Laube could not get over a certain evening at George Sand's, where Heine flattened Lamennais (whose fervent convictions of Christian socialism were anathema to him). Laube barely noticed the quiet disapproval, not only by Lamennais, but also by the hostess, of Heine's method of discourse. Heine did not know, so his Parisian friends said, when a fruitful discussion was exhausted and when a continuation of the subject became embarrassing to everybody except him (Mme. Jaubert). Among George Sand's few judgments on him is a remark in a letter of 1836: 'Heine sinks into a monomania of bad jokes [calembours].'

However, the relations between the two were always cordial and for a long time so affectionate that historians have tried to make a pair of lovers of them. But George Sand had, literally, no time for

Heine between her many other affairs. Her final judgment of him is one of the most favorable : ' Heine's heart is as good as his tongue is bad. . . . Like his poetry, he is a mixture of the highest sentimentality and the funniest mockery.' Heine, in return, considered her 'the greatest writer new France has produced,' he preferred not only her to Balzac, but also Dumas and Sue. (J. Dresch, *Heine à Paris,* 1956, from whom we borrow most of these details.) Stendhal does not seem to have come into his ken. In spite of his critical indifference, the personal relations between Balzac and Heine were good, they enjoyed talking with each other (perhaps because they talked, according to one witness, more of finances than of letters).

Heine had the most flattering introduction to the world of French letters. None less than Sainte-Beuve places him (*Le Globe,* March 1832) on a line with Börne and Menzel; the three form ' a generous league for the upholding of liberal journalism.' But as early as August 1833 (*Le National*), Sainte-Beuve combines with the most perceptive praise a series of warnings. He finds the French sense of neatness offended by Heine's diligent mixing of the genres, which interrupts the logic of prose ' at every step by rockets of metaphor.' He warns Heine not to trade exclusively in a French monopoly : ' He will be more at our French level when he has a little less " esprit ".' He would like to see a little less destructiveness : ' One would wish him a more fruitful stock of enthusiasm. His brilliant phantasy appears sometimes rather lightweight to us Frenchmen, who had a reputation for frivolousness. . . . If he thinks we are more a malicious and maligning people than appreciative, he is mistaken.' This was in a long review of the translation of *Französische Zustände,* and the subject made Sainte-Beuve feel competent to tell Heine some home truths. But Heine never became as reasonable as the foremost French critic admonished him to be. In the *Letters on the French Stage* (1838) he tried to play Sainte-Beuve against Victor Hugo. After that Sainte-Beuve did not bother about him any more. And Victor Hugo, whom he had at first flattered, left only one judgment of him : ' Wings in the spirit, envy and hatred in the spine.'

Heine's judgment of French poetry was as little advanced as that concerning the novelists. The greatest French poet, for him, was Béranger; then Musset, then perhaps Hugo (of whom he patronizingly wrote that ' he could even count as a good one among German poets, which is saying much '). Of Lamartine he noticed only that as a minister, in 1848, he was not able to renew Heine's pension. He had no sense of the sombre elevation of Vigny. But the strangest thing is the silence of all these French confrères on the subject of Heine. He was a familiar figure among them, was even the fashion, at least in 1832-35. One would like to have their opinions of him. ' There is none by Mignet, by Musset, by Dumas père, by Lamartine, by Vigny, by Thiers, by Cousin, by Delacroix' (Dresch, p. 14). No, there is an entry in Vigny's diary: 'I find him cold and offensive.' On the whole, they did not trust him, and they used the simplest weapon against insolence, silence.

Heine's reputation was that of a talker, in the good and the bad sense. Of his works, only one side was known in France. In 1844 Countess d'Agoult says (*Revue des Deux Mondes,* October) that he is known for his prose only, not for his poetry. In that periodical, it was Taillandier who most often spoke of Heine's poetry; but Taillandier was a very Victorian critic. He found even in Heine's best verse an 'irritating imitation of the worst Parisian journalism. . . . Must we get from across the Rhine what we fight at home every day?' (October, 1843) The whole edifice of German idealism is in ruins now, and 'in this general destruction all that is left is grotesque laughter and an irony that is fine, subtle, and often affected.' (January, 1845) In the July number of 1845 Henri Blaze coined for Heine the epithet 'unfrocked romantic,' which Heine relished and which has remained one of his chief titles.

His other face, turned toward the future, was less noticed by his French contemporaries. But Gerard de Nerval liked him, translated him — in spite of slight knowledge of German — very sensitively. Gautier always liked him and was almost a good comrade. And Nerval and Gautier passed on their regard to Baudelaire, who did not know him personally. It seems that Baudelaire got some elements of his symbolist aesthetic through Heine. In his first articles from France, on the Salon of painting of 1831, Heine had written: 'Sounds and words, colors and forms, all phenomena generally, are nothing but symbols of the idea, symbols which are born in the soul of the artist. . . . And the works themselves are only symbols by means of which he communicates with other souls. . . . His principal patterns are revealed to his soul as the innate symbols of innate ideas.' Fifteen years later Baudelaire's aesthetic started in the same place, before the painters of the Salons of 1845 and 1846. He knew and quoted those very words of Heine. Thus Heine passes from the 'unfrocked Romantic' to the 'herald of French Symbolism.'

'Progress is easy on the scamps (den Lumpen wird der Fortschritt leicht), but what is he to do who unfortunately has convictions?' Thus wrote one shaky mandarin to the other, old Grillparzer to old Stifter, in 1860. In the thirties, that feeling was still rare, but the convictions were there which prevented Heine's most witty and most vicious writings from being received as they deserved. Many of his compatriots took them for incendiary bombs. Few could take them for the brilliant fireworks, the illuminations of insight, the felicities of art, which they were for the author first of all, and which they have become again for posterity.

Heine knew the commercial value of scandalous poses too well not to strike them again and again. Especially when he first came to Paris, in 1831, he felt he had to live up both to his new reputation and to the old reputation of the city. He could not do better than entitle his new collection of verse *Verschiedene,* which was promptly translated in the minds of many readers as ' Promiscuousness.' Of the vast doctrine of Saint-Simonism he took most seriously the challenge to ' emancipate the flesh.' That doctrine appeared to him as the rock of a Newest Testament:

> Auf diesem Felsen bauen wir
> Die Kirche von dem dritten,
> Dem dritten neuen Testament;
> Das Leid ist ausgelitten.

The last sentence contains his actual hope of redemption, the hope that most of human suffering would soon be over, because ' the stupid chastening of the body has finally been abolished.' The fourth quatrain of the poem rises to a concise statement of this new pantheism:

> Der heilge Gott, der ist im Licht
> Wie in den Finsternissen;
> Und Gott ist alles, was da ist;
> Er ist in unsern Küssen.

Efficiently the first line starts from the orthodox view, God is light. Puissantly the second line adds the mystic view, God is darkness as well. Cogently the third line synthetizes into Spinoza's ' God is nature.' And triumphantly the last line deduces the point to be made, God is in our embraces. The little span from the first word ' holy ' to the last word ' kisses ' is as good as a syllogism.

The cycle in praise of ' Promiscuousness ' is not quite worth this Newest Testament. It contains much situation comedy, and it is very light verse; nothing sticks in the mind — until Heine hits upon the full romantic orchestration of his theme, the Tannhäuser legend. There it acquires depth and complexity, but it is no longer music according to the program, because it changes into the more crucial theme of one woman becoming the embodiment of all womanhood — no, only of all the sensual bliss it can bestow; animal, mistress, goddess of lust, Venus. Heine knows how to dramatize the theme by starting with a moment of satiety. In the initial dialogue of lust and languor almost every quatrain is memorable by its poetic simplicity and directness. Languor suddenly gets tired of the eternal travail of sex slavery, which stretches in glory and misery as far back into the past as into the future. Then the dramatic scene of Tannhäuser in Rome, stopping the papal procession with his public confession. For a quatrain or two it is confession of sin; then it turns into a panegyric of woman's loveliness; then it rises to the protestation of rapturous human bondage. and the pope can only raise his hands in resignation :

> Der Teufel, den man Venus nennt,
> Er ist der schlimmste von allen.

The Tannhäuser triptych ends with a scherzo that contains some of Heine's driest and funniest sallies.

Heine's eroticism is of a peculiar kind. Between the true Victorians, who valued sex so highly that it was sacred and unutterable — who made the inhuman condition that the fulfilment of sex should be the fulfilment of love — and the moderns who speak of it as an every-hour bore, Heine stands in an equivocal middle. He wants both the modern liberty to speak of erotic matters all the time and the old-fashioned privilege of speaking in allusions only. Even his unpublished poems keep their fig-leaves on. This constant dragging in of sex, and the gingerly pulling at its veils, have always passed for lascivious. Heine is hard to defend against the reproach, because sex is so often a joking matter for him. The gospel of the emancipation of the flesh could not be preached in that farcical way. The truth is that it did not mean as much to him as he wanted people to believe. After all, his lifelong ménage with his grisette was the most bourgeois affair one could imagine.

But when Heine takes sex seriously, even solemnly, as in 'Tannhäuser,' as in 'Ritter Olaf,' as in the middle of *Atta Troll* — passages all inspired by his ménage — it is as if he discovered an abundant spring of inspiration. It associates itself with other sources which seemed to have run dry and now suddenly flow as full as ever: historic, legendary, literary associations enrich his grand theme. But the richest supply comes distinctly from his personal feelings, individual reminiscences, even private allusions. There his poetry acquires body, which it so often lacked; it is the voice of a whole man, not of a professional jester or a political journalist. There his poetry combines what he too often kept apart; it disproves what he said to George Sand, who wrote in her diary (November 1834): 'Heine told me that love is a matter of the mind and of the senses, and that the heart has little to do with it.' Poetry, even his, had to be written with a good deal of heart. Where his love became tenderness and his lust enthusiasm, they left accents almost worth a new dispensation, a new gospel of physical love.

To the life-long Heine-reader the most long-lived enjoyment are his longest poems, the two 'epics' dashed off in that resurgence of his poetic faculties, 1842-44, which also prompted him to collect all his Paris poetry under the title *Neue Gedichte*. Heine is a poet of short breath, and it is not obligatory to like his long things best. But they have the one advantage of giving us, better than anything else, his incomparable pace. They enable us to read in the sequence in which he wanted to be read, and to abandon ourselves to his change of mood and whim. His happiest verses, his drollest contrasts, naturally also his longest developments, his most leisurely contradictions, are enclosed in these pseudo-epics, *Atta Troll, A Summer Night's Dream* and *Germany, A Winter's Tale*. They are each a cross between Byron's *Don Juan* and *English Bards*. *Atta Troll* surprises us by the exquisite nature snapshots which open almost every Canto. Queerly, the poem is directed against 'tendentious poetry' — of which Heine was the unequaled model. *Deutschland: ein Wintermärchen* is the funny account of Heine's first trip back to Germany (October-December 1843) and contains, of course, the largest collection of invectives against contemporary conditions.

Heine's poetry needs commentary less than any other German poetry, it is obvious to a fault. Yet, no other poetry has more authentic commentary. He gave it in his two critical books, *Religion and Philosophy in Germany* and *The Romantic School* (1833-36). Both books had better titles in French: *Germany since Luther* and *The Present State of Letters in Germany*. They are his two most serious, most positive works. There some of his cultural patriotism, so rarely to be detected under the forced raillery of his poems, is patent. It gives to his investigations, cavalier as they are, a genuine warmth for ideals not even his own, a genuine appreciation for historical significance, without incessant side-glances at the ridiculous side, at least without giving in to the temptation at every step.

Comparison with Mörike

The article in the *Revue des deux mondes,* July 1845, in which Henri Blaze de Bury coined the epithet of 'Romantique défroqué' for Heine, was really dedicated to Mörike. And it did justice to the somewhat inclusive title, 'La Poésie lyrique en Allemagne: M. Edouard Moerike.' With good method Blaze introduces Mörike by way of the well-known Heine. One is a little surprised to see how drily the French critic judges Heine's standing within Romantic poetry. 'In the real Romantic school [phalange] Mr. Heine would never have attained first rank. In imagination and ideas, Arnim, Novalis, Bettina herself, will always be incomparably superior to him. The cleverness of the author of *Reisebilder* consisted in creating his own Romanticism, a sort of 'critical Romanticism,' of which he alone in all Germany possesses the secret. Mix the naivety of medieval poetry with the negativity of modern society . . . that is about the procedure.' Equally surprising is the simple recognition with which Blaze turns to Mörike:

' In comparison with Mr. Heine and all the literary dilettanti of Germany, Mörike is a naive poet." But when it comes to characterize such a ' Naturdichter,' the critic is justifiably hesitant : ' To give the procedure of that poetry, however, is hardly possible. . . . Sometimes a stanza reads like prose, so marked is it by simplicity. . . . And it seems as if this poetry had within it a hidden music.'

Mörike is hard to compare with Heine, even if we choose among Heine's latest poems. There should be some approximation between the several prayers of Mörike and the parodies of prayers of Heine. But one has only to think of the terribly middle-class ' Gebet ' of Mörike. It is not only resigned to mediocrity but actually asks for it. ' Herr, schicke was du willt ' sounds like true surrender to God's will, but it ends by cautioning God not to will too much for the wretch who prays. The heart which prays there is a very timid heart, which clings to its ' holdes Bescheiden.' The mind is quite a narrow mind, for which the whole metaphysical range shrinks to a thin strip ' in der Mitten.' In comparison, Heine has an immense span and a mighty sweep. We take the first poem in the appendix ' Zum Lazarus.' No resignation there to anything like moderation and mediocrity. Instead, the most pithy statement of the imperfection of the world order. A question is put vaguely in the first quatrain, is put into pointed examples in the second, is turned into bloody sarcasm in the third, and receives the most silencing answer in the last. Popular philosophy cannot be stated with more sweep. Nihilism cannot be versified more competently.

Lass die heilgen Parabolen
Lass die frommen Hypothesen —
Suche die verdammten Fragen
Ohne Umschweif uns zu lösen.

Warum schleppt sich blutend, elend,
Unter Kreuzlast der Gerechte,
Während glücklich als ein Sieger
Trabt auf hohem Ross der Schlechte?

Woran liegt die Schuld? Ist etwa
Unser Herr nicht ganz allmächtig?
Oder treibt er selbst den Unfug?
Ach, das wäre niederträchtig.

Also fragen wir beständig,
Bis man uns mit einer Handvoll
Erde endlich stopft die Mäuler —
Aber ist das eine Antwort?

There is an inescapable ' coming to the point ' in the more and more insistent progression, ' parables — hypotheses — damned questions — no mincing ! ' There is an overwhelming crowding of incontrovertible detail in the two halves of the second quatrain, the halves clanging out into the crashing rhyme, ' the just one — the villain.' There is a satanic plausibility in the two suppositions of the third quatrain,

'Can't the good Lord help it?' 'Does the good Lord enjoy it?' And there is serpent insidiousness in the hard-hitting rhyme 'omnipotent — low-minded.' The first and third quatrains are abstract, the second is concrete, but more so the fourth, with its 'handful of earth' and 'die Mäuler stopfen' (English has nothing that vulgar and expressive: stop up our snouts). Here is the center of poetic gravity, with the compact 'handful of earth' saddled between two lines, and with the answerlessness of the question made discordant in the rhymelessness of the quatrain. Heine is as devastating in his nihilism as Mörike is satisfying in the shaping of the things within his range, 'die Wonnen der Gewöhnlichkeit,' the blessings of the commonplace — and there is no comparison.

Not to give up the fruitless attempt, let us look at one more incomparable pair. One of the most quietly revealing poems of Mörike is 'Auf eine Lampe'; one of the most self-revelatory passages of Heine is in 'Jehuda ben Halevy' of *Romanzero*. Both were written toward 1850; both may be construed as poetics.

Wie im Leben, so im Dichten
Ist das höchste Gut die Gnade —
Wer sie hat, der kann nicht sündgen
Nicht in Versen noch in Prosa.

Heine takes a precious concept of the theologians, that of divine grace, and applies it, with two strokes, to two untheological concepts, life in general and poetry in particular. He applies it in a very untheological way. For, with the third stroke, he shows the theologians what their grace needs, in order to be all that it is cracked up to be: it needs to safeguard from sin. This charisma should really be the simple consequence of the other attributes of grace. Heine, with a hypertheological consistency, boldly asserts that it works that way in his world, that it makes him incapable of sinning. And when he adds, 'not in verses nor in prose,' we get the hint. The man knows what he is talking about. Wasn't he the only man of his time equally famous for his verse and for his prose?

Solchen Dichter von der Gnade/Gottes nennen wir Genie:
Unverantwortlicher König/Des Gedankenreiches ist er.

Heine anchors his doctrine on three disciplines in which he does not believe: philosophy, theology, politics. We think it, so it is; we call him genius, so he exists. That is the specious reassurance of philosophy. He makes the title 'By the grace of God' ride pompously astride on two lines, and that is the specious unction administered by theology. But the term has mostly been appropriated by monarchs; so Heine appropriates it to the monarchs of the mind. He liked so much to imagine himself as the brother spirit of some absolute ruler, some Alexander, Augustus, Frederick the Great, Napoleon. But alas, there were no absolute rulers left, except Heinrich Heine himself, non-responsible king in a non-constitutional monarchy of the mind. For, obviously, here the non-responsibility goes with absolute power.

> Nur dem Gotte steht er Rede
> Nicht dem Volke — In der Kunst
> Wie im Leben, kann das Volk
> Töten uns, doch niemals richten.

A third time he says the same thing; how interestingly different, how insistently the same! How intricately the pseudo-religious, the pseudo-political, and the truly aesthetic spheres are mixed! Each gets a false support from the other, and thus appears incontrovertible. The great artist is responsible to (his) God only: he is (as far as the vulgus is concerned) infallible. And to make the doctrine stick, the antitheses fall as thick as hail; vox dei — vox populi; art — life; murdering — not sentencing. The privileges of art are presented in trappings borrowed from everything the poet has derided most in his life's work.

Mörike's poem on the unheeded existence of true art is in an old-fashioned verse-form, iambic trimeters. One third of the poem is leisurely wasted on describing the location:

> Noch unverrückt, o schöne Lampe, schmückest du,
> an leichten Ketten zierlich aufgehangen hier,
> die Decke des nun fast vergessnen Lustgemachs.

What is most prominently said is that this thing of artcraft is still in its right place, is here — still. The awareness of the transitoriness of art underlies the whole poem. It is said a second time, when the room is called 'almost forgotten.' But the object's function of beauty, or operation of beauty, is said three times, 'beautiful lamp,' 'delicately hung,' 'chamber for festivities'; no, a fourth time in the verb 'adorn.' Then follows, in exactly equal measure, the description of the object itself:

> Auf deiner weissen Marmorschale, deren Rand
> der Efeukranz von goldengrünem Erz umflicht,
> schlingt fröhlich eine Kinderschar den Ringelreihn.

Two materials, the marble of the bowl, the brass of the frame. Two colors, white and green-gold. But, most complacently, the representation of reality: the frame imitates an ivy crown; the bowl shows a round-dance of children. And a human sentiment comes through: 'merry.'

> Wie reizend alles! lachend, und ein sanfter Geist
> des Ernstes doch ergossen um die ganze Form —

This couplet, the first half of the meditation, gazes with understanding and response at the thing. The 'merry' feeling is expanded, 'all' is charm and smile. But with the exact compensation so characteristic of Mörike he adds, 'and yet a gentle seriousness about it all.' No doubt it is this balance of gentle gaiety and gentle earnest which earned the final verdict:

> Ein Kunstgebild der echten Art. Wer achtet sein?
> Was aber schön ist, selig scheint es in ihm selbst.

'An artifact of the genuine kind' is Mörike's stiffest pronouncement. As if he had caught himself being pompous, he makes amends in the question, 'Who heeds it?' The two half lines, the assertion and the question, together are worth a little volume. There is nothing bitter in the juxtaposition, not a trace of sarcasm. Rather there is a trace of 'it is all as it should be.' Because the genuineness and the unheededness do not stop at antithesis, they develop a synthesis which reads like this: genuine art does not need recognition; it is complete in itself; it has a blessedness within itself. But to the incorrigibly just Mörike this seems again too strong an assertion. So he adds a little word admitting that we cannot know, really, but so it 'seems.' By this time the poem seems to have become singularly soft-spoken. What started as a confident and cheerful address to a beautiful thing ends more like murmured soliloquy, almost like introspection.

Our two poets are poles apart when they speak, the one of grace and the other of blessedness. For the grace of Heine no claim is too high, too arrogant. The blessedness of Mörike consists in making no claim. No wonder that a genius of Heine's kind found the world too small. Mörike felt that he did not need the world ('Lass, o Welt, o lass mich sein'). Most of Heine's poetry is unfulfilled desires, erotic, social, political. Mörike's poetry is always fulfilled; there is a balance of powers in it which comes close to equilibrium. Strangely, the world, for which Heine cried, goes through his poetry in the shape of a thousand wraiths. The world, of which Mörike was so independent, comes to his poetry in a thousand concretions. When we come from Mörike, Heine's poetry looks sharp, thin and wan. And the other way is not possible; when one comes from Heine, one is blind and deaf for Mörike's kind. His ears filled with the din of battle cries, who can heed a pure tone, 'wer achtet sein?'

Mörike conceded that Heine 'was a poet through and through,' but also that he could not bide the man behind the poetry, 'not for one hour.' It is known what attitude Heine adopted toward Mörike. To be sure, Mörike's collected poems were only just appearing, and Heine did not know Mörike's novel with its poems. But he did not want to miss any possible friend of Menzel, so he included Mörike in a cutting libel. His publisher wrote him that he was mistaken about Mörike; so he decided to lampoon a mere anonymity: 'If you are convinced that this Mörike is rather my ally than my opponent, you may print ★★★ instead of his name, but leave in what I said about him.' (July 7, 1838) And so to this day Mörike figures as three stars in

Heine's *Schwabenspiegel*: 'I am told that an excellent poet of the Swabian school is Mr. ★★★; that he discovered himself only recently, but did not manifest himself yet; because his poems have not yet been published. I am told that he sings not only cockchafers but even larks and quails, which is very laudable. Larks and quails are worthy of being sung — when they are roasted.'

Heine's Germany

Ich bin ein deutscher Dichter,
Bekannt im deutschen Land;
Nennt man die besten Namen,
So wird auch der meine genannt.

Heine said this in 1824, a few years before it was true; and he kept believing that he had one of 'the best names' in Germany even in the years when it had again become a dubious statement. Among W. Wadepuhl's thorough *Heine-Studien* (1956) was 'Heine und Campe,' in which the whole correspondence between poet and publisher was examined for the first time. We had always believed Heine's self-estimate; Campe's letters had been largely unpublished. In the fuller documentation, Heine's popularity appears in a doubtful light. Campe made his money from better-selling authors, but Heine was his favorite and protégé, whom he paid best, and whom he pushed, because he needed pushing. Innumerable complaints from Heine (200 letters) often forced Campe into self-defense. In 1833 he had to show Heine's brother Max, from his books, that he had never printed editions larger than 2,500. Of the *Buch der Lieder,* 'the stock of 2,000 has been reduced to 800. In the last two years only it has begun to draw, because we have started to include it in shipments of *Reisebilder*. That's the way with poems. . . . In seven years we got rid of 1,200 copies, including what we gave away.' The first two volumes of *Reisebilder* had a second edition (1831). Campe tried to explain why Heine's other things did not move: 'You treat of love and of yourself and again yourself; people regard that as stinking egotism. They take the *Buch der Lieder* into the bargain to have you complete, that's all. Thank goodness, there are also the more enlightened ones. But egotism is always blamed on you, and also that you advocate debauchery. . . . Your book goes with universities and with young men, who have no money.' (July 12, 1833)

Then Heine desperately needs 20,000 francs. After many machinations, he realizes that the only publisher from whom he can get them is Campe. But the new contract is not bargained for without new incriminations, so that Campe has to review the situation: 'You overestimate the sale of your books. For ten years we have been working together, and only the *Reisebilder* have been printed twice.

Your main work, the *Buch der Lieder,* has had only one edition. Of *Französische Zustände* we still have half the edition, of the *Salon* we have disposed 1313. What is there that warrants your huge claims? ' (March 24, 1837) Things were to get worse before they got better. ' Years ago I wrote to you that we needed a third edition of *Reisebilder I.* . . . If we have enough copies left *now,* you may see how everything gets into a rut and how the items sell poorly. . . . The bans have lost their stimulant effect.' (April 18, 1839)

The book against Börne brought Heine's popularity to its lowest point. His illusions goaded Campe into the declaration of May 2, 1843 : ' Believe me, that book was your Russian campaign! Your sales have dropped by three fourths. . . . Do you think the public does not avenge itself? It does! Sure, your old friends are satisfied. But the new generation is offended. . . . Much has changed for you in Germany and not to your benefit. You know, everything has its time, in literature too. I warned you betimes; you did not listen. That you are already more a matter of history than of life — can I change that? '

Campe was a bad prophet. Heine did listen now, he had a new spurt of poetic productivity. *Neue Gedichte, Atta Troll, Deutschland,* all appeared in quick succession; the public was by no means indifferent, and Heine's was once again ' among the best names ' — in a way. The public had ceased to consider Heine a spokesman for the things that interested it most, and that was politics. Public opinion in Germany was interested in political progress more than anything. From the princes down to the craftsmen, the need was felt as if it were an atmospheric pressure. Surprising is the number of changes and signs of change which make their appearance in Germany in 1847, before the February Revolution in Paris. But when the French fought their third revolution, the Germans could no longer be prevented from starting their first. It is interesting to see how Heine reacted to that revolution, of which he had — long ago — counted almost as the foremost literary champion.

It is no less than symbolic that Heine's full physical breakdown coincided with the outbreak of the February Revolution, and that the carriage which was to take him from a clinic to his home was thrown over and used for a barricade. Any participation, active or only as a bystander, was excluded by his complete paralysis. It only remains to see what his sympathetic reaction was. He documented it precisely in a letter to his mother, written after the success of the German insurrections was well known.

' Paris, March 30, 1848. My dearest Mother: Just because it's so stormy in the world and especially troublesome here, I cannot write much. The hubbub has brought me low physically and morally. I am discouraged as I never was. I want to live quietly from now on and not bother about anything. The racket started just at the turn of my cure, and I have not only lost money but also my health. If matters should take an even gloomier shape (as I fear), I shall leave, with my wife or alone. I am in a bad mood. In Germany affairs are not cozy either, and I have no great desire to come. . . . My wife behaves. If she didn't, I would give her her freedom, as all kings give their peoples now: then she would see what's to be gained by freedom. You have no idea how great the distress is here. All the world is becoming free and bankrupt. Good bye! . . . Has our family lost much money? '

Although the letter has the touching purpose to mislead his mother about his dreadful sickness, one cannot help thinking of more straightforward attitudes. Even touch-me-not Mörike elevated himself for the moment above his privacy: ' Over the distress of the moment and my timid little existence I have been lifted into a joyous resignation. How could it be otherwise? Who has not, for a few weeks, felt himself to be bigger than he did in his whole life! ' (March 24, 1848) Eichendorff, the nobleman and loyal official, found for ' Freedom's Return ' (1848) accents of hopeful reunion, and for his greeting to Freedom his most familiar accents,

Holde Freiheit, schöne Fraue,
Grüss dich Gott viel tausendmal!

Stifter was among the men who deliberated the change in Vienna beforehand. When we hear him, a few months later, he is already worried about the future of the Revolution. ' God grant us that we realize how wisdom and moderation are necessary for building up; that, and not only tearing down, is necessary. . . . I am a man of moderation and of freedom — both are endangered now.' (May 25, 1848) Heine, however, has only sarcasm for the frantic attempts of Europe at practical progress: ' I have nothing to tell of the events of the time. It's universal anarchy, cosmic hodgepodge, God's manifest dementia! They have to put the Old One in a straight jacket, if things go on. The atheists are to blame: they made him mad.' (To Campe, July 9, 1848)

It is obvious that Heine, like other anarchists, was indifferent to the actual improvements which were the immediate results. He could not be interested in the constitutionalism which evolved so energetically and smoothly under the cooperation of the whole German nation, from the leftist elements to the governments themselves. On March 5 the first convention of 50 liberals in Heidelberg was held; on March 31, 500 delegates met in Frankfurt as ' Vorparlament '; on May 1, all Germany elected representatives; on May 18, 1848, the Frankfurt ' Parlament ' convened. It spent a year elaborating a

German constitution. Of the 600 men, 20% were teachers, 30% judges, 10% lawyers, 20% officials. It was perhaps the most intellectual parliament the world has seen. Consequently, it tried evolution, not continued revolution. Consequently, it soon had to fight against two fronts: the left-wing minority which substituted armed insurrections for parliamentary debate; and the reactionary governments, which gained force from the tension between Austria and Prussia (since the ally Metternich was gone). An Austrian archduke was elected as the executive of the parliament, but the emperorship was offered to the king of Prussia, who declined.

The excessively difficult work of the Frankfurt parliament was followed by all minds with anxious sympathy. Gutzkow (credited with the arming of the people of Berlin) issued the warning book, *Germany on the Eve of its Fall — or Greatness.* Laube (a member himself) described *The First German Parliament* in three volumes (1850). Only Heine saw nothing but foolishness: 'Everything in Frankfurt was arranged for a work of art: the unity of time, of place, and of stupidity,' he said to Fanny Lewald in September 1850. And to F. Meyer in September 1849, 'all the heroes of liberty, without exception, filled him with nausea.'

The more serious observers were filled with despondency. In Vienna, in Dresden, in southwestern Germany armed insurrections were put down by the military. Even peaceable hearts, like Mörike's, saw none but desperate means: 'I would like to know whether you see any other hope for the German cause, except a new revolution?' (June 26, 1849) Eichendorff sang to the tune of 'Dies Irae' a 'Lament of Liberty' (1849), crying Woe! over his country where liberty had been shackled so long, had been accepted so briefly, and had then been foolishly misunderstood. But he saw foolishness not, as Heine did, in the men of progress, but in the radicals of the left and the reactionaries of the right. 'Rabble rule is stupid, saber rule is more stupid; whichever way I look, I get angrier every day.' (January 25, 1849) This was written to the Prussian minister, Count Schön. These officials and noblemen were more 'men of the people' than the scoffing observer in Paris. The most eloquent laments on the atrocities in which the radicals had smothered the revolution are Stifter's. 'That was a terrible year. . . . Where clowns of state flourished, but no men of state. Every stranded writer, every flunked student, and the like, became a politician. The ideal of liberty is ruined for a long time. He who is morally free, can be free politically, no, he is so anyway; but the others cannot be made free by all the powers on earth.' (March 6, 1849) 'When I saw the course which the affairs were taking, I was seized by the blackest despondency about humankind. I followed the events with an attention and emotion which I thought I hadn't in me. When unreason, empty frenzy, then meanness and shallowness, and finally crime took over the world, my heart came near breaking. . . . Beauty, greatness, humanity gone; the soul devastated; poetry vanished. Slowly, slowly the figures come back. Rock, tree, sky begin to speak again. And noble souls are left, whom we can love.' (September 4, 1849)

Heine's judgment was not clouded by emotion, at least not by any sympathetic emotion. He had kept his unerring aim in pin-pointing the dirtiest spots in the picture. What a panorama of the post-revolutionary world we get in the poem 'Jetzt Wohin?' (in the *Romanzero* of 1851). There is a hit in every running verse. England had always been his favorite aversion, but he had never expressed it with such masterly concentration. The physical aversion is in contrast with the high political estimate of his countrymen. The radicals in Germany admired the French republic; the more numerous liberals favored the English constitution, which was one of the ideals often pointed to in Frankfurt. But there was one country which turned up as a model more often than any other in the political writings of the 1840s and in the debates at Frankfurt, that was the United States. The labors of the majority in Frankfurt avowedly consisted in an attempt to adapt American federalism to German institutions. But Heine had a dainty rhyme for the United States too:

Manchmal kommt mir in den Sinn,
Nach Amerika zu segeln,
Nach dem grossen Freiheitsstall,
Der bewohnt von Gleichheitsflegeln.

We must admire the power of besmirching with a word, with a twitch of the mouth, what was the sacred hope of most others. 'Liberty' and 'equality' were the two basic drives of the Revolution. Only on their proportion had there been a difference of opinion. But Heine brilliantly succeeds in making both sound ludicrous by the compounds 'liberty-stable,' 'equality-churls,' and by the sweeping identification of America with that caricature.

It must have been the fun of differing from everybody, which even worked when everybody execrated something: then Heine was large-minded and did not find it so bad. Russian Czarism was in Germany the hated symbol of despotism. Sympathies with Russian politics were tantamount to tenderness for the Inquisition. Thus all Europe felt it as the ultimate in shame when Austria called on Russia to put down the Hungarian revolution of 1849. Heine promptly ends the poem 'October 1849' with the remark, 'Console yourself, Hungarians, don't mind the Russ; after all, the Russian bears are decent beasts. They have beaten you, but beaten you decently. Think of what we Germans must feel when we return to the yoke of our princes. You know their heraldic animals. Wolves, hogs, and common dogs are *our* rulers.' Heine had a soft spot for Russia. As early as 1828, in a notorious passage of *Reisebilder III,* he said that 'the Russian government is imbued with liberal ideas; its unchecked absolutism is nothing else but a dictatorship to bring those ideas to life immediately.'

In many of these opinions Heine was all alone, and wanted to be. He thought it his privilege as a genius to express what nobody believed. Yet such is the charm of a great talent that the world has listened to him in the face of all the evidence, and will continue to prefer his versions to all verities unearthed since. The word of the poet is so powerful that it can change the truth.

With surprising insistence the nineteenth century came back to the question of Heine's character. The odious confrontation of talent and character would not have been repeated ad infinitum, had it not been found unavoidable. Yet we are mistaken if we interpret the verdict of his contemporaries to mean that Heine was a great artist in his works but a bad character in private. That was neither the truth, nor would they have cared. What most of his contemporaries in and outside Germany regretted was the lack of character in his *art*. The man had enough qualities to endow a few ordinary humans. He had even sublimities which amply make up for his glaring defects. If we think of his fortitude and his sheer victories of mind, we are moved to call his life one of the epics of the century. But art is not composite like life; art is personal only at its sources; its aims and its criteria must be collective: aspirations of humanity. And in that respect, Heine had a bad character. Not because of his private personality have Gundolf and Karl Kraus and Hofmannsthal considered him the worst influence in German literature, but because he cheapened poetry; because he was a blight; because he taught that (in art) the way down was as good as the way up.

It is a continual surprise to see how essentially right contemporaries are, and how posterity changes judgments quantitatively above all. Heine's greatest contemporaries had little doubt about his enormous range. Metternich wrote in his *Mémoires* (v. 8, for 1838): 'Heine is a great poet — a personality on the lowest rung of the moral ladder — and a talent of high intellectual qualities.' And Grillparzer wrote in his diary of 1836 (not long after he came back from Paris) a peculiar remark concerning his literary loneliness in Vienna: 'Since Schreyvogl's death there is no one in Vienna with whom I could talk about matters of art. No, even in Germany there would be none to suit me; except perhaps Heine — if he were not inwardly a scurvy fellow.' These two lines, 'Ja auch in Deutschland wäre niemand, der mir anstände, höchstens etwa Heine, wenn er nicht innerlich ein lumpiger Patron wäre,' are the haughtiest recognition ever bestowed on Heine. It is as if a knight were dubbed with a whack. The great ones find one another out and assess one another mercilessly.

Heine, by the way, had a high opinion of Grillparzer, correctly summarized by Laube (to Karpeles in 1847) thus, ' He has a perfect respect for Grillparzer.' The letter of 1833, ' Ich habe Sie von jeher sehr gut verstehen und darum verehren können [comprehension and therefore reverence]. . . . Sie und die höchsten Eichen des deutschen Vaterlandes,' was not polite fancy. Although the statements to interlocutors are not above suspicion individually, they are unanimous. In 1846 Heine said to Tauber (from Vienna): ' If Grillparzer were here, I'd guarantee him the first rank of German immortality; in his absence I must claim it myself.'

Grillparzer and Heine stand for the two great movements of ' historism ' and nihilism. Turgenev claimed himself, and still is often given, credit for introducing the concept of ' nihilism ' (1862). The Germans had the thing even before Jean Paul and Görres called it thus. And Heine's friend Immermann mentions ' the intellectual nihilists ' in the first chapters of *Epigonen* (1836). But in our period, the most general movement of the German mind was ' historism.' The movement concerns us only insofar as it was reflected in literature. In all the arts the time tried to establish canons of ' classic ' masters. In all disciplines of the mind the viewpoint of evolution prevailed. Historism valued ' being ' [Sein] as long as it could trace its ' becoming ' [Werden]. It was a concerted effort to justify the present by its precedents, to understand every national history from the viewpoint of organic growth. From that viewpoint the present seemed the more promising the deeper its roots were in the past. In philosophy, law, and political thought historism was the central consciousness of the century. In literature it was much less conscious. But consciously or not, Grillparzer stood for it. Heine had no part in that mainstream of German consciousness. This is his importance, that he was the antitoxin. While most of his countrymen hoped to salvage a reserve of traditional values, he was the first great nihilist. We do not know whether the movement was really more important than the countermovement. We do not know whether — from any of the viewpoints which we should command, but don't — the age belonged to the historism of Grillparzer or to the nihilism of Heine.

Part Two

THE AGE OF KELLER

PART 2

I

Gottfried Keller

G. Keller's Dialectic

When T. W. Rolleston, in the London *Quarterly Review* of 1914, called Gottfried Keller 'the most creative spirit that has appeared in German literature since Goethe,' he was far from repeating the general opinion. When John G. Robertson called him 'Germany's Greatest Living Man of Letters' (*Cosmopolis,* 1897), he was twice wrong: Keller had been dead for some years, and the judgment was loudly challenged, e.g. in the Philadelphia *American* of 1900. A more representative opinion was that of George Saintsbury, who set Keller down as 'one of the most respectable writers of German-speaking Switzerland. But if Keller be taken and read on his own merits, the sense of disappointment . . . will be curiously prominent' (*The Later Nineteenth Century,* 1907).

It has taken a hundred years for Keller's most ambitious work to be translated (*Green Henry,* New York, 1960), although from its first appearance on, there were voices that declared both its prominence in German letters and the probability of its not being popular. That was actually the trend of Keller's fame: he was, from the beginning, remarkably well thought of by the best critics; he was, to the end, remarkably little read by the public. When he finally proceeded to revise his first work, there were 110 copies left of the 1,000 of the first edition. Keller bought and burned them. And he had been a famous author for twenty years.

He was hardly a professional writer. At the age of fifteen he had been ejected from school. He became a lazy but tenacious student of painting in Zurich; then for two and a half years in Munich. Back home, his painting stagnated, but he was swept away by the new wave of German and Austrian political lyrics. He turned poet, found publishers, found political protectors who sent him to school again, to the universities of Heidelberg and Berlin. He was twenty-nine when he left for Germany (in 1848), and his interest was the drama; but what he produced was a novel and 'Novellen.' The rest of his writing career was a fitful carrying out of the plans he had laid in Berlin.

'Keller is peculiarly intangible, his excellences needing to be felt, being often too subtle for words.' This judgment of Helen Zimmern, his lonely apostle in England and America (first in *Fraser's Magazine,* 1880) is not helpless evasion, it is modest insight. There is something elementary about Keller, which cannot be analysed. But there is also a peculiar compositeness and compensatedness, which can be demonstrated. Keller himself gave us a clue in a sentence written in 1854 (to H. Hettner). 'Neu in einem guten Sinne ist nur, was aus der Dialektik der Kulturbewegung hervorgeht.' 'New, in a good sense, is only that which proceeds from cultural dialectic. . . . That is the best hint what a poet should strive for.' He saw the very basis of (his) art in a dialectic, a resolution of progressive antagonisms.

This classic of democratic literature in Germany was a doubter even in his radical youth. In a diary entry (July 10, 1843) he pondered the advances of Communism: 'However, I cannot take kindly to Communism. For one thing, it consists of chimeras which could not be put into practice without increasing misery. . . . On the other side, it seems to be the result of a spreading pleasure-seeking and indolence.' He was all for the tangible aims of Communism; 'but with your fanatic ideas go to the madhouse, if you are sincere; go to the devil, if you are merely greedy.' A few years later, in Germany, he began to doubt his own party too: 'I have never met more stupid and brutal fellows than the German democrats [Republikaner] of second and third rank. They carefully nurse all bad passions in the common people, envy, revengefulness, bloodthirstiness and lying.' (March 10, 1849) Within his democratic conviction he evolved from a radical in his twenties to a liberal in his thirties to a conservative in his fifties. And this, curiously, paralleled the evolution of public opinion in Germany, though not in Switzerland.

Keller is the glory of Swiss letters. But when he saw Helen Zimmern's capital article 'A Swiss Novelist,' he remarked, 'it has only one fault, it treats little me as a specifically Swiss literary matter. I always rebel against the view that there is a Swiss national literature. Patriot as I am, that is no joke. I am of the opinion that, if any good is to come from it, every one has to keep to the greater linguistic territory to which he belongs.' (December 20, 1880, to Mrs. Freiligrath). In his case it was no accident that he spent his decisive periods in Germany rather than in Switzerland. Even after the terrible Munich experience he wrote: 'When I came back to Zurich three years ago, it was in the hope of finding enough money to return to Munich and continue my studies with better results.' (September 16, 1845) And when he was back in Germany he wrote, 'I bitterly regret the years I wasted in Zurich after my return from Munich. . . . For a poet Switzerland is barren soil.' (January 28, 1849) 'If my tired old mother were not anxiously waiting, I would stay in Germany for a long time, for nothing else draws me to Zurich.' (September 22, 1850) Even so, he stayed for five more years. His literary associations were practically all outside the borders of Switzerland. All his works, from 1846 to his death in 1890, were published in Germany.

He was geographically peripheral, just as Grillparzer was. But Grillparzer stuck to Austria, in his private and professional life, in a half spiritless and half obstinate way. Keller was conscious of the difference, and even theorized about it: 'A certain light-heartedness was lacking in Grillparzer. This lack made him cling so anxiously to his local bureau career and prevented him from sailing freely into the world. Had he ventured abroad, the alien realms would first have naturalized him and then given him back as a made man.' (To Emil Kuh, October 23, 1873) These remarks are largely wrong when applied to Grillparzer, but they apply to Keller himself, who was never in Grillparzer's position of overlooked-plus-supercilious outsider in German letters. Fate and instinct had made Keller gain a foothold 'abroad' before he established himself at home. Indeed, only this foothold established him at home. On the basis of his German reputation his little republic of Zurich provided, intermittently, for this artist of intermittent and infinitely hesitant production, up to the age of fifty-five!

Soon after the completion of the autobiographical novel *Green Henry* in 1855, Keller published the satirical Novellen *People of Seldwyla* (1856), as if the satire of milieu had been waiting all the time, while the exploration of individuality was being carried on. The two interests intertwine in everything Keller wrote. The novel is full of episodes that have little to do with the hero and describe Swiss and Munich milieu, though less satirically than lovingly. And in the Novellen the love of the author for his heroes often outshines any satirical intent. The author has invented this town of Seldwyla in order to localize there all the foolishness of Switzerland. But in most of the stories he is forced to discover 'exceptions,' and it is to these exceptions that not only the imagination of the author but also the memory of his readers have attached themselves.

There is perhaps a relation between the public preference for the Novelle *A Village Romeo and Juliet* and the fact that he had carried it in his mind for many years. The initial vision of the two ploughing farmers is sketched in his diary in 1847, and the writing was begun soon after. It is an example of the slow maturing of everything Keller did. The pervasive dialectic in every theme of this author is manifest in this story. Before the first paragraph is over, theme and countertheme have been stated; the first unforgettably, in the figures of the ploughers rhythmically meeting and disappearing 'like constellations.' Before the children and their partly delightful, partly cruel games have fascinated us, the selfishness in the integrity of the two fathers has been insinuated. And the ample development of the first section closes with a bang when the two farmers shear off part of the field that lies between them.

The whole story is embedded in society, and every page is charged with social motivation. With unerring hand Keller traces the development of evil out of the normal. The second section is a model study of economic deterioration. But the reader is fully occupied on different levels, as in every true dialectic. At times it is breathtaking to watch how the foreseeable is told. There is constant change of pace, between lingering and precipitation; change of tone, from the solemn to the ludicrous; change of mood, now bitter now tender. And the author is simply polymorphous: he oscillates between vivid concreteness and abstract sententiousness, between the sheer image and the blunt moral judgment. Strangely, the one is not felt as the absence of the other, they too enter into a dialectic synthesis. The strongest bond is perhaps the chain of portents, signs, symbols.

The abiding symbolization is partly obvious and partly suggested. Although the author has accents of plucky realism in the speech of the farmers or of the children, these accents are fleeting as wisps. Mostly he lets people think and speak in his own idiom, that is within the whole range from articulate exposition to sheer poetry. The overall impression is that of a translation of many tongues into one idiom, rich and varied to be sure, but leaning to the side of the lucid and the expressive. Their speech almost naturally transcends into his, and his naturally shoots meteors of imagination, stirring or grotesque.

The salient contrast to the Shakespeare story is the full development of the first theme, the situation of the fathers. When the narrator has his hands free for the counter-theme, he devotes to it exactly as much space as was taken up by all the development so far. But the time left to be covered is only a day or two. We are absorbed in the tale of the two young people, but the leitmotifs of the first theme have been established so solidly, that ever so often our ear rediscovers their drone.

In the one good day which the two teenagers make for themselves, the three levels on which the story moves — naturalistic detail, conscious reasoning, and poetic fiction — are stressed successively. Hearty attempts at comedy are frequent at first. Then the social consciousness of the youngsters is illustrated to the saturation point. And finally the imagination of the poet creates some situations (the dance of the outcasts, the procession of the black fiddler, the love-death) where every throbbing page confesses unblushingly: I am a poet's fiction. The poet in Keller, the epic poet, makes us feel these 'lapses' from realistic fiction as sheer elevations. He has no system, or he changes his systems at random; but when he writes most flagrantly *fiction,* he confirms its right to rise into fairy-tale at will.

It is a story of love, but not of passion. As ruthless as the poet is in heaping degradation on the fathers, as meticulous is he in demonstrating the innocence, the chaste virtue of the children. And this is all the more vivid, because a warm sensuality pulsates in the young lovers, suffusing every incident that confronts them. The reader hangs between their subconscious sensuality and their conscious modesty and does not know which he lives more. Keller does such consummate justice to both. And the sexual union of the young couple takes place on the brink of the beyond; which is unquestionably right.

The dialectics of the story are many. That between nature and civilization can barely be touched. A simply golden light hovers over the landscape (from 'goldene Septembergegend' on the first page to 'der untergehende Mond, rot wie Gold' on the last). But louder are, within civilization, the dynamics of the 'bürgerliche Welt,' the social world. It is for these dynamics that our Victorian couple has a wonderfully sensitive ear. The poet finely attunes their ear, and at the same time rudely depreciates society. Wherever anything like a crowd, a mass is formed in this story, it is seen in an unfavorable light. The solitary heroes are always above it, estranged from it (even the word 'Verfremdung' is used). The final paragraph suggests that society sees only the wrong perspective. The poet despises society, but he wants his heroes to cherish the social ideals.

The story is so crammed with dialectic that the poet was not at all sure he had succeeded in a synthesis. Of all his stories, he doubted this one most, his most successful one. He came near excluding it from publication (to H. Hettner, April 16, 1856). He knew he had taken all the artistic risks which the story afforded. He could not be sure that it was the very soaking of every page with that mixture of observation, thought and fancy which makes the reader constantly aware of being trebly rewarded.

If we turn to the question, is Gottfried Keller representative of an age in German literature, we cannot be satisfied with the generality (stated by T. W. Rolleston in the *Quarterly Review,* 1914): 'A Swiss or a Viennese writing in German always thinks of himself and is thought of by others as contributing to German, not to Swiss or Austrian literature.' To be sure, Keller's 'Village Romeo' passes as the crowning piece of all the German village tales, so popular in the middle of the nineteenth century. But it is a village story almost by accident. Most of Keller's stories have their habitat in the moral climate of a small but intellectually cosmopolitan town. (Zurich had 30,000 inhabitants in Keller's youth, and imaginary Seldwyla was smaller.) All of Keller's heroes were consciously middle-class, but in a country where the middle-class contained also the aristocracy. Keller's *Green Henry* is (with Stifter's *Nachsommer*) the nineteenth century apex of another favorite German genre, the novel of education. But, like the rest of Keller's work, it is not in the least typical, it is altogether exceptional. And yet in its anomalous way it may be representative of a phase of the German mind: the insistence on a youth packed with curiosity and fancy vices — on an artistic career that is a failure — on the resigned life of a public servant as the salvage. Keller also passes as the master of German realism. But he is, on the one hand, a master from whom nobody learned, and on the other, one who disdained to transmit anything he saw in French and English literatures, which he knew without finding anything to admire.

It is first of all some of the negative aspects which make Gottfried Keller representative of an age of German literature. The latter was, in the second half of the nineteenth century, a desultory and peripheral affair. Political and economic matters absorbed the energy of the nation, and even in German philosophy mind was in defense against matter. In Keller's writing politics, economics, and philosophical 'materialism' occupy the foreground. Only the most robust art could absorb such coarse ingredients so successfully. But the first impression is that the ingredients are offensively present. Keller is the classic of democratic literature in Germany; political education is his theme from first to last. Keller is also the classic of economic existence; one hardly remembers a story of his where the financial condition is not nearly the *condition humaine*. And with a deliberateness that was reckless Keller made himself the spokesman of German philosophy at its shallowest (the humanism of Feuerbach). What then saved him from the jaws of all that subject-matter? The very gift of the antidote. His nature always counterbalanced. Not only the individual work is full of compensations, his career as a whole has quiet and determined gyrations. We have mentioned those of his politics. In his respect for economics he evolved from an emphasis on economic respectability to a mistrust of industrial enterprise. His bright moralism was endowed with a warm sensualism. And his humanism was more and more tempered by a deep pessimism. The little man in him, the Swiss, the bourgeois, was in sympathy with the 'progress' of his century. It must have been the tragic artist in him that saw the same development in a twilight, so that his works may just as well be counted among the classics of that cultural pessimism which dominates the second half of German 'Victorianism.'

All in all, he seems to be less obviously a representative of

German literature than of the dialectic of culture; as he prophetically said himself, '. . . was aus der Dialektik der Kulturbewegung hervorgeht.' It may be a crime against this great writer to say that he belongs less to literature than to civilization. So much is true, that he was no professional, that each of his works took an uncanny time in growing, that they grew much more in his mind than in his medium (fashioned speech), and that every volume was invariably botched in the end, because he could not stand dragging it on. But such a combination of patience, passivity, receptivity, silence, irresponsibleness, and wilfulness nursed a work in which literature, so to speak, was passed by; a work into which the cultural tendencies passed directly. The opposing forces which, secretly or publicly, constituted German life in the middle of the nineteenth century passed into Keller's work with an immediacy which we feel in no other writer to a comparable degree.

C. F. Meyer's Poetry

A German proverb says that the Swabians don't come to age till forty. The Swiss, originally of the Swabian tribe, seem to justify the proverb. Gotthelf was forty when his first book was published, Keller past thirty-five when *Green Henry* and *People of Seldwyla* gave him a reputation, and Conrad Ferdinand Meyer was forty-five when his first valid poems appeared. He was the slowest in growth, and not only as an artist — he married at the age of fifty. The life which this rich bourgeois of Zurich tried to lead could be called drab, were it not interned, so to speak, between two chasms: the insane asylum at twenty-seven and the insane asylum at sixty-seven. The timid bourgeois held himself so stiffly, because all his life he walked under a shadow.

The slow growth of his art is simply phenomenal. In his student years he was so untalented in everything that his mother gave him up as hopeless, and that he hid himself from the eyes of people, living as a recluse in his room, emerging at night for long solitary swims in the lake. Aimless and without a profession he spent those years. His 'early' poetry (when he was about forty) was uniquely undistinguished and ungifted, as in the case of no other major writer. Yet Conrad Ferdinand Meyer is *the* German poet of his time. Rarely did anybody make so much of so precariously little. With endless effort he altered and substituted, added and, above all, rejected in his poems, from year to year and from edition to edition. Nobody ever rejected so much. And in the direction of his efforts this man without talent had genius; his endless alterations were always improvements. While a much more gifted man like Keller impaired many of his poems by later corrections, Meyer always mended, refined and purified. Perhaps the very mediocrity of the initial stages left him only one direction to move. At any rate the final result was sometimes superb.

In Meyer's poems nothing is natural, everything is artificial. They do not contain, they are not the expression of, his deepest drives. His dominant drive was that of perfection, and he sternly muted, ruthlessly mutilated everything for that. Hence there is a curious sense of distance from the organic, of being left with the synthetic. The unity, even in his shortest poems, is not in the natural spurt of an emotion or an inspiration, but in the patient addition, substitution, or mere suggestion of motives, the aggregate of which makes the small units complex and rich, makes the larger units consist of beautiful fragments within an indifferent context. Indifference is even an adopted tone and attitude for him. Indifference or impassibility is a curious attitude to strike for a lyric poet, but Meyer insists on it. In the preamble to his poems he insists that his soul is not bound up in them, but remains free and above them.

Und ergötzt sich drüberhinzuschweben.

In the proem to the most personal section, 'Love,' he insists once more than in all these poems there was less reality than playfulness.

Und alles war ein Spiel.

That was an exaggeration, a pose, a mannerism, and Meyer had many. He adopted them with a candor and thoroughness which make them over into honest character. He almost had to adopt them because he was a man of too many choices. He had no fate, no life which held him under compulsion. He spent many of his formative years in French Switzerland, and for decades he was under the spell of French literature; he thought he would devote his life to it. In his mature years he leaned heavily toward Germany and German politics, he admired Bismarck wholeheartedly. But his highest literary models remained those of French classicism. And when a penetrating contemporary (Spitteler) wanted to characterize him succinctly he said, 'that is French!' Others, Frenchmen among them (R. d'Harcourt) have confirmed the impression. And indeed, C. F. Meyer reminds us of nothing in German literature so much as he reminds us of his French contemporaries (whom he ignored), of A. de Vigny, of Leconte de Lisle, of the essence of the Parnassians.

It was not only between French and German civilization that he was able to make an option (and he chose both). The same happened between past and present civilization. All his grand Novellen aggrandize periods of past history. He has been persuasively but variously identified with a Renaissance man, a soul of the Reformation, a seventeenth century 'mannerist,' a Baroque type. He has been ably documented as a representative modern Decadent or Esthete. But there is in all his art such a preoccupation with ethics, with flagrant crime and saintly virtue, with subtle and with brutal questions of conscience, that one marvels at this shifting alliance between a great esthete and an indomitable moralist.

An example of the esthete in Meyer is the much-admired 'Roman Fountain.' The eight-line poem is of an almost irritating objectivity. There is so little of the emotional subject in it that the interpreters have been forced to recognize in Meyer the protagonist of a new type of poetry, the object-lyric (in contrast to the *Lied,* the 'natural' outflow of subjectivity). The poet is only observing, contemplating; and the fountain rises and falls before our mind's eye astoundingly recognizable and true to itself. In the last of many revisions, the poet transposed the accent upon the first syllable, and this last stroke is evidently the master-stroke which heightens the rising sensation of the first half of the first line:

> Aúf steigt der Strahl, und fallend giesst
> Er voll der Marmorschale Rund,

— We see the water jet first, see it rise, then fall. We see the marble basin only when the water hits it. At once we see the top basin being filled, see the curious beclouding and flouncing action which takes place as the water enmeshes itself to brim over. The grammatical subject has changed to the basins, because they, more than the water, shape the flow from now on:

> Die, sich verschleiernd, überfliesst
> In einer zweiten Schale Grund;

Every couplet focusses, not on one basin, but on a transmission from one to the other. This is most amply done in the third couplet, where there is room to state the 'becoming too rich,' the 'giving' and the 'swelling' separately:

> Die zweite gibt, sie wird zu reich,
> Der dritten wallend ihre Flut,

— But it is the last couplet which wonderfully trebles the 'simultaneousness,' the 'giving and taking,' the 'streaming and resting,' thus satiating the process:

> Und jede nimmt und gibt zugleich
> Und strömt und ruht.

The last word contains the biggest surprise. It is not, like 'streams,' a summary of the foregoing poem; it is the whole thing under a new aspect: all this movement is, for the mind, a closed circle and therefore at rest. And all the time, this underlying restful truth was accompanying the poem in the alternating rhymes in '*u*,' the stillest of the German vowels. In the initial 'Aúf — steigt der Strahl' we can now hear the wilful interruption of the circle. We can also hear the resolute arresting of the motion in the broken-off half-line 'Und strömt und ruht. . . .' This ending in an audible pause was, like the beginning on an ejaculatory accent, a last-minute touch. And if one adds the circumstance that Meyer reduced the poem from 16 to 8 lines, one gets the measure of the superiority of his execution over his inspiration.

Many of Meyer's poems tell of dramatic actions. Many others describe scenes, inanimate objects, art objects. The reader does not easily find the central tenor of a Meyer poem. From so many influences, possibilities and options resulted an eclecticism of attitudes, themes and tones which the reader feels as the lack of something compelling, or as the presence of something synthetic. It would be just to speak of something polyphonic. The recognizable simple melody of the *Lied* is not there; the poem relies on the polyphony of several motifs; and if the reader has been attentive to them, their symphonic union, usually in the final climax, is a fulfilment.

Although Meyer knew many more parts of Switzerland, and much more intimately, than Keller (who was a ' Stubenhocker '), and although the poems are full of the Swiss locale, the voice of that locale sounds muted. To him it seemed that the light on the Alpine peaks was omnipresent in his character and in his poems :

In meinem Wesen und Gedicht
Allüberall ist Firnelicht,
das grosse stille Leuchten.

This is said so beautifully that one would like to find it true. One is much more inclined, however, to accept his own thinning-down, which he modestly manages in the final line :

Ein kleines stilles Leuchten !

The voices of Switzerland are modulated into his own voice of a modern man. This is true even in his long poem-sequence *Huttens letzte Tage,* which is full of the atmosphere of the Lake of Zurich, but fuller of the moral, confessional and political interests of Meyer. The idyllic Lake laps its rhythms into many another poem. But even when the circumstance is as reliable as the schedule of the ' Spätboot,' the last one of the little steamers plying between the shore towns before turning in at Zurich —

Hüben hier und wieder drüben dort
Hält das Boot an manchem kleinen Port

— the reality is overshadowed by the mood and symbolism. We have quoted the middle of the 7-couplet poem. It continues,

Bei der Schiffslaterne kargem Schein
Steigt ein Schatten aus und niemand ein.

The atmosphere is so thin that the dubious word ,' Shade ' suffices to make us think of the shades of the underworld; and we are confirmed rather than bothered by the incongruence that this is a boat where the ' shades ' do get off.

Nur der Steurer noch, der wacht und steht!
Nur der Wind, der mir im Haare weht!

There we have Charon, erect and solitary, and there we have the lonely passenger, the poet. All human companions have gone, he is alone with the wind and the water, and Charon.

Schmerz und Lust erleiden sanften Tod.
Einen Schlummrer trägt das dunkle Boot.

Three kinds of death are attained in this final couplet. What is stated is only that the passenger falls asleep. What is implied is only that 'pain and pleasure' are stilled. But what the whole poem has prepared us for is the calm expectation of Death, for which the other two deaths are only practice.

Meyer is a master of evasive moods, evasive in their formulation only; their duration may turn them into obsessions. It is these obsessions which, under a hundred chaste veils, form a rather sombre, rather tired, but longing life beneath the poems. There is much of modern man, but little of the Swiss people. In spite of the grand figures which Meyer likes to sketch in his Novellen, in his ballads, it is not they whom we remember, it is just their moods. Neither do we look for Zurich there, nor for the Swiss landscape, nor for its 'lakescapes.' It is 'soulscape' that the poems communicate, and soul itself is here a skeptic, eclectic, and synthetic concept. Here we are at the opposite pole from Keller. Meyer is the voice of no one civilization; rather a voice of modern civilization itself. He is so civilized a soul that it remains mysterious how it remained a poet's soul after all.

The Master of the Novelle

Keller lived from 1819 to 1890, Meyer from 1825 to 1898, both in 'little' Zurich (which in their lifetime grew from the size of Weimar to 150,000). When Keller died, Meyer outlined his sentiments. 'I state that I felt reverence for Keller, not a conventional but a true and deep one. Not only for his incomparable talent, but no less for his heart and character. From our very first meeting, I was struck by his ethical weight.'

On several occasions Meyer insisted on the ethical weight of Keller. Why he had to insist so much is not obvious, except that Keller had a local reputation for indelicacy and uncouthness. One finds traces of such reservations even in the foreign reviews during his lifetime. His habits of a bibulous celibate did not help, and his lack of a profession made him almost suspect among his industrious compatriots. Then something memorable happened. After the seven years in Germany he had dawdled at home for seven more years. In 1861 he meddled more than usually in politics, making himself especially obnoxious with the majority and the government of the County of

Zurich. But his well-wishers prevailed on him to apply for the position of secretary to the administration [Staatsschreiber], and he got it. It was one of the best-paid offices in the state of Zurich, but time-consuming too. The man who for forty-two years had been a passable example of a good-for-nothing suddenly proved to be a devoted official and justified the extravagant confidence which a few enlightened politicians had placed in him. For fifteen years he served faithfully, and they did not even prove a sacrifice for his writing career; for toward their close he readied three volumes for publication, *Seven Legends, People of Seldwyla II,* and *Züricher Novellen.* It was these three volumes which brought him, in his fifties, a solid fame.

C. Spitteler has an expert paragraph on the causes of Keller's late success. On the hundredth anniversary of Keller's birth, he said: 'Today we ask, how was it humanly possible that a book like *Green Henry,* where poetry shines forth from every pore, could remain unknown for decades? . . . Many things had to come together to bring recognition to Keller: Verse had to lose its reputation and novel and Novelle come to the top; the poetic dignity of humor had to be recognized; the two best-known and most-read story writers [Auerbach and Heyse] had to honor him publicly and with grand modesty; a literary pope [Vischer? Hettner?], year after year, had to drum Keller into the minds of his students, i.e. of the future professors; an omnipotent publisher [Weibert, of Goeschen] and a powerful periodical [Deutsche Rundschau] had to take him under their wings. Then it worked.'

Moreover, German public opinion, in the seventies, was a national-liberalism which felt not a little flattered by the stories of Keller (from *Seven Legends* on) as well as by those of Meyer (from *Hutten* on). And Swiss public opinion could not help seeing that, with all their German sympathies, these two writers still placed their *little* country far above everything. C. F. Meyer was not alone in defining the core of Keller's authority thus: 'Most and mightily impressed was I by the position he took toward our little country; it was indeed the position of a guardian spirit. He watched and taught, preached and warned, frowned and corrected paternally.'

But that was only one side, the public side of Keller as a man of letters. There was a very private side to him, which the fastidious Meyer did not want to touch upon. It is of course the very lonely and loveless life which the passionate man led between an old mother and an ageing sister. Short, ill-favored and slightly grotesque, he had an agonizing taste for perfect women, tall, intelligent, and good. He never inspired more than friendship. His intellectual mastery of his fate, his decorous disguising too-intimate truth with ready invention, these together form the fine texture of his love-stories. Apparently he knew that he had satisfied the longings of his heart with the creation of exquisite feminine figures ' such as the bitter earth has not nursed.'

> Doch die lieblichste der Dichtersünden
> Lass nicht büssen mich, der sie gepflegt:
> Süsse Frauenbilder zu erfinden,
> Wie die bittre Erde sie nicht hegt!

His accomplished feat in this direction is the heart-piece of the *Züricher Novellen,* 'The Governor of Greifensee,' where he tells the *five* luckless lovestories of a man, in a row and even in anti-climactic order, and manages to interest us throughout. Moreover he risks ruining his pieced-on story by regular interpolations of chapters in local history.

On some patriotic occasion, the forty-two year old Governor, Salomon Landolt, is reminded of his five past loves. He is on such cordial terms that he can invite each of them to his castle. We have hardly caught the rare tone of his relationships — a blend of courtesy and comradeship, respect and intimacy — when we are set on a different track by the pathetic story of his old housekeeper. On such changes of tone Keller builds the continuation of the precarious story.

The first episode is of a 'normal' engagement, a perfectly suitable match, matured in a perfectly pastoral idyll. As contrast Salomon exaggerates his unreliable family traits, and his over-honest description frightens the reasonable girl into marrying a more solid prospect. Landolt finds ' he has escaped a danger.'

There follows the most 'abnormal' affair, one of the high points of Keller's fiction. Placed in the very family of the official moral censor of the city, the elemental spirit of Figura is of such gaiety that her lover nicknames her 'the Buffoon.' This strangest of the episodes is most heavily loaded with pages of cultural history. The poet's infatuation with the past sprouts into delightful scenes where censor and censored are matched in joyous 'evildoing,' topped by another scene where the dullest facts of literary history are converted into a scherzo which enfolds the tragic dénouement: the Buffoon fears hereditary insanity. After the complacent dallying the muted rapidity of the concluding paragraphs is very effective. In reality nothing is concluded: the best of men stays in love with the gayest and most unhappy of women.

Nothing can happen to Landolt's heart for seven years. Then he begins to specialize. He falls for sheer beauty. Keller is incredibly resourceful when — in each of his books — he paints the Fata Morgana which the mind of a man sees in the perfect body of a woman. Then, after having loved first youth, second spirit, third form, Landolt falls in love with taste, or something that passes for it.

The fifth time, he falls in love with true love — for another. He becomes the distinterested helper of the couple.

Keller is nice to a fault, whereas his contemporaries, and his French critics including Baldensperger, sometimes reproached him with coarseness. In the *Züricher Novellen* we actually miss any trace of it, likewise in all of his lovestories. He revenged himself on the unresponsive sex in only one, generous way: 'Süsse Frauenbilder zu erfinden/Wie die bittre Erde sie nicht hegt.' He did not like it at all when Auerbach characterized his women as 'bachelor dreams'; but it was fitting, because he was in love with so many specimens that he did not know 'human bondage.' In his dozen stories of married life he was never interested in the 'Physiologie du mariage'; he thought that took care of itself. But he was sensibly interested in all the other compromises. There is an inexplicable, rare understanding for womanhood. Keller gave himself away when he confessed in his first love-letter (at twenty-eight) that 'ihm schon mehrere eingeleuchtet haben.' This focussing on 'becoming evident' reveals how fair, how objective, how directed at the girl's *raison d'être* he was even in such a circumstance. Hence perhaps the excess of light which he throws on his women figures. They emanate such a good feeling that we are ashamed to admit with what complacency we would like to stay them, with what bourgeois ease we like to linger round most episodes of Keller, with what an un-Faustian sigh we say, 'Verweile doch, du bist so schön.'

With instinctive compensation, the finale of 'The Governor of Greifensee' has the five invited (and well-preserved) beauties attend a session over which Landolt presides as justice of the peace. Here the seamy side of marriage forms the needed counterpart to the former rosy episodes. And the fair guests 'gradually turned rather timid, from the sureness with which they saw this bachelor know and treat matters of marriage.' The counterpoising intention is equally clear, when at table the Governor tells them the gloomiest pages in the history of his district. The reunion ends with a mock parliament, where his former rebuffers vote whether he should marry his little maid or his old housekeeper. And the Novelle ends with lingering epitaphs, the last one, queerly, to that honest housekeeper.

At each reading one becomes slower, more absorbed, more wondering. Keller's humor and his pathos are equally dry, that is why they mix so cleanly. On every page invention and observation play a game with each other, but not against each other. C. F. Meyer was especially struck by the part of observation. 'Keller had no liking for aesthetic generalities . . . but he liked to analyse the individual case, the particular motif. . . . His definition of beauty is well-known: truth presented with fulness.' 'He searched — often too meticulously

— for the real things long " before he read Zola." How often I heard him say, " That *is*! I've seen it! I've experienced it myself! " ' We are perhaps more struck by the undiminished splendor of invention. The contrast to ' modern ' fiction is evident. Keller's is the classical way where the ' story ' probes deeper than analysis, or instrumentation, or built-in commentary, and not the other way. In classical fiction the turns of the narrative are the real revelations, the fully symbolic events. Keller's pages are so spiked with fictions that it hurts our thin skins. In the following half-century several first-rate writers (James, Proust, Joyce, Mann) made models of the modern novel of their impotence to create stories. In Keller, analysis is undisguised and terse, but a means of fiction, not its master.

In this predominance of ' pure ' fiction over the other ingredients, Keller is representative of the German Novelle, which genre dominated German literature in the whole ' Victorian ' period, 1830-1890. It is not the rise of almanacs and periodicals which fostered the rise of the Novelle. In England and France the same vehicles gave rise to the instalment novel. The German lending libraries, the chief feature of the literary market then, lived on novels (half of them translations), not on Novellen. It must have been a morphological decline of all the ' great ' genres — of the lyric betrayed by Heine, of the drama deserted by Grillparzer, of the epic shunned by all real poets — which benefitted the Novelle. All those moribund genres heaped their legacies on this half-legitimate relative. The German Novelle cannot be understood as an undersized novel or an overblown story; it can be understood as the prose-epic, the prose-poem, and especially the prose-drama of the period. Almost every outstanding writer contributed some masterpiece to it, but four other authors made it their chief vehicle, each excellent in a different thing: Gotthelf in natural substance, Stifter in intense still-life, Storm in lyrical mood, Meyer in well-staged drama. So many writers, so many forms. But with Keller it is: so many stories, so many forms. He is the easiest inventor, he has stories within Novellen, and anecdotes within stories. All his fiction reminds one of the original meaning of anecdote, ' unedited.'

But Keller shares the essentials of the Novelle with his co-Victorians; first of all the lyrical character. Storm, Meyer and Keller were lyric poets; yet they did not intersperse their fiction with poems, as the Romanticists had done. They infused poetry into it, and the result was a lyrical quality of the protagonists, which became the rule in German Novellen (while it is the exception in French, English and Russian novels). Then there is the heritage of the drama. The comedy, and especially all the tragedy (three of our five are basically tragic) results from the clash of individuals set at each other by society — if only in the sense that society is the cage which forces one individuality to live on the others. In the legitimate drama the clash leads to the destruction of the most valuable individuality. In the compromise drama of the Novelle the tragedy is reduced to a 'harmonious' resignation on the edge of society.

With all that, the vague entity of the Novelle is still a picture of the *liberty* of form so dear to German literature, where 'innere Form,' individual form, escape from form has been paramount. The Novelle can range from ten to a hundred pages, a mere publisher's whim can call it short story or novel, and almost all German fiction has room within it. The Novelle can simplify itself enormously (with Gotthelf and even more with Stifter), and it can divide and multiply itself internally (with Keller, especially *Green Henry*). But one negative character unifies it, the absence of a center of civilization. After all, it was not France and England and Russia which wrote the great novel of the nineteenth century, but Paris and London and Petersburg plus Moscow. But in Germany it was the *country* which wrote the Novelle, and the tiniest German country most of all, since Switzerland alone furnished three of our five provincials. If the modern novel pictures the man of cosmopolis, or whatever it pictures from a window in cosmopolis, the German Novelle depicts man *before* cosmopolis, and seen from the inside. Hence the infinite variety of scenery, society, and oddity. It is the *ancien régime* of mankind. Who has not breathed its fictive air, n'a pas connu la douceur de vivre. Once they called it realism; but to us, as we read it, it is nostalgia. There is an unbelievable oecology of people and ideals, of not unsalvageable cranks in not insoluble societies. There is man in a society which is still *sui generis,* that is, individual. It all has acquired an air of fairytale. Yet these Novellen are the truest picture we have of the great diversity that was the Germany of the nineteenth century. And this extra-literary value must be admitted as their best. As their world receded from every other surface of the earth, the pages of these Novellen have become irreplaceable.

C. F. Meyer's 'Soulscape'

C. F. Meyer is a writer so full of reticences that even for his intentions we had better look somewhere else than in his own words. One might say that the program of his poetry is best stated in an essay of a poet unknown to him, Leconte de Lisle's preface to *Poèmes antiques* (1852). 'This book is a collection of studies. . . . The personal emotions have not left many traces here; contemporary passions and events don't appear. . . . That explains the impersonalness and objectivity of these studies. . . . We are an intellectual generation; instinctive, spontaneous, fertile youth is irreparably lost. Poetry will find its only realization in art, will no more engender heroic actions or inspire social virtues. . . . O Poets, if you do not want to be wiped out, your future is in isolating yourselves more and more from the world of action, taking refuge in a life of scholastic contemplation, in a sanctuary of quiet and purification. . . . The mind of humanity has its periods of arrest and reflection. Let us say loudly that nothing seems sillier and sadder than the empty agitation of originality which is proper to the bad periods of art. We are at such a point.'

Meyer could not have been nearly so precise nor so defiant as his French contemporary. He was never proudly aware of being different, he rather tended to incorporate himself in what he called ' die Kontinuität . . . die Tradition.' In his conscious thought he was open to all the progressive tendencies of his time; it was the waves from his subconscious which threw him back to a position of reactionary, which gave him, occasionally, the voice of timeless uniqueness. The paramount spiritual current of the mid-century was the religious skepticism of which Keller is the example. Meyer underwent the current, but was not swept away. ' For despite all my efforts to emancipate myself from Christianity or at least its logical conclusions, I feel led back to it by something stronger than myself, more every year, in spite of all criticism and philosophy ' (to F. Bovet, January 14, 1888). In his Novellen the religious questions are fought out, under the masks of his characters, often with violence. In his poetry they often reveal a curious equilibrium, made in equal parts of affirmation and resignation, of Christian faith and of a stoicism which is more late-Christian than pre-Christian. One of the successful expressions of such an equilibrium is the eight-line ' Säerspruch,' a blessing without faith, where the sower rather casts his bread upon the waters. At least, he first thinks (in lines 3 and 4) of the seed that will die:

> Dort fällt ein Korn, das stirbt und ruht.
> Die Ruh ist süss. Es hat es gut.

The tone of stoic detachment is not in the reasonable expectation that some grain will die, but in the immediate readiness to see the blessing in such a death, the immediate coupling of ' dies ' with ' rests,' and the almost pleasurable insistence on the statements, ' Rest is sweet. It is well off.' However, these sentences of sweet content have a brevity which is near acerbity. And this insinuation of controlled indifference is plainly fortified when the statement of the *opposite* eventuality is welcomed in *identical* terms:

> Hier eins, das durch die Scholle bricht.
> Es hat es gut. Süss ist das Licht.

That is impartiality, one grain (of pessimism) there, one grain (of optimism) here. And both are greeted by the same adjectives, ' good,' 'sweet.' The plain craft of Meyer, however, shows in the simple shift of rhyme; there the dark vowel of 'ruht,' here the bright vowel of 'Licht.' The negative and positive possibilities are perfectly neutralized in the last couplet, which also audibly balances 'Weltfrömmigkeit' and 'Gottfrömmigkeit,' the two parties of piety which then divided the votes between themselves.

Und keines fällt aus dieser Welt.
Und jedes fällt, wie's Gott gefällt.

Not only the truism of every true religion is confidently claimed ('And not a grain that falls out of the world'), but the subsumption of every fall and case and accident ('fällt') into the arbitrariness of God ('gefällt') is verbally 'hit.'

The most pregnant formulas for Meyer's poetry were coined by F. F. Baumgarten (in 1920). 'The poems are loneliness become manifest.' 'It is a poetry of moods, not of feelings.' 'He composed, not his experiences, but his memories.' 'His is a Book of Images and not a Book of Songs.' 'Meyer was most disloyal to his actual experience and most loyal to its perfect and suggestive expression. He betrayed his experience to his form.' 'Meyer's development was from the folksonglike poetry of feeling to symbolist poetry.'

The last claim, the symbol content of Meyer's poetry, should be obvious as soon as we look at some of his best poems, which have long been anthology pieces. In the four couplets of 'Eingelegte Ruder' (Oars at Rest), the symbolic situation stated in the beginning, of a man suspended motionlessly between the abysses below and above him, is so plastic that it threatens to outdo the rest of the poem.

Meine eingelegten Ruder triefen,
Tropfen fallen langsam in die Tiefen.

This suspension is so teeming with possibilities, that we regret that the poet has to single out one of them to continue.

Nichts, das mich verdross! Nichts, das mich freute!
Niederrinnt ein schmerzenloses Heute!

The puzzling exclamation marks are not really exclamatory, they just mark the words as three escaping sighs, in contrast to the statements before and after. Other things are puzzling too; but what should be obvious is that the poem has managed to state itself, fully, four times. Each line has 'contained' the whole! 'My locked oars are dripping' (1) is the entire visible situation. 'Drops are falling slowly into the depths' (2) would be merely a more leisurely restatement, were those 'depths' not to be opened later. 'Not a thing that saddened or gladdened me' (3) is the entire invisible situation: the lack, or loss, of emotive experience. 'A painless day is dripping down' (4) would be a mere contraction of the dual (3), if the verb were not there to reinstate the full image of (1), and if the contraction were not giving away the world view of the weak or the convalescent: Absence of pleasure-plus-pain is felt as freedom (from pain). The somewhat forced past tense of (3) recalls the past participle of (1), suggesting that active life (rowing) had just stopped.

One does not look forward to what more the poet will add to his reiterative poem. The entire second half is at first a disappointment:

> Unter mir — ach, aus dem Licht verschwunden —
> Träumen schon die schönern meiner Stunden.
> Aus der blauen Tiefe ruft das Gestern:
> Sind im Licht noch manche meiner Schwestern?

When we apply the principle of organization which was thrust on us by the first two couplets, we find that it operates here too, though with less apparent force. Lines 1-4 were under the aspect of the present. Lines 5 and 6 modulate into the aspect of the past: 'The better of my hours are already dreaming below' enlarges the scope to a retrospect over a whole life, embellishing the dream of the past at the expense of the present. Lines 7 and 8 bring the whole under the aspect of the future, with 'Yesterday's' query whether there are any 'sisters' left to live. The world below which was rendered negatively, 'vanished from the light' (5), is compensated by being positively restated as 'the blue depth' (7). The seemingly bleak present-plus-future is compensated by being, after all, identified with 'the light' (8). And the feeling which finally gains the reader is one not of apathy but of serenity. Future, past, and present are equally tolerable; certainly not enjoyable as life, but evenly enjoyable as reflection or meditation or art. The art here is, in the choice of words, of a supreme simplicity; in the distribution of references, of a superb sophistication. It takes only the " blaue Tiefe ' (7), so natural in German for 'water of a beautiful lake', to re-establish the originative image of the poem. Even 'aus dem Licht verschwunden' (5) has a vague reference to underwater darkness. But the raison d'être of the second half is that it gives the first half its dimensions, in space and time. Indeed, when we look back at the beginning, we realize that we have read 'Eingelegte Ruder' backwards all the time, that it is a poem which we cannot read *except* after having scanned its sequence first, and hearing, so to speak, all the eight lines simultaneously as an eight-part canon. But once we read it that way, the eight lines with their swinging 'soft' endings (a rarity in Meyer) impose themselves as a little masterpiece of concentration, the hard core of which is the symbolic situation itself, 'eingelegte Ruder.'

We understand that Keller spoke of Meyer's poetry first of all as if it were an especially fine old instrument. 'In his verses you will be struck right away by the unusually fine and fine-grained tone [schöne und kernige Ton].' (To Th. Storm, June 5, 1882) Or 'the lyrical part has that peculiarly noble tone quality [eigentümlich edle Klangfarbe] which is so rare.' (To the publisher J. Rodenberg, Dec. 7, 1882). The whole difference between the two realms of poetry gapes wide when we hear Meyer characterize Keller: 'But what a depth in spots, what a natural force, what sweetness, and what refined art of detail.' The correspondent, L. v. François, questioned the 'Süssigkeit,' and here the devotee of Keller will passionately assent to Meyer. 'Süssigkeit' is the helplessly elementary expression for the pith of poetry. (A great critic, Grillparzer, used the same helpless term for what was to him the most irresistible poetry, Lope de Vega's.) This elementary 'Süssigkeit' could never be claimed for Meyer, while Keller possessed it, even when writing prose.

Meyer had little of such elemental endowment. He knew it and said severely, 'my trifles become tolerable only by some semblance of perfection.' (To H. Lingg, Aug. 31, 1887). That is why he thought too little of his poetry and too much of his Novellen. The lyrics did not offer enough food for his ethical craving, which demanded actions, moral issues, characters. That is why he protested, 'I am not at all "artiste." On the contrary, I never write but when a moral fact hits or shakes me.' (To Bovet, Dec. 31, 1881). Meyer misjudged his true talent. Keller grievously misjudged Meyer's character (in the notorious letter to Storm, Dec. 21, 1881). But with infallible instinct he put Meyer's lyrics above his ballads and his poetry above his Novellen. To be sure, Meyer's Novellen have not paled much to this day, but his poems have immensely deepened in color. Only when he resigned himself, even in the form, the compressed form of the lyric, did he find the commensurate expression for his essentially weak, pathetic, and pathological personality. 'I believe that in his concise manner, sharpened to a point, lies his measure, and that he has no more to say than he says, in spite of his intelligence and poetic gift.' (Keller to Heyse, Dec. 25, 1882).

Keller's Switzerland

'The uniqueness of Keller is the combination of two things; on the one hand, the specific patriotism of a Swiss and his still upright ethical qualities of honesty and dutifulness, on the other hand an unusually strong fantasy with its whims and extravagances. It is a rare mixture which will hardly be duplicated.' Thus C. F. Meyer in 1890. Keller combined such odd qualities not only in his work but in his public life too. When he was appointed county secretary, a Zurich newspaper wrote: 'The appointment makes a deeply discouraging and demoralizing impression.' (Sept. 20, 1861). On November 1, the same newspaper said: 'Public opinion was hugely wrong about Gottfried Keller. If he continues like this,he may well be one of the best secretaries Zurich ever had.' He must have been; for even when the administration which he had faithfully served (and to whose conservatism he had adjusted) was overthrown in 1869, he was kept on against all expectation. But in the next few years the completion and success of *Seven Legends* (1872) and *People of Seldwyla II* (1874) made him yearn to be nothing but a writer; so he resigned in 1876. His farewell present to his little state, so to speak, was the *Züricher Novellen* (1877).

The political life of little Switzerland has been given considerable treatment in Keller's works, yet the treatment is so charmingly fused with the human and often the humorous aspects of the stories that the unpolitical reader often remains unaware of the deep seriousness of purpose. This seriousness is documented early in the Gotthelf articles which he wrote for a German periodical between 1849 and 1855. 'When the Swiss people, by the new federal constitution of 1848, had for the time being found a conclusion to the long battle for the best accord of centralisation and federalism . . . there began in the counties a merry revising of their individual constitutions . . . For twenty years they had been making constitutions, had been protecting, attacking, breaking, patching, and revising them, and had shown in this business a proficiency which is rightly called political education . . . True political maturity is not revealed in the celerity with which a people devise and adopt a law, but in the honesty, seriousness and determination with which they apply it.'

His own contribution to this period of reconstruction is the heartwarming tale *The Upright Seven* (1861), in which he describes the events surrounding one of the celebrated shooting festivals. Later (in the autobiography of 1889) he characterized 'the opus as an expression of satisfaction with national conditions, and with the new federal constitution. It was the good moment when you are not yet aware of the inexorable consequences in the wake of things and when you look at the world as good and complete.' A more direct postscript is in a letter to Storm (June 25, 1878). '*The Upright Seven* is now obsolete; the patriotic satisfaction, the old-fashioned liberalism have practically vanished; social discontent, speculation and bankruptcies, interminable rush, have taken their place.'

The reverse of the picture is shown in the last Novelle in *People of Seldwyla*, 'The Smiles Gone' [Das Verlorene Lachen]. This tale starts with a singing festival and its hero, Jucundus. At first the subject seems to be the difficulty of making a match between the unprosperous Jucundus and the rich Justine, both distinguished by a smile of rare beauty. But a purposeful motherly campaign has soon concluded this episode, when the economic condition claims all the interest. Jucundus' timber deals make him regret the spreading deforestation. Things come to a head when a millenial oak is threatened, a landmark of the county. Trying to save it as a national monument, ' he bought the oak himself and the acre around it, cleared the ground and placed a bench under the tree, from which there was a fine view of the distance; and everybody praised his action and enjoyed the view. But from that moment too, everybody tried to abuse and to cheat him, as a gentleman, to whom no quarter is given.'

Keller is adept in showing the contrast of this innocent one and the corrupt business world. The day of Jucundus' sell-out in Seldwyla sees also the fall of the old oak on the horizon. But when we have followed Jucundus to the factories of his wife's family and have wondered at his growing ineptness, the religious issue crops up, and the liberal but proselytizing movement of the church seizes his wife. Jucundus' free-thinking more than his nonsuccess leads to the break with his wife.

The eddies of the story have already slowed down to form chapters of a novel, but we are only in the middle. Here we enter the discussion of democratic politics. It concerns the overthrow of the conservatives (representative government) by the radicals (direct self-government). The conservatives ' considered the world and the state, in their present condition, as complete and good, and refused any considerable changes, withdrawing into a constant activity and gradually improving the existing. By this resistance they gained the reputation of enemies of progress. But as they administered the affairs effectively and honestly, it was hard to find the opening of a big action against them . . . But a people or republic is never long at a loss about a beginning, when it absolutely wants a quarrel with its administrators. The people simply faced the persons and said : ' we don't like your faces any longer.'

Then Keller details a campaign of calumny, which would be a bitter satire of demagogy, were it not also a funny Seldwyla prank. At any rate, the figure of honest Jucundus, who believes everybody, is beautifully worked into this muddle. And by one of those accidents which Keller prepares so generously, Jucundus who is after political truth and his wife who is after religious truth are generously brought face to face — and cured of their fanaticisms. Smiling again their fabulous smiles, they solemnize their reconciliation in front of a huge tree nursery : the Swiss forests will grow again.

' The Smiles Gone ' is one of the best examples of what Keller dared to do to the Novelle. He packed into it all the virtues and vices of the novel. Precipitations and retardations; poetic, metaphoric short-cuts and prosy dissertations; dependable cultural history and reckless yarnspinning; leaps from realism into fairytale; sudden transitions from the tender to the grotesque, peripateias from comedy into tragedy, but also sudden turnings from tragedy into idyll. He is often hard to follow, as he leads us from room to room, each decorated in a different style. But those who follow him will soon see that it is the variety of a huge talent, which in the end forces all contrasts into a powerful synthesis. We have only to look at the way his individual stories have of complementing each other in a cyclical fashion, in the *Züricher Novellen,* in the exquisite *Epigram,* and above all in his most difficult and heterogeneous *Green Henry*. The mysteries of cyclical composition apply also to his individual stories: they too are loosely constructed, somehow more spacious than their outward dimensions.

In politics, the queer synthesis of provincial patriotism and liberal large-mindedness shows itself in two ways. One is the interpenetration of criticism and optimism. Keller never ceased to believe in his little country, its democracy and its destiny. Even his last work, a rather gloomy political novel, was supposed to have a positive second volume. But criticism there was too, from the preface to *Seldwyla I* (intensified in the preface to *Seldwyla II*) and from the first version of *Green Henry*. F. Baldensperger gave 'l'helvétisme' first rank among the qualities of Keller and summarized it impartially. 'We have here a phase of his work which an alien can only half appreciate and which even for his countrymen suffers from datedness, loss of interest due to time-bound tendencies. But the helvetism of Keller also shows in the more general and durable aspects of his work: the care to give good advice, to teach or suggest a useful and sane truth, the instinct for ordinary life as subject-matter. Even more than the status and adventures of his heroes does their psychology betray the influence of the national milieu. The best are gifted with that Tüchtigkeit, that latent devotion to civic life. . . .'

However, there is another synthesis, that of Swiss patriotism and a large sympathy with the German nation in the wider sense. His ties of friendship with both Austria and Prussia were many. The decisive assessment of his worth came from those quarters. The first substantial article on him came from the arch-Prussian Treitschke (1860). The public congratulation from Berlin on his last (the seventieth) birthday found special favor in his eyes 'because Moltke's name headed the list of signers' (Petersen's memoirs). In literature he maintained, like Grillparzer, that Swiss and Austrian were hardly separable from the whole of German literature. In politics he believed, like Meyer, that the emerging German 'empire' was only a redress of former wrongs. He found their politics and warfare far superior to their literature. 'I would never have believed that the writers and poets could lag so far behind the soldiers in *Tüchtigkeit* and intelligence as is seen now' (to Emil Kuh, Nov. 9, 1874). In a way, he considered his very Swiss predilection for the ethical a common German burden. He comments on his comic epic, 'Apothecary of Chamounix' thus: 'It is a kind of death-song to the Heinean licentiousness, because that, mixed-in with sentimentality, holds no promise to us Germans. We ought to be clear, true and naive — without having to be asses' (to Freiligrath, April 22, 1860).

It is surprising both how many pages in his works are given to sermonizing, and how these meditations are lost in the other riches. They are converted; they reach into the fictional substance and dignify it; the fiction reaches into them and makes them poetic. Keller is never theoretically sure of his means, but practically he uses them with a sort of compulsion — which afterwards he finds hard to justify: he abounds in deprecating, even harsh judgments of his works. He alternates his means because he does not aim at a single vision, but rather at a whole, fictional world. And the relation of that fictional to the real world is not at all that the former imitates the latter, but rather the opposite, that reality please learn a lesson, now and then, from fiction. Therefore his only steady rule is to make the fictional world as rich and spacious as he can.

Religious and moral questions gradually took more space in his work than political issues. In this he was perhaps a protagonist of his age, for religion remained a problem for more minds. What Keller tried to do — in his last story of *Seldwyla,* in the last of *Züricher Novellen,* in the last story of *The Epigram,* and in several episodes of *Green Henry* — was to change the problem from a question of the mind to a question of character. To sacrifice traditional religion and to enhance traditional morality by the very sacrifice, almost to sanction it thereby, that was the hopeless task, of which the utopian pursuit is not the least charm of these stories and episodes. What had been a rather platitudinous religion-substitute in the hands of D. F. Strauss and L. Feuerbach, became in Keller's modern fairytales a series of experiments in combining delicate hearts with sturdy characters.

The more the social, moral, and religious history disproved his theories, the more devotedly did this pious atheist work at making amends in his fictional world. His sacrifice was acceptable, because it was not mere morals which he infiltrated, it was a poetry of the heart and a poetry of character. Nowhere else is it so apparent that he had the secret of converting anti-poetic elements into figures of fiction, into colors of his palette, into chords in his score; he made music with morals. To be sure, his Novellen were only a diluted sort of music, a dietetic or digestible sort of poetry (compared with richer and younger periods); but in the world of nineteenth century fiction they are still audibly musical, visionlike, poetic, boldly beyond the measure and the criticism of reality. And his music of morals was also the simple bread and the rich wine which satisfied the hunger of many minds that were not primarily aesthetic.

To many Keller represented first and foremost the essence of the middle-class. The solution of his great novel was intransigently bourgeois: renounce art, better renounce all ' higher ' aspirations, do what others need to have done, and you will be safe. Much in Keller looks like this solution, on the surface. But it is only the modest brown into which all bright colors flow together if we mix them. Seen as they are, his canvasses are made of the brightest and boldest colors. The main impression is perhaps that of *Buntheit,* variegation. In none of his stories do we find an affinity for the monochrome, everywhere colorfulness made by contrasts. His whole work is a set of paradoxical compensations. His preaching was only just as good as his deflating. He was sometimes the most fanciful and whimsical, but more often the most earthy and humorous. This apostle of normality was also the chief crank of the time. He was both the most bourgeois and the most bohemian, the most civic and the most artist.

II

The Metaphysicals

Schopenhauer's Iconoclasm

'To shout Schopenhauer /From the top of a tower' (as an awful limerick of Rossetti has it) was a mission of his friend Franz Hueffer. We need this Wagnerian and music-critic of the *Times* to tell us about the first article in English on Schopenhauer. In the *Fortnightly Review* of 1876 Hueffer speaks of the thirty years of silence which shrouded the life-work of the philosopher. 'Success came at last, and from a quarter from which it had been least expected, and perhaps most coveted. This quarter was England . . . The attention created [by Schopenhauer's *Parerga*] would most likely soon have subsided again, had it not been for a foreign voice suddenly and loudly raised in testimony of the neglected philosopher's merits. Such voices are listened to with particular eagerness in Germany. I am alluding to a paper called 'Iconoclasm in German Philosophy.' . . . It soon transpired that the author was Mr. John Oxenford, the well-known dramatist, critic and scholar. The article is masterly in all respects, combining perfect grasp of the subject with lucid exposition and interesting treatment. It may be called without exaggeration the foundation of Schopenhauer's fame, both in his own and other countries.'

This report of Hueffer's hardly exaggerates anything. Schopenhauer's work was published in three far-spaced instalments, which might be compared to three concentric rings: in 1818 the massive nucleus of *The World as Will and Idea;* in 1844 the volume of supplementary essays, *Will and Idea II;* in 1851 the outer circle of essays, *Parerga and Paralipomena.* Only after this final instalment was there an echo in the periodical press; and the English did not wait for the German press. As early as April 1852 J. Oxenford had a few incisive pages in the *Westminster Review*: 'German philosophy has never come in contact with a more savage adversary than Arthur Schopenhauer; nor, if he meets the attention which his acuteness and erudition deserve, with one more decidely dangerous . . . His book is chiefly interesting as a complete "show up" of the German philosophers since the time of Kant. His scurrility, which is worthy to be compared with that of Swift . . .'

Hueffer's remark that success in England was 'perhaps most coveted' was not much of a misstatement either. No German philosopher read the English writers with as much relish as Schopenhauer did, none quoted English poets and thinkers as copiously or with as much approval; and for current information he relied not on German papers but on the daily reading of the *Times*. The English were not only his chief source on India and the Orient, he even shared their prejudices, for instance against America. It was also true that Oxenford's anonymous and unexpected article in the *Westminster Review* (1853) impressed Schopenhauer more than the contemporary German articles. Oxenford's ' Iconoclasm ' had the ring of a fanfare that could not be overheard. Besides, it shrewdly pointed both to the incomparably broad education and to the English leanings of Schopenhauer, calling him a ' student of philosophy who, having devoted himself to the wisdom of the Oriental world, to the dialectic of the Greeks, to the acuteness of the French, to the hard, common sense of the English ... He first comes forward as a special admirer of the common sense of the English. Hobbes, Berkeley, and Priestley, whose existence has been almost ignored by the modern German teachers, are at his fingers' ends, and he cites them not only as kindred souls, but as authorities.'

The main service which ' Iconoclasm ' did was to point to Schopenhauer as a writer for the average reader, which was what he turned out to be in the next sixty years: ' He is one of the most ingenious and readable authors in the world, skillful in the art of theory building, universal in attainments, inexhaustible in the power of illustration, terribly logical and unflinching in the pursuit of consequences, and ... a formidable hitter of adversaries.' ' While Schopenhauer's teaching is the most genial, the most ingenious and, we would add, the most amusing that can be imagined, the doctrine taught is the most disheartening, the most repulsive, the most opposed to the aspirations of the present world, that the most ardent of Job's comforters could concoct.'

With the last statement we have come to a consideration of Schopenhauer's doctrine. Contrary to his own claim and to the conviction of his true disciples, it is not necessary to read all of him in order to understand any part. His novel strength lay in the very opposite, that you can read any of his volumes or single essays without any more preparation than an open mind. To this day the many essays of his last volume, the *Parerga,* are far more popular than the central work. But it is a misfortune that *Will and Idea II* has been under the shadow of its first volume. In the middle one of the three instalments the author is perhaps at his best, equally far from the long-winded systematization which he constructed in his youth, and from the scattered dispersal of his thoughts which he collected in his old age. We will take an example from that middle volume, *Will and Idea II:* 'The Metaphysics of Sex.'

First, the philosopher wonders why he has no predecessors in the treatment of so paramount a problem. Then he begins to find answers. 'It is no trifle that is in question here, no, the importance of the matter matches the earnest and ardor of the business . . . What is settled there is nothing less than the makings of the next generation.' Again and again Schopenhauer finds the telling words to make obvious that it is the least private affair of all. 'It is not a question of individual weal or woe, as in all other affairs, but of the existence and constitution of the human race in the future . . . What speaks to the individual consciousness as the sexual impulse is not aimed at a definite individual of the other sex — it is simply the will to live itself.' But when Schopenhauer describes what mates a certain male and a certain female, he is so rich in making sense of every phase of love-making that one would have to copy pages to give an idea of the realism of his observations and of the cogency of his interpretation. 'The growing fancy of two lovers is already the will to live of the new individual, which they are able and desirous to beget. In the very meeting of their longing glances its new life is kindled and announces itself as a well-composed future individual. They feel the desire for a union and fusion into a single being.'

He is positively irresistible when he persuades us that the sexual instinct is the stronger, the more nature finds it necessary to conceal the sole concern for the species under the apparent interest of the person. Further, that the general tendency is to procreate the *ideal* human (the best balanced). Hence the supremacy of beauty, health, strength in all questions of sex. Then he consummates the first act of the chapter by describing the after-effect. 'Every lover will, after enjoyment has finally been attained, experience the strangest disillusionment. He will be astonished that what is devoutly wished for does not accomplish more than any other sexual satisfaction would have. That wish was proportioned to his other wishes in the proportion of the species to the individual: an infinite to a finite thing . . . Therefore every lover, when at last the great work is consummated, finds himself cheated . . .'

In the second half of the essay the analyst only sets out to prove what he propounded in the first; and the strange thing is that he keeps interesting us — evidently *not* because he proves what we have already realized, but because he makes us realize new consequences, especially when he comes to variable preferences. 'Each loves what he lacks . . . All sex is one-sidedness . . . The most manly man will seek the most womanly woman . . . Little men have a decided penchant for big women, and *vice versa* . . .' There are pages of easily verified observations. On the mental side, it seems to be the will-power of the man and the intellect of the woman which matter and match. The mere sexual impulse, unindividualized, quantitative and without much regard for quality is vulgar. 'But a considerable passion . . is, so to speak, by special order of the species.' 'The high and ruthless passion of the future parents for each other: indeed an unparalleled illusion which makes a lover give everying in the world to sleep with this one woman . . ."

We pass over the third part, in which the philosopher reviews the tragedies and comedies resulting from sex, 'to which *alone* honor, duty and loyalty yield, if they withstand every other temptation.' 'It even seems that the illicit lovers are conscious of a higher right than the interest of individuals could confer.' We hurry to the conclusion in which Schopenhauer relates this topic to his general 'metaphysics.' The immense business of sex proves to him (1) 'the indestructibility of the essence of man.' (2) 'the essence being more in the species than in the individual.' Nothing else but the upkeep of these two principles could make sex the highest concern, for every one 'the affair of the heart.' It is only the world of appearance which lets individuals seem important. But underneath all appearance there is a nucleus of reality, and underneath our consciousness there is a subconsciousness of that reality; because the core of reality and the core of our consciousness are one, the thing-in-itself, before and behind the 'principle of individuation' one and the same in all individuals, and nothing else but 'the will,' the will to live.

It is not hard to see why Schopenhauer has always given so little to philosophers, and so much to the non-specialist reader. It is so easy to doubt his system, because his sense of reality and his powerful imagination constantly incorporate elements antagonistic to his system. It is easy to find fault with his method, because his sense of the ultimate oneness of the world and his sense of the phenomenal struggle in it express themselves in a dynamics of speech which oscillates from cool abstractions to glowing metaphors, and operates with both as with realities of the mind. He can afford to build his books with blocks of those inspired exaggerations with which Poets build their works. 'The Metaphysics of Sex' is one such magnificent exaggeration. In a sense Schopenhauer is the first philosopher who did not believe his own system. (Hence the obstinacy with which he accumulated proofs for it during a lifetime.) And his public discovered him as soon as it was sufficiently skeptic for a philosophy which did not have to be believed in to be rewarding, meaningful, and helpful. The generation after 1850 realized that the explanation of the world as will and imagination was ingenious; but that ingeniousness was little compared to the richness of the manifold picture of the world. The philosopher satisfied that generation by the very fact that in his world everything was multivalent.

It is not a single aspect of Schopenhauer that was responsible for the circumstance that the egregiously unread thinker of the first half of the century rather suddenly became the most widely read of the second half. It is his power of combination. He combines the metaphysical quest of German philosophy for a heart of the world with the suspicion of modern science that this heart may simply be a principle of dynamics. He combines the idealism of poetical minds with the materialism of cynical observers. He combines an unparalleled humanist culture, which endeared him to generations of ' Edelbürger,' with a broad snicker of vilification, which made him accessible to generations of ' Spiessbürger.' His general assumptions are the most plebeian, his intellectual outlook is the most aristocratic. His style of writing is downright demagogic, his manner of quotation recondite, for the modern ignoramus even esoteric. His human range, not only in his personality but also in his writings, is from the loftiest to the vulgar and petty. In the frightful loneliness in which every line of his work was written, his depressions distilled themselves into exultations. Under the atmospheric pressure of a thousand solitudes his heterogeneous experiences synthesized themselves into a fluid cosmos, where all the hierarchies intercommunicated. His age sensed the floating relativity in him and recognized it as its own. It recognized especially his Promethean attempt to explain the universe in terms of our own instinct (Wille) and consciousness (Vorstellung), to construct a cosmology in terms of an anthropology, or, as he beautifully put it, to match the microcosm by a makranthropism.

Not all of this can be seen in the one chapter, ' Metaphysics of Sex.' But to verify the picture we have only to proceed to the next chapter, ' The Pain of Life.' It starts: ' Awakened out of the night of the unconscious into life, the will finds itself an individual, in an infinite world, among innumerable individuals, all striving, suffering, erring; and he hurries, as through a bad dream, back to the former unconscious. On the way, however, his wishes are unlimited, his claims inexhaustible, and every satisfied desire gives birth to another.' We are, of course, at one of Schopenhauer's favorite themes, the one which never fails to make him so eloquent that people who like to simplify have forgotten all his other themes besides his pessimism. It would not have inspired his most splendid pages, if it had not given him the satisfaction of contradicting his three pet enemies, the state, the church, and public opinion. As it is, he wrung from the sombre theme his most sweetly saturated and almost surfeiting chords. ' Everything tells us that happiness is meant to be frustrated or recognized as an illusion . . . Life reveals itself as a continued cheating. If it made a promise, it does not keep it, except to show how worthless the desired thing was. When it gave, it was only to take away . . . Happiness lies always in the future or in the past. The present is like a little dark cloud which the wind drives over a sunny plain : in front and in back of it everything is bright, only itself always casts a shadow.'

We cannot continue, because he is inexhaustible in new paraphrases of the feeling that existence is a constant struggle to maintain existence, and that life is a business which does not repay the cost. Like all subjective truths this one gets its impact mostly from the personal intensity of perception and sentiment which is behind it. But Schopenhauer commands also a little arsenal of psychological proof. 'We feel pain, but not painlessness; we feel worry, but not the absence of worry; fear, but not security . . . Only pain and want can positively be felt, they announce themselves; well-being is negative only. Therefore the greatest boons, health, youth, and freedom, are only perceived when we have lost them : they too are only negatives.'

Schopenhauer sometimes uses logical deduction, frequently induction, but his best weapon is analogy. Sometimes he uses it as an insistent simile, like the one suggested by the irritating 'life is a present.' No, he says, 'on the contrary, it has all the earmarks of a contracted debt. Its instalments are collected in form of the pressing needs, torturing desires, and endless distress inherent in existence. The normal life is spent to pay off that debt; but life pays only the interest. The amortisation of capital is effected by death. And when was the debt contracted? At procreation.'

The rest of the chapter is polemics against the professors of optimism and a little anthology from all those who have considered life as guilt or pain, from the Old Testament to Leopardi. We must be satisfied with the short quotations, although they cannot give an idea of the writer's main strength : the dimension of his developments, which have something massive in their orchestration, something dramatic in their tempo. Even less can we give a picture of the dramatic structure of the whole work, where the intellect, although born a slave of the will, has the chance to emancipate itself from the will; where the will itself, although powerfully determined, has the secret desire to negate itself. Add to this that the artist treats the two tendencies and their reversals not in a compound where the four could neutralize one another, but in four large blocks, a tetralogy so to speak, where each part forms a drama of its own, consisting of many vivid scenes. The dramatic impression is not only in the lively presentation which frequently caps the dry discourse; it is an attribute of the system. Instead of accepting the intellectual disappointments of the nineteenth century, Schopenhauer dramatized them. His almost maniac awareness of the spiritual heritage of the past and of the trends of the present raised them into struggling dualisms. He constructed intellectual tragedies, which do inspire pity and fear; but first and last they arouse the transports which art generates.

Hebbel's Tragedy

The real tragedies of the middle of the century were written by Friedrich Hebbel (1813-1863). It was he who expressed, like no one else in the nineteenth century, its tragic situation. He lived and enacted Schopenhauer's philosophy: it was more *his* nature, one might contend, than the other man's. His life, his art, and the fate of his art were tragic. He came from the poorest of circumstances. Yet as in the case of Keller, it was soon recognized that he had the gifts to which society owed an education, so there were always people who secured one for him. Then there was the state — in his case Denmark, for Germany's northernmost province was under Danish rule at that time — which gave him traveling scholarships, so that he could spend years in Munich, Paris, and Italy. But mostly there were women, from varied strata of society and in variant relations to him, who again and again helped him to survive. However, all these aids barely made him get through. To the age of thirty-three his struggle for survival was fierce, his sense of poverty and humiliation was chronic, and hunger was his most frequent state of mind.

His state of hunger was more than physical. Everything about Hebbel was charged with an acute and hurtful awareness of himself, of his circumstances, of the people about him, which made his life a continuous experiment, as tortured as it was honest. The monstrous proportion of intellect in his constitution, the fund of penetrating self-analysis in his works and diaries, made him a favorite object of good critics. By them he was fully appreciated even in his lifetime. It was not personal experience only, it was almost a valid historical judgment, when the sensitive Emil Kuh, in his first letter to Keller, stated that for him the contemporary sky contained only three stars of the first magnitude, Schopenhauer, Hebbel, and Keller. Yet this man, who can be ranked with the greatest of representative Germans, has not touched world literature, and has only a precarious foothold in German literature.

He was of such striking originality and force that, as soon as he appeared, he could not be ignored. He was never in doubt about his specific superiority and never at a loss to impose it. But all his victories, early and late, were inforced and not consented, were short-lived, and had to be won over and over. His first drama was performed in Berlin, when he was twenty-seven. Nearly all his plays were performed during his lifetime, nearly all with chilling success. Hating the theater, he wrote for it all his essential work. And he practically married into the Vienna Burgtheater, when its finest actress became his wife and gave him security (1846). But the Burgtheater was only intermittently hospitable to his dramas. His satisfaction had to remain in his self-contemplation and in the admiration of a small circle of enthusiastic friends.

One cannot read a page of Hebbel without being stunned by his grasp, his penetrating insight, and his force of expression. But the way he has always affected his readers is a paradox in itself. One can best circumscribe it by the sensation of very hot and very cold in quick alternation. Few minds find his a human climate, most find that the demands both on their intelligence and on their emotion are too great, and many shun him as too exacting a master. To this day the truest tragedies of the nineteenth century find only lukewarm audiences.

The most human of his plays is *Maria Magdalene* (1844). With stupendous originality he creates a tragedy with the elements of the middle-class mind. Morality, religion, honesty, thrift, frugality, duty, a good name, these powerful stabilizers of society can just as well become terrible when one of them appears in absolute purity; for every individual thing is destructive.

One does not know what to admire first, the oppressive atmosphere of the mild resignation in most characters, or the meek rebellion in others; or the pathetic closeness of family ties, the constant deflection of every thought by the regard for others; or, behind this, the abuse of all dialogue as dialectic, with everybody constantly refuting and correcting everybody else, everybody ' alone ' being right, everybody else so terribly wrong.

It is the language which soon fascinates and disquiets us. There is nothing simple about the language of these simple people. In every dialogue, in every monologue, they are ' witty ' in the Metaphysical sense. And though their metaphors are all from the middle-class sphere, their frequency and insistence comes from insufferably active minds, and their sustained hyperbole from intolerably tortured souls. How the normally wordless suspicions become articulate here! How these people watch, or expect one another. Each cannot help making exaggerated claims on the other, each cannot help making sure of his automatic disappointments. Shortly before the first catastrophe the father says: ' That which a man gains in the sweat of his face, he must honor, esteem, and value. Or he must disbelieve himself and find all his dealings contemptible.' He points to the intense compulsion of giving value to something. In the next scene, his son is arrested as a thief, the sickly mother dies of grief, and one of the most compact and hard-hitting first acts is over, made of nothing but ordinary circumstance.

Hebbel's dramas are full of sensual passion, yet the sensuality is smothered in what its owners know about it and think about it. Klara, the heroine, expects a child by a man she does not care for. What she cares for most is her father, Meister Anton, and he is the real hero of the tragedy. What gives these two petty protagonists the dimension of representatives of Victorianism is their desperate urge to make the individual existence agree not only with their social instinct but with their image of the world. They want to *live* their ethics; in that they can't be fooled, and do not try to fool anybody else.

Act II of *Maria Magdalene* is constructed of nothing but imaginings, nothing at all happens. But Klara's position between a former sweetheart, an independable fiancé, and a father whom she is sure to kill by any disgrace, becomes more hopeless than any action could make it. We realize with dismay that not one of these people enjoys the blessings of a limited horizon; they are all in the universe. There is not a trace of saving stupidity in them. They know too much about themselves and guess and foresee and forefeel too much about each other. Their anomalous awareness gives them such an abundance of motivations that their speeches are fairly crammed with them.

The main difference between the nice people and the villains is that the former feel *for* the others. What happens to others happens almost more to them, and they imagine this to be true of the others as well. They try to hurt in the way it hurts the least. This reflectiveness makes an unlikely number of them psychologists. It is a peculiarity of Hebbel that his nice people are more interesting than his villains, more complicated, more motivated, and more elaborately drawn. (Keller dwells on his villains with more interest and sympathy, enjoys them more, often has some hope in store for them.) It is simplification to say that Klara's motivation is to do everything for her father. But as a dramatic fatality it is almost true that his *thinking* that she is all he has left, and her *thinking* that she must save his manner of thinking drives her to suicide. This ends three (or five) existences in a doom that leaves us stunned, although it has hovered in the metaphor-charged atmosphere from the first speeches on.

There is no question that the excess of psychology would have been more suitable for novels. It did discharge itself in great novels at that time, outside of Germany. Hebbel's dialectic mind probably had no alternative but the dramatic form. In subject-matter he had all the choice in the world, he never repeated himself, and nobody in that century chose more interesting subjects. The 'bürgerliche Tragödie,' which he abandoned with *Maria Magdalene,* rose again only with Ibsen, thirty years later, less concentrated and more digestible. (Ibsen himself wondered 'why the Germans got excited about his plays — it was all in Hebbel before.')

Hebbel always forced the issues. He treated each subject with such violence that to say he raped it would be nearer the truth than to say he loved it fiercely. The popular complaint about his 'monstrosities' was always well deserved. His heroes do not outherod Herod without good reason. He felt with infallible instinct that he had to strain his voice, if the tone of 'high tragedy' were to be preserved at all — after its time was really over. But splendor of classical language and ripeness of form conceal only overconsciousness, overripe intellects, the very existence of which fills us with such doubts that we can never suspend our disbelief long enough to assent to the drama. These monsters of awareness generate so much light that there is not enough mystery left for the genuine play of emotions. The heroes overexplain themselves, until we no longer believe in them. They are so full of motivation that we stop listening to them. The best example is probably the climax of *Herod and Mariamne*. The king has just been foiled in one attempt to find out whether the queen would kill herself were he to die. A *second* chance offers itself: and the partners play the infernal game again. The greater monster is the queen, for while Herod only guesses her almost correctly, she knows him to transparency. 'Jetzt werd ichs sehn,' she drones; 'wir werden sehn,' he keeps on, a hundred lines later. Once more they go through the whole ordeal, while our whole response is: not again! A magnificent act is wasted on us. Here the undeniable truth that it makes a great difference whether something is done in passion ('im Fieber der gereizten Leidenschaft') or in cool determination, proves to be wrong dramatically. The dramatist has fallen into the temptation of showing us both sides of the truth, each in a complete action. No matter how different they are for our intellect, they are only a deadening repeat for our sensibility. His heroes want to know, where feeling should have been knowing too; *we* want to feel and cannot, because there is too much to know.

The very sin of Hebbel is his intellectual overcharge. The loading of his tragedies with metaphysics was admitted by Hebbel in treatises which are philosophic in their formulation. Hes best-known remarks are from 'A Word on the Drama' (1843) and 'Preface to Maria Magdalene' (1844):

'A drama's content is the life-process as such ... It presents the dubious relation and opposition of the individual to the universe; the original connection has been loosened, the individual is incredibly free, yet it is still part of the whole.'

'In a philosophical drama, all that matters is that metaphysics is derived from life.'

'All that remains to be done is to throw the dialectics into the idea itself.'

'Only where there is a problem has dramatic art any business: where the cracks of life show, whereas your mind sees the idea rejoin the lost Oneness.'

'Art is philosophy in actuality, as the world is the idea in actuality.'

We had better say it again, these are not the philosopher's words but Hebbel's. Schopenhauer is simpler when he expounds the aesthetics of tragedy; but in some of his concepts Hebbel reminds one very much of Schopenhauer.

The Ethics of Schopenhauer

One must not imagine Schopenhauer's work to have become a best seller once he was discovered. There remained too much about the work that was aloof, overbearing, and almost forbidding. His *Welt als Wille und Vorstellung* did not reach its third edition until 1859, the year before his death. For *Wille und Vorstellung II* (the 'Supplement' of 1844), that was the second edition. And his so-called popular work, the *Parerga* of 1851, attained a second edition only posthumously. But in comparison to the thirty-year quarantine previous to 1851, this was popularity.

In England and America articles in a dozen journals betray the interest during the seventies; but there were no translations before 1883. Both volumes of the *World as Will* were done by R. B. Haldane and J. Kemp, and published in three volumes in London and Boston from 1883 to 1886. 'We have had nothing but a few fragments of Schopenhauer in English up to the present time,' writes W. M. Payne reviewing the first volume in the Chicago *Dial* in 1884, and he is quick to predict that Schopenhauer will prove very difficult: 'The work is much more comprehensive than any English philosophical system . . . and makes such demands upon the reader, that it will be slow to win for itself the regard . . .' The reviewer himself is enthusiastic about Schopenhauer's style, less so about that of the translation, but most of all he has confidence in the contents: 'There is perhaps no other writer of whom it may as truly be said that to read his works is itself a liberal education.'

When the Haldane-Kemp translation was completed, a reviewer in the New York *Nation* (1886) made some shrewd remarks about the relative readability of what we have called the first (1818) and the second (1844) *World as Will*: 'The first volume, which was issued three years ago, did not excite much attention . . . it embodies the skeleton of his metaphysical system . . . But in the succeeding volumes his metaphysical hobby becomes less and less obtrusive, until it finally assumes the form of an inconspicuous thread on which he strung his pearls.' The second half of *Will and Idea II* was then the third volume, and ' it is in the third English volume that the reader will find the most inviting themes and the most brilliant treatment.'

These early sentiments were not heeded in subsequent publication. That the Haldane-Kemp version has remained the only one and is reprinted by several publishers to this day, is in part due to its high standard. But that the first half is more often reprinted than the second can only be explained by a certain blindness to the superiority and self-sufficiency of *Will and Idea II.* Even Thomas Mann, in his brilliant ' Presentation ' of *The Living Thoughts of Schopenhauer* (1939) reprints only as a climax, not as the core, some chapters from the later volume. That is the volume which would warrant a rejuvenation in the rhythms and phrases of the twentieth century.

The fourth and last part in the treatment of 1818 as well as in the addition of 1844 is Schopenhauer's Ethics, the importance of which lies not only in its sizable proportion, not only in its position as the final stage in his system, but also in its comparative plainness. Perhaps he is easier to know in his ethics than in any other aspect of his thought. The ' Will ' may have something mysterious in the first parts of his system, where it is really a term for *all* forces in the universe, the whole cosmic dynamics. But when we come to his Ethics, the ' Will ' is simply the human will and has nothing obscure for anybody. Indeed his ethics is so little esoteric that we could often substitute ' morality.' ' My philosophy is the only one which gives morality all its due,' he says in the beginning of the chapter entitled ' More on Ethics.' 'Moral problems are more important than any other.'

Schopenhauer hears two voices in nature. One speaks from the center of the individual and says, "the all-important thing is myself." The other speaks from the consciousness of the whole and says, ' one individual is nothing.' This leads to ' the great difference between what we are in our own eyes and what in those of all others; it entails the egoism which everybody sees in everybody else. Our basic error is that we are not-I for one another.' Schopenhauer derives all virtue from ' the instinctive knowledge of the metaphysical identity of all beings.' ' To be just, noble, kind is nothing else but translating my metaphysics into action.' 'It is the same as the brahman formula " tat twam asi — that is you ".' (Here is the source of that partiality to animals which expresses itself so impulsively in Schopenhauer's writings and biography, and in the case of Hebbel likewise.) At the last the philosopher defines ' sympathy ' in the widest sense as ' the empirical transparence of the identity of Will through the physical plurality of its phenomena.'

With that, everything essential has really been said; and if we are disappointed by it, it is because we find nothing that is strange and nothing that is revolutionary. Schopenhauer is the first to acknowledge this, and his next chapter, 'More on the Denial of the Will,' expatiates on the dogmas of the most widely accepted religions, which his doctrine only restates. He finds that 'the core and spirit of Christianity is the same as that of Brahmanism and Buddhism . . . They all teach a guilt-through-existence-itself . . . Our only true sin is original sin.' While this may seem meta-ethics to common morality, a curious parallel with Hebbel makes us pause here. Hebbel, who as a true dramatist should not have been able to operate without personal guilt, despised it as a true philosopher. With impressive stubbornness he preached the dramatic importance of original guilt and the insignificance of personal guilt in 'Mein Wort über das Drama': 'Individuality and its inherent excess . . . in the excess lies the guilt . . . This guilt is an arch-original guilt, not separable from the concept "man," it is essential to life. It winds as darkest thread through the traditions of all peoples, and "original sin" is its Christian derivative. It has nothing to do with the good or bad bent of our will. . . . The highest drama has to do with *that* guilt. And it is not just immaterial whether the hero perishes from a wicked endeavor or a good one; no, the latter is necessary for the highest pathos.' Such a congruence, in thought much more than in expression, suggests that both Schopenhauer and Hebbel had the deepest instinct of their time for a metaphysical ethics.

Just as simple as Schopenhauer's distinction of only two basic tendencies (the egoistic and the anti-egoistic) is his derivation of the moral virtues. They are again only two: justness and kindness. They have their source in the individual's finding himself out, 'seeing through' himself. They are symptoms of the fact that 'the dis-illusion of the will is setting in; one might say, it is flapping its wings, ready to fly off.' The just man refuses to shift his burden onto others; the kind one takes on more than his share of the burdens. Both acknowledge themselves in others. Although we are here at a point where Schopenhauer's Will sublimates itself into pure Idea, and in that sense at the most dangerous and questionable point of his system, we may refuse to see anything dramatic here and find only the old identification of morals with wisdom. And it is true of Schopenhauer as it is true of most Victorians that their best efforts were put to finding new reasons for old values. They tried once more to invest the plain old virtues with all the dignity which philosophical or artistic inventiveness could contrive.

To exploit his concordance with the moral teaching of the great religions, Schopenhauer caps his volume with the chapter 'Die Heilsordnung.' That is a term lifted from theology, of which the ugly translation 'dispensation of salvation' would render nothing. Actually the pseudo-theological flight is genuinely aesthetic, and indeed the concept of tragedy crops up very soon. ' The specific effect of tragedy is that it shakes our inborn delusion, that it exemplifies the frustration of human striving, that it discloses the deepest meaning of life. That's why it is the highest genre of poetry.' When Schopenhauer establishes suffering as the true destiny of life, he keeps thinking of the *normal* life as a tragedy. ' The course of life is basically tragic. . . . As a rule fate crosses a man's essential goals radically; thus his life takes on a tragic tendency.' The aesthetic and religious analogies easily concur here. ' Suffering is mostly the only process of purification by which man is purified. . . . Death is so to speak the final sanctification or canonization.' But all of this ' salvation ' against our will is only ' the minor mode,' the way of sinners, ' as we all are.' Another way is the way of the elect, those who ' see through ' the world early, the saints. At the end of every book of Schopenhauer stands the saint, sometimes documented in quotations from all the scriptures, sometimes evoked in dithyramb, sometimes only briefly silhouetted in his quiet inaccessibility.

' Morality is the very law of the universe,' Hebbel wrote (1846); and ' in its moral core Christianity is above all other religions ' (1857). The almost fanatic adherence of these men to a radically Christian ethics is in glaring contrast to their indifference to the rest of the Christian doctrine. And no matter how original they are as thinkers otherwise, in that dilemma they are only spokesmen of their time. The more the second half of the nineteenth century saw the Christian cosmogony endangered by the scientific world view, the more it seems to have become anxious to preserve the Christian ethics. If it had to live without a Christian universe, it was afraid to live without the Christian way of life. Perhaps they are not far wrong who claim that Schopenhauer's sudden appeal to many minds lay above all in his ethics, in his apparent success of laying a very pagan foundation for a quasi-Christian ethics.

Those who hearkened to Schopenhauer were above all aesthetically gifted minds. But they did not listen for the aesthetic presentation, although by it they were won over unconsciously. They may often have read him the way one reads *belles-lettres,* and looked for truth the way truth is found in poetry, that is in context only. But they ended by believing in what he had to say, not in how he said it. The most articulate among this kind of readers, Thomas Mann, made most explicit this conversion of Schopenhauer's persuasiveness into convincingness. ' That one never forgets what Schopenhauer has said may come from the fact that it is not tied up with the words he uses, that one could substitute other words. And still a nuclear sentiment would remain, a realization of truth, so acceptable, so invulnerable, so right, such as I have not found elsewhere in philosophy. With it one can live and die — especially die. I dare assert that Schopenhauer's truth is apt to last in one's last hour — without effort, without cogitation, without words.' [The passage was omitted in the English version of Mann's essay.]

Hebbel's Ethics

After the first year in Vienna, Hebbel wrote in his diary, 'I am married, and not with Elise in Hamburg; that tells it all.' No, it takes more than the whole, long New Year's meditation to tell it all, although Hebbel dissects himself mercilessly. 'With a different suit I become a different person.' One does not know what to wonder at, Hebbel's inability to have illusions about himself, or his ability to see the highest morality in the height of egoism. 'My conviction in all eternity will be that the whole man belongs to his foremost energy; it alone is the source of his own happiness and of all use he is to the world.' To his refusal to choose a tragic life (when he had a choice) he probably owes his last fifteen years and the series of near-masterworks which they produced.

The great experience of his Viennese years was the revolution of 1848, which in Vienna was more marked in its outward phases, more full of reverses, than anywhere in Germany. At the end of 1848 he had learned several lessons. He hoped that absolutism could never come back; but he also experienced 'What a thing chaos is.' 'Nobody remembered how hard it once was to lay the pavements of society; now we appreciate them again.' It was this experience which colored his next tragedy, *Agnes Bernauer* (1851).

There was something violent in Hebbel's grip; he forced the form of the drama overpoweringly; but he could not prevent the form's resenting it. There is always a secret battle between his form and his subject-matter. It is more glaringly the case with this prose tragedy about love and politics. If *Maria Magdalene* had something to do with the progressivism of the forties, *Agnes Bernauer* has a great deal to do with the conservatism of the fifties. In no other German drama is the conflict of the individual and the state faced so inquisitively. This drama is pure dialectics: there is no villain to suggest any issue between good and bad. There are only principles which fight each other and eliminate the individual worthy to be their obstacle.

This time any accepted notion of how a drama should be constructed — so that we are aware of its leading motifs all the time — is brutally set aside. The first half is given over to the happiness of the individual, the love of the young duke Albrecht of Bavaria for 'the Angel of Augsburg.' As if he were illustrating Schopenhauer's 'Metaphysics of Sex,' Hebbel builds Agnes up as the ideal woman for that ideal man, so that they only have to see each other to fall irrevocably in love. The only fault with the first two acts is that everybody thinks too quickly and talks too splendidly. There is only the gradation from the concentrated prose of the expository speeches to the dynamic explosions of the climactic statements. Once Agnes says: 'What happened to me last night took my speech away; what has happened just now gives it back to me.' But it's the only untruth she ever utters. These people are never speechless with emotion; their strongest feelings inspire their wittiest conceits; the wildest passion makes them most articulate. It's their only fault.

In the later acts, which are more and more given over to considerations of state, the splendor of language is noticeably abated — apart from a heavy chain of sombre premonitions which garlands its symbols from scene to scene — we are in an old man's world, not ruled by beauty but by honesty. There is something scrupulous, punctilious about the old Duke's and his old Chancellor's efforts to find a solution which will prevent civil war without sacrificing the happiness of the young couple. The simplicity of the old men's habits and thinking, but also the intricate ways of political chess (even in the fifteenth century) receive their due. The old men try long delays and many means, including the giving away of the succession in Bavaria. When the last attempt fails, the fate of the barber's daughter is sealed, she must die to save the peace of millions. There is no high-sounding praise of the state, there is only worried scrutiny of necessities and anxious calculating of probabilities. And the actual triumph of the state consists in long-meditated abdication and bowing of heads.

Agnes Bernauer may be the most dialectic German drama; however, among Hebbel's plays it is probably the one with most body. The world of the fifteenth century is evoked with a fulness which no other background of his dramas has. And the architecture of the play shows nothing of a clumsy bipartition. The theme of beauty and love goes through a mighty decrescendo from its dominance in the first act to its last stand in the last act, when Agnes prefers to die as Albrecht's wife rather than to save herself by an annulment. The theme of the common weal goes through a proportionate crescendo from the warning in the first act, 'Denkt an Kaiser und Reich!' through the many pleadings and entreaties which swell to an almost national chorus in the last.

But this drama, with all its perfections, has always had a crack for every unprejudiced viewer. It is a drama that should not be. There is something intangibly but essentially wrong with all its order and resignation. The accounts do not balance. Probably, because every problem is from the beginning raised to its metaphysical exponent. Whenever the lovers are at the height of their passion (and they are so rather constantly), they think of God. Whenever the statesmen are deepest in their ponderings, the name of God seals their direst plans. It is almost as if the shortest definition of the deity were ' tragedy.'

By 1848 Hebbel had arrived at a concept of morality which reads as if it were a short-cut through the ethics of Schopenhauer. He assembles in a few sentences not only the eternal antagonists: individual and universe, and necessity as the thing that relates them. But he stresses another, more humanly charged relation, that of understanding, of personal insight, of the process of resignation and liberation; and he even identifies this with the cherished German concept of self-realization — Bildung: ' When Man has understood his individual relation to the universe in its necessity, he has completed himself [seine Bildung vollendet]. He has, in a way, ceased to be individual. The concept of his necessity, the capacity to penetrate to it, the force to hold it: this is the universal in the individual. It quells all excessive egoism and liberates from death by anticipating it.' If Schopenhauer had seen this (it is a letter of 1848), he could not but have been moved by a quiver of recognition. The last sentence is a parallel to those codas of Schopenhauer's books where he points to the higher human road, the one of true liberation, the miraculous power of sainthood.

But we do not find anything of this liberation in the dramas, although they are painfully charged with moral issues. The finest of his heroines, Agnes in the *Bernauer* play, the queen in *Herod and Mariamne,* Rhodope in *Gyges,* are veritable monsters of morality. But they do not spread the blessings of sainthood, neither on their fellow creatures nor on us readers. While Schopenhauer's saint embodies reconciliation with the universe, the saints of Hebbel spread destruction and are adepts in suicide. There is nothing exemplary in their being; ' it moves us not ' it does not even tempt us to put ourselves in their places. In the great tragedy, from the Greeks on, a sort of sanctification is achieved for the heroes, and in a ' minor mode ' for the onlookers. Hebbel's tragedy is strangely devoid of it. Perhaps he was too curious about the psychology of his heroines ever to let them find that saving simplicity which could elevate them into the religious sphere — and extricate them from him and his complications.

There is something brutal about all his heroes, something slightly loathsome about all his subjects. Although no German wrote a more Shakespearean language, we cannot stand the blustering of all his supermen. Their swagger seems closer to Falstaffs than to princes. Should it really be true that Hebbel never outgrew the lack or belatedness of his education? that he never made up for his unfamiliarity with good society? There is something uncivilized, not about the thoughts, but about the speeches of his finest characters. They slightly but relentlessly grate on our nerves.

Hebbel is at home in pre-civilization worlds. The more he goes back to early or mythological ages, the more his grip becomes steady and powerful. Perhaps that is why his apparent concordance with Schopenhauer's ethics could not be transferred to his dramas. It was genuine, perhaps even spontaneous, in his thought and theory; it could not be transplanted into those primitive worlds which his imagination preferred to create. Schopenhauer is eminently civilized, Hebbel is a genius of a barbarian. Schopenhauer is — in the structure and culmination of his work — if not actually religious, at least lingeringly post-religious. Conversely, Hebbel's dramas could be called 'pre-religious,' and in the notorious scraps of religious message which he patches into *Judith,* into *Herodes,* into the *Nibelungen,* he really 'seweth a piece of new cloth on an old garment . . . and the rent is made worse.' Schopenhauer's is an eloquent and sometimes a stirring ethicism; Hebbel's heroes are the more believable the more they are pre-ethical, mouthpieces of a passion that has as much in common with volcanoes and hurricanes as with morally motivated human beings.

Certainly this is not all of Hebbel but only one powerful and dangerous tendency in him. It may explain why a work that is stamped with the seal of greatness almost as if it were its trade-mark chills us wherever we touch it. G. Keller, at the time when he was most interested in the drama, felt distinctly both the power and the essential un-modernity or anti-modernity of Hebbel. After seeing *Judith* (in Berlin, 1851) he had simply 'a great impression. It is a drama full of power and depth. . . . The wrestling of prehistoric man [Vorweltmensch] with the gods whom he shaped in his primary creativeness offers a majestic spectacle.' Keller saw philosophy shine all through the play; during the whole performance he had to think of his favorite philosopher Feuerbach. But a few years later (1854) Keller thought of Hebbel mainly as an example of mistaken wilfulness: 'There is no individual and arbitrary originality. . . . Hebbel is a genius, but because he wants to be novel by any means, he invents such abominable plots. New in a good sense is only that which proceeds from the dialectic of civilization.'

The Art of Literature

Just as the Haldane-Kemp translation of *The World as Will and Idea* has remained not only the standard but the only one to our time, so T. Bailey Saunders' translations of the *Parerga and Paralipomena* are being reprinted to this day. They are in a nimble style; and from the beginning (about 1890) they had the advantage of being available in small volumes, such as *Counsels and Maxims, Religion and Other Essays, Studies in Pessimism, The Wisdom of Life*. The selection that seems to have been reprinted most often is *The Art of Literature*. This little paperback contains essays largely from the last part of Schopenhauer's last book. They approach the domain of literature very much from the outside, from the viewpoint of a disgruntled *grand seigneur* who condescends to discuss the right of the miserable scribes to exist. His bad humor is roused by the excess of trash over the worthwhile. Although some pages in the chapter 'On Style' are simply polemics against the depravation of the German language, there are numerous passages which afford us insights into Schopenhauer's own stylistic endeavors. The savoriness of his prose was only in part a gift — 'style is the physiognomy of a mind.' In equal part it was a product of reflection and work. And it showed some evolution from his preference for long periods in the *World as Will* of 1818, through the widest range of effects in the *Will and Idea II* of 1844, to the sometimes shrill sententiousness of the *Parerga* of 1851.

On the subject of style, Hebbel was a more intimate observer. At the close of an article written in 1844 he set down a description, which really seems to be a characterization of his own dramatic style: 'At every step it takes, this language feels crowded by aspects and relations, which point backwards and forwards, and all of which it has to take along. The voices of life mingle and cancel out each other. The thread of thought breaks before it is spun through; the sentiment capsizes; the word emancipates itself, turns up a secret meaning which paralyses its ordinary sense. For every word is a die with several surfaces.' It takes only one such quotation to realize that Schopenhauer and Hebbel are just superficially contemporaneous. Hebbel has the linguistic sense of the nineteenth century, while the other harks back to the eighteenth.

The polemical side of Schopenhauer's literary essays is climaxed in 'On Men of Learning.' The essay would be vastly amusing, if it were not so devastatingly true. For fear of quoting too much of those savage attacks on the drawbacks of the university system, we shall quote nothing at all. The positive counterpart is the essay 'On Thinking for Oneself.' Here we have to listen, for Schopenhauer is speaking of men of his own kind. 'Anybody can put his will to reading and learning; but not so to thinking. Thinking must be kindled, like a fire by a draught, by an interest in the subject. . . . Objective interest exists only for heads that think by nature, to whom thinking is as natural as breathing. They are very rare. . . . Reading is nothing more than a substitute for thought of one's own. . . . Reading is thinking with someone else's head instead of one's own. . . . The thinker speaks from direct and "immediate" comprehension. That is why all those who think for themselves do, in the last analysis, agree.' Schopenhauer admits that a modern philosopher's reading must be enormous, but that he needs a proportionate time to assimilate it. That reminds one of the enormous walks that were part of his mental diet. One might say that he — and Hebbel too — was a voracious walker. He might have said, as Hebbel did, 'if you take my legs away you take my head.'

'On Some Forms of Literature' is a section of Schopenhauer's last essay on aesthetics. His view of high tragedy, which 'turns our will from life,' is well known. But his view of the novel is stated only here. 'A novel will be of a higher order the more inner and the less outer life it represents. The ratio between the two will be the criterion for all grades of novel. . . . Art consists in using the smallest expense of outer life to set the inner in strongest motion; for it is the inner life that really excites our interest.' The section closes with such a praise of books — 'a high degree of culture leads us to seek entertainment almost wholly from books and not from men' — as is scarcely compatible with the preceding section. But that is just the attraction of Schopenhauer that he does not stick to a few opinions. He develops so many lines of thought that all the differences in the world are possible consequences of his system.

The sections 'On Criticism' and 'On Reputation' are probably not worth ranking among his popular writings. They are as full of quick insights and pithy formulations as any of his essays, but they are so personal that they can hardly be read in the right frame of mind any more. We must not forget that every last one of these essays was written before the ice had broken that had encased his own reputation. Therefore these essays constitute a final bitter, and sometimes sour, self-consolation. They were a soliloquy, entirely and haughtily true at the time of composition, but not ringing as true when taken as teachings for posterity, and by his very fame invalidated when taken as a testament.

When Hebbel visited Schopenhauer — the one and only time, in 1857 — the old man spoke to him of 'the comedy of his fame.' He felt like a stagehand on whom the curtain had opened before he scurried into the wings. Hebbel wrote to his wife afterwards that Schopenhauer and he would without question become friends, if he lived in Frankfurt too. Other friends told more details about the visit. The old philosopher (he was seventy, Hebbel forty-five) praised the 'pith and truth' of *Maria Magdalene*, but attacked its Preface. If one can believe the very reliable friends (Jordan and Kuh), the philosopher went so far as to congratulate the robust constitution of a poetry that was not smothered by so much complicated reflection, and then he argued against philosophy bringing forth poetry, maintaining that the reverse was always true.

It is certain that somebody misunderstood something there. For on that point there could be no argument. All of Hebbel's philosophy came from and after poetry, all of his reflection was derivative of his imagination. (It is true that the heroes he imagined were too conscious, too reflective, too intelligent, especially with the brutal and primitive tempers he gave them.) But it is also certain that Schopenhauer was very much on the poet's side, since the entire third book of *Will and Idea* gave art a place such as no philosopher had ever claimed for it.

Whereas the last step (the fourth) in Schopenhauer's system is the turning of the will against itself, the liberation through ethics, the third step is the liberation through the intellect. But this 'pure subject of cognition' which perceives ideas, and not mere concepts or relations, is such a combination of philosophic intuition and artistic imagination that the whole area, this true 'World as Idea,' is nothing but Schopenhauer's Aesthetics. If we look at the second *Will and Idea* (1844) and open the 'Third Book,' we soon forget the warning of the first sentence that the liberation through aesthetics is (in contrast to the fourth step) 'not a liberation for good, but a reprieve, an exceptional disengagement from the service of the will.' We are, throughout the book, wafted on Schopenhauer's wings of enthusiasm through a higher region. The more he knew how temporary such flights are, the more he made them sustained here. He deals with the triumphs of art and of philosophy alike; indiscriminately he claims for both the *imagination* as the main tool, 'indispensable to genius.'

He suddenly springs on us an ethical principle. One big difference between ordinary men and genius is that the former take care of their own affairs, the genius of the affairs of the world. They consider creating and thinking a means, he considers them his sole purpose. 'He sacrifices his personal good to an objective purpose; they do the opposite. Therefore they are small, he is great. . . . Great is only he, who in his activity, be it practical or theoretical, does not seek his advantage but an objective purpose. Even if his purpose should be erroneous, even if it should be a crime — that he does not seek himself and his advantage, this makes him great, unconditionally. . . . Only the true hero and the genius have a right to that predicate. It means that contrary to human nature they have not lived for themselves but for all.' Schopenhauer is almost at a stammer of excitement on this grand page ('On Genius'). It is one of the points where his third and fourth book communicate, where his artists stretch their hands out to his saints, and touch them.

'Not only philosophy, the arts too work in the last analysis at solving the problem of existence.' This common task inspired Schopenhauer to maintain himself, throughout the third book, on a line where it is indifferent whether he speaks more from the viewpoint of art or from that of philosophy. Perhaps the very indetermination gives those chapters their atmosphere. 'What is life? — Every genuine work of art gives, in its manner, a correct answer to this question.' The whole array of the arts is looked at by Schopenhauer with fresh and loving eyes. Because (as he says in that other essay 'On Genius' extracted from his *Parerga*) 'the masterpieces of past and contemporary men of genius exist in their fulness for genius alone.' It is difficult to say which art stimulates his thoughts best; perhaps music, or perhaps tragedy. 'As the seventh chord demands the fundamental chord . . . so every tragedy demands an existence of a different kind, another world, which can only be apprehended negatively. In the tragic catastrophe we obtain, better than anywhere else, the conviction that life is a bad dream from which we ought to awake. . . . What gives the tragic its peculiar impetus and upward flight is the dawn of the discovery that world and life offer no true satisfaction, are therefore not worth our attachment. That is the tragic sense, it initiates into resignation.' How close he is again, as at all high points of his aesthetics, to his ethical bias, is seen in the fact that here as there he prefers the Christian product to those of his beloved Antiquity, Shakespeare to Sophocles. 'Antiquity simply had not reached the summit and destination of tragedy, nor of philosophy.'

The fascination of these final vortices, into which he draws all the material that is within distant reach, lies probably in the ease which they afford us to operate with sentiments instead of with concepts, to substitute analogies for distinctions, and to wallow in a welter of references, recalls, and reminiscences. The similarity with the way poets generalize calls up Hebbel's term 'Gedankentrauerspiele' for all important creations of the human mind (in the letters to pastor Luck, 1860). 'I could not be inimical to religion; that is not possible for a poet, if he deserves the name. . . . Religion and poetry have a common source and a common destination. . . . Neither in the anthropomorphisms of religion nor in the doctrines of philosophy can I see anything specifically different from the great creations of poetry. They are three kinds of *Gedankentrauerspiele* (tragedies of the idea), in which now the imagination and now the intellect preponderates.'

In Schopenhauer's case, the three sequences of his opus offer each a tetralogy which owes not a little of its appeal to its dramatic qualities, to effects not of analysis but of synthesis, such as suspense, climax, peripetia. The latter especially, the 'Umschlag,' is tried and achieved so regularly at all the high points of his system that one must claim a lasting affinity of Schopenhauer for that kind of mysterious conversion, transmutation, or rather reversal, which makes it possible for the will to become consciousness at a certain point, for the selfish consciousness to become pure intellect at another point, and for the blind will to become all-understanding non-will at another. Those may be the greatest weaknesses of his system, but each time he commits them, a pang of recognition goes through the reader: those are the grand scenes in the great drama, the incredible modulations in our attunement to the universe, the impossible sudden salvations of our humanity.

Schopenhauer's work is not, like that of other philosophers, characterized mainly by deductibility, coherence, and consistency. It has those qualities in the more aesthetic guise of coordinance, harmony, and correspondence. He claimed to be a mind that had only one thought; we notice more that he applied that thought to a thousand striking situations, a thousand themes which by their very appearance delight us. There is, to be sure, one criterion by which we judge philosopher and artist alike, the criterion of range. Schopenhauer's documentation is equally copious from classical philology, from modern science, and from the history of religions. But what likens Schopenhauer most to an artist is that he not only shares the artist's way of looking at things — responding to each image of the world as if it were more than an illustration, as if it were rather the whole once again — but that he also shares his language. With good reason has he claimed metaphor as the preferred language of genius. His own indiscriminate power lies in using metaphorical, even mythical terms on the same level with abstracts. He revels in his power of analogy. Hence the lack of impact on abstract minds, hence also his appeal to those who think in his kind of language. They see flash-like intuitions in his similes, they hear delightful accelerations in his analogies: 'Schopenhauer can do no wrong in my eyes: I no more quarrel with his errors than I do with a mountain cataract. Error is but the abyss into which he precipitates his truth. The more wide-minded men like the beauty of speed.' (W. B. Yeats to T. S. Moore, January 1928)

III

The Critics

Nietzsche at Thirty

Nietzsche was not, like Schopenhauer, 'discovered' by England. The earliest English articles, in the middle of the eighteen-nineties, all point to his established fame in Germany and France, although there that fame was of very recent date. What catches our attention first in those early English articles is a tone of soberness, of quiet discrimination between the admirable and the unacceptable in Nietzsche. A tone of sound criticism applied to this supreme critic seems to have remained a mark of English and American Nietzsche literature from that time on.

The situation was complex enough to inspire mixed feelings. Then, Nietzsche was insane, and pity for the man toned down any invective against the philosopher. However, the last of his works were translated first, and their intransigence warranted any reluctance. Besides, the critics were acquainted with the first biography of Nietzsche, by his sister (1895) and were suspended between its irreplaceable facts and its more questionable interpretations. Moreover, they were quick to discover in Nietzsche himself an abnormal multiplicity of viewpoints. M. Wallace in *The Academy* of August 1896 called him 'an adept in allusiveness and insinuations *pro* and *contra*. . . . Through the abrupt turns and winding sweeps of a dialogue between the two, or rather the two-and-twenty, selves that struggle for victory within him. . . .' But no matter how heterogeneous the elements were, one thing was not among them: 'Nietzsche's safeguard and glory is a delicate perception which revolts at anything gross, vulgar, heavy, luscious. There may be storm and waste, abyss and war in his haunts, but there is nothing mean, foul, petty.'

In an anonymous thirty-page article in the *Quarterly Review* of October 1896, 'The Ideals of Anarchy — F. Nietzsche' are dutifully questioned, but largely ascribed to Darwinism, or simply to 'science.' Everywhere we find sensitiveness to Nietzsche's 'headlong, iridescent style.' 'But this, certainly not too sane, philosopher, who could not write a book, was, to repeat his well-warranted self-praise, Master of the Sentences.' 'This "mystic maenad soul" was original rather in temperament than in theory, and most of all in manner.' The outstanding American article in this early crop, F. Schiller's in the New York *Book Buyer* of 1896, also does justice to the style: 'The writings of Nietzsche will long be read for the excellence of his style and the brilliance of his epigrams. . . . As philosopher, I should be inclined to rate him less highly . . . his views seem too fragmentary, unfounded, and unbalanced to win much permanent influence.'

Indeed, after the first flurry of interest, there seems to have been a lull. The first three volumes of translation found no successors. Only Nietzsche's death in 1900 revived the controversy. It had become almost a controversy between Nietzsche's vulgar disciples and his true interpreters. The epitaph in the London *Academy* (September 1, 1900) deliberately closes with the remark that even in insanity Nietzsche 'retained his natural dignity, elegance, and sweetness.' The London *Athenaeum* (June 15, 1901) is more insistent: 'At present the writer lives chiefly in the heads of anemic, over-nicotined, over-absinthed students in France and Germany. . . . But of course there is a better side in Nietzsche's teaching than this. Essentially it may be said to be an appeal to the honesty of individual conscience from the dishonesty of conscience hypnotized by "journalism" and public opinion so called.' The outstanding American article in the year of Nietzsche's death may well be that of G. Crawfurd in the New York *Nineteenth Century* (October 1900), which is full of reservations against the later Nietzsche, but full of tolerance for the earlier one. 'Like Schopenhauer, Nietzsche arrived at his mastery in the art of expression by . . . considering language as an artistic instrument . . . of course, it is the best and highest method.'

It is strange that the soberest of Nietzsche's books, *Human, All-Too Human* (of 1879) was then, and has always remained, the one of least interest to English and American readers. Yet it is the book in which not only we can find out most easily his way of thinking, but also he, in his own opinion, 'found himself.' Friedrich Nietzsche had been a professor of Latin and Greek at the University of Basle since 1869, since he was twenty-five. Distinguished in his teaching rather by gentleness and courtesy than by force and impressiveness or anything like success, he had soon become known beyond the small circle of his students by a restless expansion of his field. His publications concerned not Greek literature, but a philosophy of literature, which easily enfolded a philosophy of civilization. Then they attacked contemporary trends in German civilization or interpreted leaders to a higher civilization: Schopenhauer and Richard Wagner. But when Wagner's work was finally crowned with public success, and the Bayreuth theatre was opened (1876), his most eloquent disciple, Nietzsche, withdrew. He began writing his huge though disguised recantation, his change of heart and change of mind, *Human, All-Too*

Human.

The book is a huge collection of ideas, in three layers, (for three years). And in each of the three layers we distinguish three foci: (1) a probing into the genesis of philosophies, morals, religions; (2) a probing into the criteria of 'higher' civilization and the function of art therein; (3) a probing into various topics which camouflage the most personal topic: 'Der Mensch mit sich allein,' Nietzsche's self-analysis.

(1) In each of the three layers the thought wanders to a serene acceptance of both the traditional and the revolutionary. In morals, everything has developed and must still develop. New habits, of simply comprehending, of neither loving nor hating, of seeing-through, grow on the very soil of our mistaken virtues. And mankind grows towards a new innocent irresponsibility (I, 107). 'Do you think that all good things always have a good conscience? Science (certainly a good thing) came without a good conscience, secretly and deviously, veiled and marked, like a criminal or at least like a smuggler. . . . Everything good was once new, against nature, immoral' (II, 90). 'If all goes well, the time will come when people will reach rather for Socrates than for the Bible in order to educate themselves morally and rationally. . . . To Socrates can be traced back the different philosophical ways of life, ordered by reason and custom and directed to enjoying life and enjoying one's self' (III, 88). These are the serene endings of the three successive layers. They conclude three series of attacks on everything the Victorian age held sacred.

(2) The centre of each of the three parts is devoted to questions of art and civilization, and it is here that we can grasp best the peculiar turn which Nietzsche's mind was just taking. It was a sudden suspicion of art and its motives, its lack of veracity, its retrospection, its infantilism. Art is the last refuge of metaphysics. Modern music is mainly a counter-Enlightenment. 'Scientific' man is the higher development of the species 'aesthetic' man. Art seems so intense now because we see its after glow. Then he speaks of 'higher civilization.' It requires the decadent, the skeptic, the subversive. The free-thinker is the answer to an abnormal need. Retrogressions in civilization are possible: the German Reformation was a retrogression from the Italian Renaissance. We are not sure of our progress, we are only sure that we don't want to turn back. We are getting more curious, and the world is getting more interesting. Higher civilization does not mean more happiness. One demerit of our civilization is the lack of contemplation. The sign of the higher species is a refined heroism.

The centre of the second part is introduced by one aphorism (II, 99) which may stand for all the rest, because it is unusually comprehensive:

'The Poet as Guide to the Future.'

'As the poets once continued the figures of gods, so the present poet should continue the picture of man, inventing those cases where, in the midst of modern reality, the beautiful and great soul is still possible, where it still arranges itself in harmonious and orderly conditions, through which it acquires visibility, durability, and typicalness; so that, by creating envy and imitation, it creates future. The works of such poets would seem sealed against the hot air of passions. All our incorrigible faults, all shattering of the human stringed instrument, everything tragic and comic in the old fashion would look old-fashioned, coarse, beside this new art. Strength, kindness, mildness, purity, and an inborn measure in persons and actions, a level ground which offers rest and pleasure to the foot; a luminous sky reflected on faces and affairs. . . . This would be the golden ground for the painting itself, the painting of growing human dignity [Hoheit].'

Is it wrong to think of Gottfried Keller's work here? Not because Keller wanted to call one of his collections 'Auf Goldgrund'; but because so many of the adjectives and nouns of Nietzsche's paragraph are just the ones which have occurred naturally to many viewers of Keller's art. And because the very idea that poetry may educate a higher type had the sanction of the pedagogical democrat, who wrote (on account of his 'Sieben Aufrechten') 'I consider it the duty of the poet not only to transfigure the past, but to embellish the present and to strengthen the germs of the future. . . . The national stock is always healthy; but we must keep showing it as even better [than it is].'

To think of G. Keller was not far from Nietzsche's own mind. In the third part (III, 109) he raised the question what the nineteenth century had contributed to the lasting treasure of German prose, and he came up with only two names: Adalbert Stifter and Gottfried Keller. There were just as few critics then who could have subscribed to that verdict as there are now who would dare contradict it. We may add here that Keller was not equally well disposed towards Nietzsche. He was not willing to see the budding genius in him. Later, in 1884, the relations became more than courteous, according to Nietzsche's sister even cordial. But no document exists of a conversion of Keller to the young incendiary.

(3) The third focus of *All-Too Human,* the only one which is clearly put at the end and climax of the three instalments, is 'Man Alone,' where Nietzsche talks, more or less unreservedly, to himself, about himself, or against himself. The dominant note is one of methodical doubt, of methodical change of opinion, for the sake of change, for the sake of liberation. The synthesis of these moods is in aphorism I, 638, where Nietzsche introduces for the first time 'the Wanderer,'

the figure which he himself was to resemble more and more in the following years:

'He who has attained intellectual emancipation can regard himself only as a wanderer, though not as a traveller towards a goal, for there is no such thing. . . . He must have in himself something which takes pleasure in change and transitoriness. To be sure such a man will have bad nights. . . . And the day is almost worse than the night, but then there are the compensations.'

Nietzsche succeeds in laying himself open to all impressions, to such a degree that this collection of his thoughts becomes a welter of irreconcilable attitudes. We frequently wonder whether we hear the same man speaking. He is his own antagonist. Since this is the book of his beginning solitude, all its voices are his own; but they mimic the discordant voices of the whole world, in so far as it penetrated into his solitude. 'With these I have come to terms, when I have long wandered alone'; and he enumerates Epicurus and Montaigne, Goethe and Spinoza, Plato and Rousseau, Pascal and Schopenhauer (II, 408). If one adds that the book is dedicated to Voltaire and crests, so to speak, in Socrates, one is stupefied by the multitude of patron saints; they are incompatible. And indeed, the book has nothing to do with consistency. The heterogeneity of its sources is matched by the heteronomy of its methods. He could think from more diverse viewpoints than anybody before him, the very essence of his thoughts was diversity. 'Changing opinions is for some natures as much a demand of cleanliness as changing clothes' (III, 346).

The dazzle of the freedom of his thoughts soon turns into a dizziness from lack of firm ground. His craving for liberty becomes a craze, to which he eagerly sacrifices everything, a veritable holocaust. In a hundred passages his language betrays that he is sensitive to the dominant fear of Victorianism: that the tenuous consistency of the moral order was barely holding together, and that any jolt might be destructive to it. Nietzsche is fully aware that it is so, but he does not fear the jolts, he provides them.

This freest of minds, which practised a thinking regardless of consequences, also discovered for itself the form in which such thinking without consequences was possible, the aphorism. The schizophrenic genius found his schizophrenic form, where one thought does not lead to another, where the next one can refuse to know its neighbor, can forget its predecessors and can ignore its successors. On every page, Nietzsche starts afresh, with new premises, that is with no premises. Paragraphs of from two lines to two pages are the units of his book. The accidents of his poor health — besides his admiration for the French 'moralistes' and their 'maximes' — helped him find this form. Severe eye trouble kept him from writing continuously.

Severe headaches kept him from meditating coherently. So the aphorisms only ignite a thousand flashes of insight. Most other books have a steadier and milder light, all other books have a warmer light than Nietzsche's; but what other books are not dull in comparison to his?

'The best in us is perhaps inherited from the sentiments of former times . . . the sun has gone down already, but the sky is still aglow from it' (I,223). Victorianism was a rearguard action. Half the charm which its ideals exert on us is due to the *Abschiedsstimmung,* to the softening of our hearts at parting. The best of his time knew it and felt it; Nietzsche knew it and refused to feel it. In his earlier sallies he had attacked only the excrescences of Victorianism; now he attacked what was best in it. It was vulnerable: just the notion that all things, all men, hang together, and do not merely amount to mediocrity. It was tenuous: just the hope that the average human being can partake of the true, the good, and the beautiful. It was precarious: just the assumption that those three nebulae may create some world, if we let them. Nietzsche, with the savage joy of a young scientist who values his experiments beyond all experience, subjects all the delicate phantoms to vivisection. They die under his scalpel, and he is triumphant. When his sentiments were found acceptable, Victorianism was dead.

In the first English treatise on Nietzsche, the first essay in Havelock Ellis's *Affirmations* (1898; the essay itself was written in 1895), the book *All-Too Human* receives its due perhaps more handsomely than in any later criticism. H. Ellis too is under the influence of the earliest biography; but he is a very good reader of the early and middle Nietzsche, whose qualities he sketches thus, 'clearness, analytic precision, and highly organized intelligence: light and alert' (p. 41); and he competently marks the main targets: 'His whole significance lies in the thorough and passionate analysis with which he sought to dissect and to dissolve, first "German culture," then Christianity, and lastly, modern morals, with all that these involve' (47). 'In an age in which moralists desire to force morals into every part of life and art . . . the "immoralist" who lawfully vindicates any region for free cultivation is engaged in a proper and wholesome task' (76). Thus this championing yet very discriminating first English essay on Nietzsche arrives at the general verdict, 'From first to last, wherever you open his books, you light on sayings that cut to the core of the questions that every modern thinking man must face' (79).

Fontane's *Entanglements*

'My whole production is psychography and criticism, creation-from-the-dark, arranged in the light.' It was not Nietzsche the supreme artist of impressionist philosophy who said this, it was an old journalist about to write the best impressionist fiction, Fontane to his wife, (May 14, 1884). The end of Victorianism is almost 'caused' by the works of Friedrich Nietzsche; it is described in the works of Theodor Fontane. Yet the two took no notice of each other. The fame of old Fontane (1819-1898) came so late that the younger man could not hear of it; the notoriety of Nietzsche was of such a violence that the old pacifist had to turn a deaf ear.

Fontane was, with more right than Nietzsche, proud of the strong admixture of non-German blood in his veins. Although this was largely French, the country that made most impression on him was England, where he sojourned three times. It was after years in London that he said, if he had an option between writing prize-winning tragedies and leading articles, he would choose the articles (September 20, 1858). No German in Germany would, at that time, have voted that way. Fontane was the first German who became a writer by way of a journalist career. To be sure, he did not get to write the leaders he may have dreamed about, destiny confined him to literary and theatrical criticism. And this, strangely, did not spoil him for creative writing but confirmed him in it.

We may find an access to his own dainty and delicate fiction through his criticism. In 1875, while working on his first novel, he asked in a review the question, 'What's the purpose of a novel?' The first noteworthy thing in his answers is the form 'er soll' with its connotation of duty. 'Avoiding the exaggerated and ugly, it is to tell a story in which we believe. It is to speak to our imagination and emotion. . . . It is to let us live among people who are either pleasant or interesting, whose intercourse aids, enlightens, and instructs us.' Nothing could be more Victorian. He is, indeed, so much an admirer of the English novel that this sounds like a hasty defence against French Naturalism, which he did not yet know, which he was never to know well.

We discover a little more about Fontane if we pursue his criticism of Keller, written between 1875 and 1883. Although never looking to Keller as a model, he never failed to realize the excellence of the Swiss story-teller, who was exactly his age, but had achieved fame a generation earlier. 'Never has there been more meticulous, careful, loving workmanship.' This is not true, in the same sense, of Fontane. Not only is the work of his last twenty years, with its sixteen short novels, more voluminous than all the work of Keller, it is also more uneven, more left to accident, and some of it is casual. ' Every one of his tales is *sui generis*.' This too is less true of Fontane; his tales have less profile, more family-likeness than Keller's. ' Gottfried Keller is, *au fond,* a teller of fairy-tales.' That is a very striking remark, it tells us much about Keller, and it is said from a profound feeling of otherness. Fontane was to become the best of German realists because there is *no* fairy-tale left in his stories, the probabilities of psychology are minutely observed and resignedly accepted. But the most differentiating remark is the following: ' He has a fairy-tale language, essentially unchanging, in which old and modern time, high and low participate.' This is pertinent criticism; Keller could not, or would not, differentiate the speech of his people enough. All of his people say things of which they would not be capable unless the poet prompted them. Here Fontane is half a century more modern: his people characterize themselves, more and more, by their speeches. What they say and how they say it: that and nothing else is their character.

One of the best examples of his art is the novel *Irrungen Wirrungen* (Entanglements, 1888), in which a segment of Berlin society of the eighteen-seventies is sketched with an incomparably light hand. The entanglement is between an officer of the Prussian nobility and a seamstress of the lowest middle class. The interest is on so many other things that one feels he has to do with a many-sided author, not only with the superb maturity of a seventy-year old, but also with a thorough training in different branches of literature. The strikingly short chapters (26 for only 150 pages) remind one that Fontane had first earned recognition as a ballad writer. And in many of the bittersweet chapters we might see a sort of bourgeois ballad, where a certain fatalistic mood would be heavy, were it not safely enclosed in concrete detail. First place in this detail is held by the locale of Berlin and its environs. Here Fontane is simply unique. He made the modest features of the capital of Brandenburg yield many appeals; he had practised just this art in volumes of *Wanderings in Brandenburg,* descriptions and local stories, which had occupied him for decades and had been the chief source if his reputation. Both the ballads and the travelogues had had their original inspiration in England and Scotland. But their pervading sentiment was so unmistakenly Prussian-patriotic that Fontane also became the semi-official chronicler of the three wars in which Prussia was engaged between 1864 and 1870. And even this almost official side of the many-sided man is not altogether absent in *Entanglements,* where it is noticeable as the gentleness of his criticism, the absence of social caricature, the tolerance for political needs.

The novel opens on so light a tone of assent (to everything seen or said) that we may expect a story marked by two absences, one of emphasis and one of antagonism. People and things are likable by the absence of anything hateable, they are curious by the absence of anything categorical, they are interesting by the absence of anything obvious. The author has a wide focus, he seems to hesitate as to who will be his heroes: meanwhile he makes everybody interesting. He seems to hesitate as to what his story will be: meanwhile his people talk themselves into a story. But they do not tell us much more than ' decent ' people, people not in a novel, could. They do not say what isn't said. And so all the wonderfully natural conversation only lets us *infer* that there is a liaison between baron Botho and seamstress Lene. And when we finally have Botho in the circle of all the little people, we infer that he is happy with all of them, trying to make everybody like him, and succeeding.

But as soon as Fontane has made us infer that the two lovers are as right as they can be, they themselves make it clear that they do not expect their happiness to last. Before they have time to insist, the narrator bounces us into the milieu of Botho, his relatives, his friends. And their (slightly) luxurious pastimes and conversations are as natural to them as they are incommensurable with the other world. Then follow two (modestly) elaborate scenes of the pleasures of Botho and Lene, first in company, then alone, on a weekend trip.

We have come to the middle of the story, and we may venture to summarize our impressions. It seems that the most ' interesting ' scenes or questions are ignored or neglected or simply understood. But what is not ignored is the opinions which everybody has about everything. It is a world of opinions generously poured forth by everybody. The contrary opinions do not refute each other, they compose a concert of voices, in which each opinion can lead and each can accompany; each colors the others and is tinged by the others. These people like to hear themselves talk; but they also like to hear each other talking; they enjoy each other in speech. Practically all Fontane's characters are impressionable, many are self-explaining, apologetic. Few take themselves quite seriously. Most — whatever their social status — combine a penchant for irony with a capability for self-irony. There are many half-sentiments and half-statements; but that is not so much the result of incompleteness as it is the product of mutual limitation: these people get most of their lighting from each other, via a good impressionistic technique. But they also get a curiously scant and unimpressive lighting from their paltry Berlin surroundings.

Touching are the raptures with which they view their flat Brandenburg vistas. A corner of a park, a semblance of a hill, a movement of a canal, such nothings can elicit at times a pang of aesthetic appreciation. These moments are invariably slight and right — because Fontane was a friend of Menzel? because he painted only what he had felt on the spot? No, because he conditions everything on the spot. Every moment is an exception, every impression is transitory and soon replaced. And most of the time, in most of the observers, there is a little fond irony for the very littleness of their satisfactions.

The story has reached its expected crisis when Baron Botho faces the need to save his family's future by marrying a girl of his own class. Then follows the marriage, and Botho is as happy with his baroness as he deserves. His friends even find that he does not entirely deserve her, because he is not perfectly happy. Slightly tragic Lene does find a good husband, a pietist from America. He is terribly reasonable, and when honest Lene has warned him of her ' past,' he goes to Baron Botho and asks him what it is all about. The scene is certainly the boldest in this novel in which nothing is risqué, and it reflects as much honor on the baron as on the pietist. When the story has ended several times (it seems), there is another conversation in which Botho preaches to a younger comrade not to follow his example. We have gathered that he will continue to be an exemplary husband, but that his heart will remain incurably entangled with the image of ' the truth, the reliability, the honesty ' of Lene.

The big words, then, are not entirely avoided; but they are repressed as long as possible. And when they come, they come with a blush of embarrassment that makes them hard to resist. The great sentiments are as unpretentious as the rest, because pretension is the one thing Fontane does not allow. None of his characters show a trace of it without being made fun of! But although everybody is so conciliatory, so contaminable by everybody else, many things are left unquestioned; or they are tinged with doubt without being extinguished. And yet many critics, at the time, saw in the book radical realism which excelled in depicting the ugly. Fontane could only shake his head; he found Botho and Lene simply likable.

We find that if Fontane erred, it was in painting too pretty. People are more vulgar and mean than he lets them be. He cannot help dwelling on their sunny side, just as he favors the sunny hours and good-weather days of his none-too sunny climate. Objectively there is much too little drizzle, slush and cold in his Berlin. Likewise there is too great a proportion of good in his people, in all classes. His low-class folk are neither dreary nor unhappy. His aristocrats are neither arrogant nor pretentious. As a matter of fact, they are more affable, courteous, unassuming than the others. This is the more surprising as the old Fontane developed a growing dislike for the Prussian nobility and its superannuated functions in the Prussian state. Fontane was not ' at home ' in their world as he was in that of the middle classes; but he was not an alien either. He could remark, parenthetically, ' he had been told by three German emperors that he was their favorite poet ' (May 17, 1889). He got at the best sentiments of the nobility; but he was sensitive to the failings, and to the absence, of nobility *especially* in the aristocracy. Yet in his novels he almost cast an after glow of tenderness over that very class.

Like other things in Fontane, this reminds one of his contemporary Henry James. James is even more engrossed with an aristocracy that is rather one of sentiment, refinement and awareness than of social standing. The aiming at awareness is the strongest bond between the two writers, and in both it expresses itself in a mellow culture of speaking. The pre-occupation with degrees of consciousness is characterized by a gingerliness in matters of sex, and yet in both authors sex is forever unobtrusively present. What people think of their situations matters rather than the situations themselves. That is why there is so little dramatic change in the situations. The material itself, in its concreteness, is repugnant to these authors. They almost abhor thickness, massiveness. Their delight is in a progressive rarefaction. Yet with all the similarity, James is more thin-spun, Fontane has more substance. His atmosphere is simply thicker, his people are concerned with more facts of life, from politics to food, than the supersubtle phantoms of his greater rival. His books are, in spite of his selectiveness, informing chapters in cultural history.

The main impression is one of immense fairness, one of people steering a course between the contempt for hypocritical conventions and the respect for deep-seated norms. His people are neither revolutionary nor reactionary. That is so honest about Fontane, that his experiments are carried on without prejudice. His favorite characters try to live a ' new,' an unconventional life. It is life itself which teaches them that they are wrong. Not before, but after the experiment they are allowed to say, ' Tradition governs our actions; he who obeys it may fail too, but he fails in a better way than he who fights it.' Even the true pietist in the story professes the very Fontanean faith, ' The one way is good, and the other way is good too ' — as long as there is, on either way, ' the truth, the reliability, the honesty.'

Zarathustra

While Fontane, who thought so much of the English, and who grafted their kind of Victorianism so successfully on his French stock, was almost overlooked in England, Nietzsche's largely anti-English and fully anti-Victorian writings took root in England, through successive waves of translation. The first project of a complete translation had stopped after three or four volumes, about 1897. But by 1913

Oscar Levy had completed the eighteen-volume edition, done by nine different translators. The most noted and the most debatable translation was *Thus Spake Zarathustra,* done by Thomas Common.

For a long time the forced poetic style of *Zarathustra* was pursued mainly in the direction of archaism. Although the attempts were frustrating, they were continued. Even Common's translation did not seem antiquarian enough. ' Everyman's Library ' went back to A. Tille's translation (of 1896), and when M. Bozman revised it in 1933, it was in the opposite direction from modernization, it was ' to assimilate the English version more nearly to the prose rhythm of the German original, and to preserve more consistently the archaic style.' The breakthrough for *Zarathustra* came only with the nineteen-fifties, when we suddenly get three rival attempts to emulate not the archaism, but the freshness of the original — the three translations which have made Zarathustra feel almost at home in English: the Viking translation by Walter Kaufmann (1954), the Gateway translation by Marianne Cowan (1957), and the Penguin translation by R. J. Hollingdale (1961). Around them a whole crop of other Nietzsche translations has sprung up, to the effect that it now looks as if Nietzsche were the German author most fully represented in English paperbacks.

In Nietzsche's own development *Zarathustra* is such a deviation that we try in vain to explain it by way of biography. In 1879 protracted illness forced him to resign his professorship at Basel. University and city proved very generous to the young emeritus. One is reminded of the casual yet ample way in which another Swiss city, Zürich, provided for her prodigal son Gottfried Keller. The liberality of Basel to the stranger Nietzsche, who had served, rather unsuccessfully, for only ten years, was still more striking. Several pension funds together provided him with a yearly income of 3,000 francs. It was providential, for it was materially on this income that he became ' the most independent man of Europe ' — although he meant that only intellectually. The incomparable abundance of work which he now produced, between his 35th and his 45th year, is due not a little to the liberty with which he could follow the vagaries of his health. And the spotty beauty of that work is not a little due to the beautiful spots which his ailments made him seek for relief: Venice, Marienbad, Genoa (1880); in 1881 he discovered Sils-Maria high in the Swiss Engadin; then again Genoa, Messina, Rome, Naumburg (the home of his family) in 1882; Rapallo near Genoa, Rome, Sils-Maria (1883); Nizza, Venice, Sils-Maria (1884). With that the first three waves of *Zarathustra* had passed; but the wandering life continued for all the following books. In all these places Nietzsche lived thriftily, even shabbily, the restlessness itself consumed his means.

The frequent pains of sickness were accompanied in those years by the pangs of an emotional crisis. Ever since his one-sided break with Wagner in 1876, Nietzsche had noticed that all his personal associations began to cool. While he became more and more the one he wanted to be, the echo to each successive publication became weaker. The friends became fewer, and their assent more guarded. It was the opposite of what he felt he deserved. He craved enthusiastic response; he was waiting for, he was wooing disciples. His most notorious attempt at association or partnership, with the young Lou Salomé in 1882, led instead to a general clash, even with his mother and sister. Perhaps the increasingly personal and poetic elements in his writings were unconscious straining for the personal response which was withdrawing from him. At any rate, it was after the years of greatest physical pain and emotional trial that he found his one exceptional utterance, in which his universal views and his personal desires, his boldest ideas and his most intimate art fused into an incomparable whole, *Zarathustra*.

It is still a book of aphorisms, but they have emigrated from the region of expository prose. They inhabit a higher region, somewhere between philosophy and poetry. And how vast the region is, not a thin borderline between two vegetations, but a broad zone with its own paradisic climate; in spite of its elevation, which is differentiated by further heights; and in spite of its austerity, which is its proper beauty. Even if one knows that each of the first three books was written in ten days, and all three within one year (1883), one is unwilling to believe it. The inner dimensions of the book are those of a lifetime, or those of a mountainous peninsula of the mind, vast and varied. All the unceasing lapses of Nietzsche were converted here into a sustained success.

At every step one is afraid that the different elements will cease to be held together by the sorcerer. If the curious rhythm failed him, by which he rocks us from chapter to chapter? Or the elemental imagery by which he freshens the abstractions? Or the 'supply' of thoughts, which conveys all modern life into the mountain haunts of Zarathustra, to be mere combustible for his sarcasm or his prophecy? Wherever one of these elements becomes thinner, the ground vacillates under our feet, and the mountain landscape threatens to collapse. But the self-certainty of the sorcerer holds it up, and we wander on to new vistas.

Nothing better can follow the 'Preface' with its perfect unity of situation, doctrine, and sentiment. Zarathustra has even given away his best: teaching the superman rather than the 'last-and-least' man. But when Nietzsche lightens the narrative masquerade in 'Zarathustra's Speeches,' the charm is not gone. It is something more intimate than epic camouflage; it is a new texture: less written, more spoken than anything else of Nietzsche. A figure, Zarathustra, is built, not in our mind's eye but in our mind's ear. A man grows out of the mere rhythms, intonations, waves of his speech. The rhythms are made of smallest units: nearly every sentence is self-contained. The intonations are characterized by a blending of sermon and sensual image: nearly every sentence is couched in imagery. The radiations are negligibly intellectual but overwhelmingly emotional: an endless assault of appeals, wooings, imprecations. Here a terrible loneliness overcompensates itself by soliciting ecstatic intimacy.

Not a little of the richness of *Zarathustra* is due to the abnormal tension of its polarities. The thoughts and attitudes are too contradictory to be at home in one living organism without endangering, bursting its unity. One thought does not limit the other, as it does in a normal mind. The conflicting attitudes have, as it were, more space between them than there is in one mind. Zarathustra can prefer now an icy intellectualism, now the enthusiastic feeling; now the science of evolution and now the legend of the golden age. He makes fun of art, but he is nothing if not an artist, 'only a fool, only a poet.' He looks down on saintliness, but he behaves like a saint. He derides priesthood, but he is himself a high priest. Of what? Sometimes of the highest civilization, sometimes of a new barbarism. You can interpret half the book in the sense that all morality is despicable: but then you must interpret the other half as the pursuit of the highest morality. And the whole book reads as if everything revered by 'the others' were vain idols; but the whole book also reads as if only veneration, reverence, worship constituted human value. And besides the many permanent contradictions, there are the many reversals of feeling which, instead of being masked, are dramatized.

As in former books, Nietzsche cannot end. Every half year another layer of sermons is graded like a higher tableland above the former. The progression is something like this: Book I, Zarathustra to the multitude; Book II, Zarathustra to his disciples; Book III, Zarathustra to himself; Book IV, Zarathustra to the elect. The specious sentiment of climbing higher is largely achieved by the arrogant rejection of former views. Hardly have we become familiar with a set of sentiments, when a new Zarathustra declares them suspended, spurned, left behind. It would be intolerable, if there were not the irresistible chapters where only the poet Nietzsche murmurs, where his insanely burning glance implores us to understand how uncertain he is of everything, how ready to accept anything, us, the world, and any truth. That is where the sources of his language are deepest and purest; that is where he is untranslatable. 'The Night-song' and 'The Quietest Hour' in Part II are fine instances of this most human, insecure, loving and lovable Nietzsche. But he is perhaps his most soft-spoken but most lyrical self in 'The Other Dancing Song' Part III. This one chapter may be taken as an epitome of his powers. After he has done his worst in section 1, his worst in artificial excitement and lightness and grace, there comes this incredible section 2, where his partner 'Life' simply ends all his artifices by stopping her ears. And he has to listen to *her*:

> '"The two of us are a couple of ne'er-do-wells and ne'er-do-ills. Beyond good and evil we found our island and our green meadow...."
>
> Then Life glanced thoughtfully behind her and around her and said softly: "O Zarathustra, you are not faithful enough to me!
>
> "You don't love me nearly as much as you say; I know you are thinking of leaving me soon." ...
>
> ... And I whispered something into her ear, right through her unruly yellow foolish tangled locks.
>
> ... And we looked at each other and at the green meadow over which the cool evening was just running, and we wept together. And at that time Life was dearer to me than all my Wisdom ever was".'

This is followed by section 3, the poem of the Midnight Bell, '... But all joy wants eternity ...', the end of the original three parts of *Zarathustra*.

It is a book that delights speaking in riddles, that triumphs by speaking in symbols, that toys with the most daring ideas and gets away with it, because it so superbly, so satisfyingly plays with words. The words suggest the images and the images suggest the ideas. Analysed as ideas, they are just as incoordinate as Nietzsche's ideas ever were, contradictory, self-confuting, discordant as no other philosopher's thoughts ever dared profess themselves. But he uses the dissonances as a musician does — and everything falls into a larger harmony. There is music in his insistent rhythms of word, verse and chapter; music in the use and abuse of echo and refrain, of variation and rondo; music in the movement, the rushing, gushing, welling, swirling motion; music in the constant recall of the major themes, not as thoughts, but as leitmotifs, insinuating, sensual, audible, easily remembered leitmotifs. Musical is even the introducing of everybody's saws and sayings as if they were novelties: they are, in their new modulations. And musical is the composing of 'movements' out of conflicting themes; the more contrast, the better the polyphony. Thus it is that mainly such people have admitted the spell of *Zarathustra* who resist its musical modulations less than the rocketing of its ideas.

This wonderful world is an exotic, extramundane world. If it makes the most brilliant show of criticizing reality, reality in return criticizes the book and its tendencies devastatingly. Reality refuses to be more than playfully implicated. It is probably to the detriment of reality — for the Zarathustra world is of a unique elevation, purity, austerity, generosity — but reality has the superiority of existing, at any rate existing in more dimensions. Fontane criticizes the same reality, but so that reality recognizes itself and even compares itself. The Zarathustra world is incomparable.

Nietzsche and Fontane are both witnesses to the same vanishing Victorianism, but Nietzsche has for it the perspicacity of hate, Fontane the insight of sympathy. Zarathustra has only one consistency, the immense drive and power to be different. Hence the pervasive symbolism of elevation, height, rising, which is present on every page in the book. Just this sentiment is shunned by Fontane, who makes the best of the horizontal, the plain with its small accidents, the lowlands with their modest undulations. Nietzsche makes mediocrity a crime — as if it could be helped. Fontane also sees mediocrity everywhere, but tolerates it for the sake of its honest efforts. Which is more philosophical, Zarathustra who claims excellence as a norm, or Fontane who claims that excellence must forever be the exception? When he says ' Purity and virtue are like Bismarck and Moltke, that means they are rare ' (*Entanglements,* ch. 23), more reality is caught than in any one verse of *Zarathustra.*

It is not natural to compare the two, the one who knew only the virtues of heroism, and the other who cultivated all the virtues of compromise. But the epoch upon which they tried to act, the eighteen-eighties, allows the juxtaposition. No doubt, Nietzsche was the profounder diagnostician, but he cared so little for the patient that he gladly helped to kill him. Fontane was not much of a physician either, but he was a kind nurse, who recognized every patient's right to live. Yet he admitted ' the truth of the Nietzche word about " the common herd " ' — one of the few times he mentioned Nietzsche (to his daughter, August 9, 1895). Zarathustra, who had learned so much from so many sources, who had learned parallelism of the Old Testament and gentleness of the New, refused the wisdom of either. In that way he was blinder than one of the foolish women in *Entanglements* (ch. 3) who was taught by life : ' the best way is still that of the catechism.'

The Berlin Bourgeois

That *Frau Jenny Treibel* (1892) is Fontane's most authentic masterwork is far from generally agreed. It has not been translated into English, whereas *Irrungen, Wirrungen* was translated as *Trials and Tribulations* by Kath. Royce for the 'Harvard Classics' in 1917, and

Effi Briest was translated by W. A. Cooper for the ' German Classics ' in 1913. Apart from those two favorites only the *Journeys to England in Early Victorian Days* (1939) found some English interest. *Effi Briest* (1895) is, to be sure, Fontane's most serious bid for a masterpiece. It is a highly successful anti-Mme. Bovary; that is, all its independence cannot make the reader forego the constant comparison with Flaubert. As a chapter in social and moral history, it stands the comparison very well; it is probably even superior in these regards. But how could it rival the other book as imaginative fiction! Its double subject, the bad conscience of adultery and the bad conscience of moralizing, has something wingless and weary. It is a wonderfully mature, kind and sad book. But only one who is already a Fontane-convert will get the oblique effect which the autor aimed at and achieved.

For a book like *Mrs. Treibel* Fontane has no rival. As an exposé of Berlin bourgeoisie in the 1880's it has no equal. As a sequence of conversations and speeches it is the most felicitous among Fontane's novels. And as fiction it has the obviousness and pointedness which make us unwilling to regard it as different from things which we have experienced in ' life,' It suffers, if at all,from a certain overabundance. The short novel creates such a wealth of characters of obvious potential that it does not quite know what to do with them. When the whole story is deftly concluded, one keeps wondering what happens to most of the characters. They have been endowed with an excess of life, and cannot live it out in their allotted span. Their handicap, however, lies not in Fontane's circumscribed form; it is the very limitation of life in society. Fontane's novels — in this they are perhaps less like other novels and more like life — allow one individual only as much time as the other individuals can spare, which is very little. Everybody has his turn, no more; because the others wait for their turn too. And thus this novel, with its leisurely loitering, looks in the end like a system of abridgements.

More than other Fontane stories it gives an illusion of reality. The types which it selects as foreground figures were not the vanishing nobility so dear to Fontane's imagination, nor the rising working class so dear to his heart. They were the masters of the moment, the rich or newly-rich bourgeoisie, exemplified in the Treibel family. Their foil is the household of Professor Schmidt, a high-school teacher. And the joke is that rich Mrs. Treibel pretends that ' kleine Verhältnisse, a life of small means, is the one source of happiness.' Professor Schmidt's poor daughter counters with the insolent wish to be as rich as her maternal friend. That is in the first chapter. The next ones are devoted to letting us taste the good life at ' Kommerzienrat's.' where a formal dinner is given for a visiting Englishman. Although in several chapters of tabletalk we get as many chapters in the history of Berlin civilization, the main experience is the overwhelming impression which the professor's daughter makes on those sitting close to her, especially the Treibels' very eligible son. And the wicked girl, on the way home, discusses her strategy with her cousin, who is in love with her too. Everything is beautifully frank and yet hardly malicious. But before we are conceded more of the intrigue, we are treated to the counterpart of the Kommerzienrat's dinner, namely Prof. Schmidt's evening, largely with colleagues, where the conversation is no less enjoyed, but the simpler fare even more. 'I'll bet those men of high finance don't talk about a turtle soup with half your zest, dear Schmidt.' In the Treibel circle the best speaker is the Kommerzienrat himself. He says somewhere (ch. 3), 'I see the life-task of the wise man in the achieving of what is called harmony.' Similarly the best speaker in the Professor's circle is Schmidt himself. He says (ch. 6), 'The highest imaginable viewpoint is that of irony.' Both sayings are quite incidental, and that reminds one of Nietzsche. Harmony and self-irony are so often invoked by him, because they are essentially alien to him. Here, in the Treibel & Schmidt worlds, they are so much at home that we are positively surprised to find the people aware of them at all. We have discovered them as their second nature long before they accidentally stumble upon their formulations.

Here lies one value of Fontane's books; they form a weighty counter-document to Nietzsche's slanders of Victorian civilization. To be sure, Fontane prettifies a little, but not nearly as much as Nietzsche vilifies. To gain the towering altitude without which he does not want to breathe, Nietzsche has to belittle everything he sees around him. All the differences and degrees between good and bad, wise and foolish, honest and false, generous and petty shrivel before Nietzsche's eyes into insignificance. It is the smiling observation of these small differences which makes Fontane so amusing. And it is a rather high degree of civilizedness which manifests itself in the lively exchanges of opinions between his characters. To be sure, we see their psychology in its Sunday clothes: it is remarkable how marginal their actual work is in these novels. We hardly ever watch them at work; yet they are all professional persons to the core; even if they are mere housewives. But businessmen or teachers, bosses or servants, they share a high degree of interest in each other and tolerance for each other, of respect for judgment and common sense, of appreciation for the beauties of nature and the comforts of civilization. It is a sane world.

It is a Berlin world, because nobody in it is naive. Fontane simply cannot invent a figure unable to see in perspectives, that is, to change perspectives. Nietzsche may have been right in claiming that he had brought perspectivism to philosophy, but it is inborn in Fontane's Berliner. Even as an artist Fontane had perhaps too much of it. In *Mrs. Treibel* he is so reckless with his story that he tells the whole outcome in advance. Or rather, Prof. Schmidt knows Mrs. Treibel, his long-ago sweetheart, too well. When his nephew is worried that he will lose his cousin, Schmidt predicts how mother Treibel will prevent any mismatch between her son and his daughter. 'She continually plays the liberal and the sentimental, but it's all a farce. When it comes to an issue, money will decide and nothing else . . . We may be uncertain of everything else, one thing we can rely on, the character of my friend Jenny. And if my daughter should outdo herself in tomfoolery, let her; I know the outcome of this story.' (end of ch. 7).

We are made to forget the prediction in the next chapters, where the intrigues within the Treibel clan, the political aspirations of Treibel himself, and an excursion to the Grunewald hold our attention. At the end of the excursion, the professor's daughter has no trouble in steering the Kommerzienrat's son into an engagement. Then we are treated to an entire battery of speakers' duels, between Mrs. Treibel and her son, between Mrs. Treibel and her husband, between Mrs. Treibel and her son's fiancée. And if we have admired so far in the social talk the amiability without triviality, we now admire in the single combats the malice without coarseness which distinguishes almost one and all.

The variety and yet purposefulness of these conversations, their wealth of incident, their light tone yet weighty substance, make them the distinctive feature of Fontane's art. Each character has a facility of speaking 'ad hominem,' of illuminating more the interlocutor than the speaker. But from that mutual illumination results a wonderful intimacy and community among the characters. They understand each other perfectly, and they have a passion for quoting from one another. Fontane does not cultivate the 'Vorbeireden,' the talking past one another. In his novels conversation = compromise. Thus, no matter how many idiosyncracies are brought into play, the result is always the strengthening of a certain 'middle,' a mixture of interests, a meeting-ground of viewpoints, an average humanity.

Once Fontane had observed that G. Keller's figures talk too much alike; he took the greatest trouble to make his own figures talk each according to type. If there is one class consciousness in Fontane it is that of 'speaking classes.' To be sure, he knows no other classes, but there is a hierarchy among them: he has use for them only according to how well they speak. One example is the housekeeper at Schmidt's, widow Schmolke. The real embroilment of the story is literally wrapped in two conversations between the housekeeper and the high-minded daughter of the house. We are required to believe that the daughter is a genius. But nothing she says has the punch of the policeman's widow: 'Schmolke used to say, "modesty is good, and false modesty — it *is* more or less false — is still better than none".' It is the widow Schmolke who, after watching for a week or two the stalemate resulting from the capricious engagement, talks sense into the girl and sets things on the right track again.

The justice which everybody does himself and others in all these playful conversations is in striking contrast with the insistent arbitrariness of Nietzsche, who would find all this compromising contemptible, all this golden mean a mediocrity. Where Fontane is all mutual exchange, Nietzsche is all self-assertion; where Fontane is all moderation, Nietzsche is all vehemence. His fault is his heroic temper; he has to fight. And since he never had a worthy interlocutor, his whole work is a huge monologue, in which the multitudinous voices within him fight it out. Philosophic soliloquy is the most unsocial of all forms. It never gave Nietzsche a chance to develop an extroversion. He was not incapable of it. There is an unbridged gap between his personal intercourse, so warmly remembered by literally everybody, and his literary utterance, so domineering, presumptuous, monomaniacal. But the form of the novel gave Fontane all for which his inmost nature had waited for a lifetime. The novel proved in his hands, as it had not yet done in German literature, to be the supremely social genre.

When looking at *Mrs. Jenny Treibel* one feels inclined to think of an operetta in the usual three acts. We have the same all-around pleasant situation in the first act, the same well-arranged complication in the second, the same easy re-arranging in the third. One is a little taken aback when the adjustment is so very simple, quick, and reasonable. A fine counter-intrigue had been prepared, a faithful cousin too was waiting to be fully recognized, and reason prevailed everywhere, while fun was made of everybody and nobody was spared. But if the general settlement and reconciliation seem especially easy, they are hardly an exception to Fontane's usual management. His people are so very manageable, in comparison with much of the species of *homo fictus*. He creates no people who live by making life miserable for each other. They are not only interdependent, but they acknowledge it, and they behave accordingly. Every little world, each of his little novels, is like a prism, where the colors complement each other, because they are by nature complementary, because they are originally and intrinsically related. His stories, although never without suspense, always unfold as a matter of course.

We rarely feel that we are moving in an invented plot: it is too typical to stand for less than a thousand cases; it is too unassuming to raise any doubts. Fontane must have been aware that the *petit fait* assumed in his technique an abnormal displacement. He incorporated (ch. 7) an allusion which has caught the eye of many a critic:

'"Those are Schmidt specialities. You are always for the anecdote and the genre-painting. I value in history only the great, not what is little and incidental." "True, the incidental does not count when there is nothing in it. But when it is meaningful, then it becomes the main thing, because it gives away the human element . . . The Poetic element — provided you understand it differently from my friend Jenny — is always right; it far surpasses the historic element". This was a favorite theme of Schmidt's.'

It is strange that Nietzsche, the man who wanted to see all Victorianism terminated, felt such a strong attraction for the genre-painting of Stifter and Keller, yet despised it as a trend of the time. A thousand instances in his work betray his feeling for the modestly and picturesquely human. Yet he pretends to 'value only the great' and universal. The difference is probably in the two genres of writing. The philosopher has to focus on universals; he can at best expect that the little human facts will not refuse to blend into the margin of his panorama. The novelist has to focus on the unusual case; only if he is lucky will the general truths condescend to be implicated. In the case of Fontane, one is tempted to admit that the universal did not condescend to incarnate itself in his novels. They are somehow *too* accurate. The best in them is bound to time and place. They are somehow provisional — mirroring complacently a transitional society — and provincial, in spite of Fontane's English and French preoccupations. Nietzsche was from first to last a great European. Fontane was the least objectionable of Berlin bourgeois. But he succeeded in translating his limitations into a fictional world, which now stands as a monument to a capital and a society that have vanished.

It is preposterous to compare a professed cultural critic's truth with that of a professional fiction writer. It is even more preposterous to find that the fiction is truer to the cultural reality than the picture drawn by the philosopher. But that is the case. Nietzsche's more and more truculent criticism did not correspond to a degraded Germany but only to his heightened, exasperated claim. Old Fontane's gentler criticism was the more representative self-criticism of at least a segment of Germany. As his awareness of his own competence as a society mirror increased, his definition of the modern novel became more definite: 'The task of the modern novel seems to me this: to give a picture of a life, of a society, which is an undistorted reflection of the life that we actually lead' (1886). This is also the main difference he feels between the admired G. Keller and himself. After reading Keller's *Epigram* he notes in his diary (1881): 'There is something absolutely superior in it . . . Still I don't know whether these are the tasks one should undertake . . . An exact description of actual life, the presentation of actual people and their destinies, seems to me the higher task.'

Nietzsche at Forty

The curve of Nietzsche's writings offers a simple pattern : a prologue and five acts. *The Birth of Tragedy* (1872) is the prologue. Of the five acts *Zarathustra* (1883-5) is the center and summit, in spite of the later works. Around the summit are grouped the books that criticize the ' highest ' values, the books of the *All-Too Human* period (1878-82) and the *Beyond Good and Evil* couple (1886-7). As acts I and V we have the early polemical works, *Thoughts out of Season* (1873-6) and the late polemical works, the four or five volumes of 1888, of which *Ecce Homo* was not published until twenty years later.

The post-Zarathustra books show not only an incredible rapidity of succession but also an undeniable superiority of writing. Their stunning sweep, however, does not cancel out the impression that in them Nietzsche turns back, turns down to former themes and modes, even though he handles them now in a superior way. *Zarathustra* was to be his main message, although he tried hard to outdo it in the hectic production of the few years remaining before the onset of insanity. (1889).

The contrast is great between the over-all feverishness and the relaxation of the individual page. Although Nietzsche was now reduced to having his books printed at his own expense, although every one of them was a new attempt to raise his voice to a higher pitch and to force himself upon unwilling ears, the confidence of having fulfilled himself in *Zarathustra* never left him, and the assurance of being able to say the most awkward and questionable things with mastery and ease never left his writing. The relaxation has the effect of a new intimacy. This is civilized talk, the ' Plauderkunst ' of Fontane, only in the superlative. Not only the ease of transitions, the comprehensiveness of view, the length of breath are there, the eloquence and effusion, exuberance even. Nietzsche shares with Fontane's talkers especially that most communicative quality of perfect talk, the certainty of being perfectly understood. That is the queer thing about the works of the more and more isolated Nietzsche, that he takes us more and more into his confidence, that he talks to us as if it were to disciples already won, that we listen under the hypnosis that he ' talks our language.'

One wonders sometimes whether Nietzsche does not, after all, fit into that world of Fontane. Most of his paradoxes were dictated by the dwindling faiths and the rising fears of his generation. They would not have been within reach a generation before, they would not have been worth his while a generation later. But against the background of his time he looms as the figure of the deliberate negator. He chose to refuse the realities which all the ' realists ' about him acknowledged. By his fight against them he acknowledged them: but their existence only, not their right to exist. It was a question of temper and not of insight. He chose to kick over the moralities which the others chose to hold up. He did not lack a realisation of how long it had taken to build them up; but he was impervious to the worry as to what would replace them. He flatly refused all the possibilities of the Victorian age. He did not shrink from the idea of starting a Kulturpolitik with nothing but impossibilities — as if politics were anything if not 'the art of possibilities.' If we take the gentle critic Fontane as one exponent of late Victorianism and the devasting critic Nietzsche as the other, we may say that their main difference lies in the fact that Nietzsche had no sense of synthesis.

It is as easy to reduce the general purport of *Beyond Good and Evil* to truisms, as it is difficult to give an idea of its individual detail. A modern anthropology must be a morphology of self-assertion (=Wille zur Macht). Our good and evil drives condition one another (end, ch. I). The future philosopher is 'thankful for god, devil, sheep and worm in us; almost criminally curious, almost cruelly inquisitive' (end, ch. II). Christianity, sublime as it is, has wrought a degeneration of the white race (end ch. III). 'Society has reached a point of decrepitude, where it even takes the side of its spoiler, the criminal, and where punishment seems to it unfair' (end ch. V). The last chapter, 'What is Elite?' starts with 'the desire for larger dimensions within the soul itself, the evolution of higher, rarer, wider conditions in it, the raising of the species Man, the continuous self-overtaking of Man.'

No matter how much we may have the illusion that he talks our language, we have no illusions that he thinks our thoughts. The bold trajectories of his thought are far beyond the finest flights which Fontane, for instance, dared invent for his speakers. It is an almost cosmic beyond-atmosphere, without weight, without breathable air, and especially without resistance. At the end of *Beyond Good and Evil* he describes his type of philosophizing: 'A philosopher, that is a man . . . who incessantly experiences, sees, suspects, hopes, dreams . . . who is struck by his own thoughts as by events and thunderstrokes; who is perhaps himself a thunderstorm pregnant with new flashes; a man around whom there is always an ominous grumbling, rumbling and crashing.' Modest Fontane would adapt to himself the adage of every novelist: 'Je suis un homme pour qui le monde réel existe.' Nietzsche was struck by his own thoughts as by events and thunderstrokes. He rarely struck a happier image for the concreteness which this his imaginary world had for him. And he confidently expected the world to be shaken by his imaginary thunderstorms. Fontane was more genuinely sceptic; his scepticism started with doubting his own possible influence. Although Nietzsche did not originate the principle of 'Wille zur

Macht' (it was the "libido dominandi" which he had inherited from Pascal, La Rochefoucauld, and Burckhardt), it was *his* dominant trait. No philosopher was ever so little concerned with understanding the world and so much with changing it.

In 1886 Nietzsche wrote five prefaces for a re-edition of his earlier works. These prefaces present a belligerent and almost exultant retrospect. They are masterpieces of interpretation, yet they do no objective justice to the earlier works, only to his then current views. In these prefaces he re-interpreted himself in such a wilful way that many things which were tentative in the earlier book were made to look assertive and doctrinaire, and that many things which were hardly there were made to look like the secret meaning. The books which were formerly polemics *for* his gods, were re-interpreted as polemics *against* his old idols. He could not compromise with his former teachers any more than with his own former ideals. He did not listen to his own former voices objectively enough to understand them correctly. He took the revaluation of values seriously enough to revaluate all his own. He had too little respect for coherence and too much for freedom. And as far as morality *is* agreement, coherence, consistency, it was easy for him to be the great 'Immoralist.'

The very counter-image of this polemical, immoralist, non-compromising Nietzsche is the Fontane who was able to make peace with himself and the world as he inherited it. The most complete statement of the Fontanean creed is probably in a letter to his daughter of August 24, 1893: 'I am a man of peace and compromises. Whoever does not know the art of compromise may as well be buried. . . . All the great words in the Sermon on the Mount have something bourgeois; but if their wisdom is practiced, not in cowardice but in quiet courage, they are the only truth . . . Everything may burn, if only ten or twelve norms remain on which human order rests (not the system of the world — we don't know a thing about that) . . . Beware of dissecting the feelings of others, of ferreting out the 'real' motivations . . . If something is lacking, I add a little faith, charity, hope . . . Schopenhauer is right: the best we have is fellow-feeling. But the other feelings are a shaky business. All the same we need them, need to believe in them. And even where there is nothing, we must not see this nothing. Who stares at this nothing turns to stone. Truth is death.'

Nietzsche was satisfied to be a ruthless truth-seeker. He had no time for compromises, because he was too busy with his ambivalences. All his intransigencies were shifting, none of his absolutes stayed put. It was this constant loss of identity which toward the end alienated his friends. And they did not even know the full extent of his constant self-transgression, because the final and finest statement among the recurrent re-interpretations, *Ecce Homo,* was not published then. In the longest, central section of this last of his books he interpreted all ten of his former books. Since nobody else had said of them what he wanted to hear, he said it himself. And the miracle is that this paroxysm of self-approval did not miss the mark, that this self-canonization has not made him perennially ridiculous, that this insane self-idolatry has come closer to the essential truth of his work than anything that was ever said about Nietzsche. All subsequent (after 1908) serious discussion of Nietzsche is but approximation to these dictatorial decrees. The intolerable intensity of this feverish self-assenting is at the same time the deepest penetration of self-scrutiny. And what makes this impossible pretention bearable is that it is creative, it does not leave the former books unattacked — although it attacks them as a lover. If it violates his earlier books, it violates them passionately, voluptuously, procreatively. He cannot touch himself without masterfully changing himself. *Ecce Homo* is the revaluation of all Nietzsche.

The section ' Why I Write Such Good Books ' ends in his most violent indictment of the Germans, whom he despises for their historism, their moralism, their Christianism. ' All the cultural crimes of the last four centuries are on their conscience,' he cries when he thinks of the Reformation, of Idealism as philosophy, of the war of liberation against Napoleon, and finally of their disgusting sense of equality, their democratic sense. All these qualities are seen under their Victorian aspect. Some of them *were* nothing but the Victorian aspect of German culture, but the invectives hit them as if they were millenial vices. Nietzsche is good at invectives; but they do not sway us as his dithyrambs do. His enthusiasms are catching, his phobias leave us cold. He probably wanted it the other way round, he insisted on his antagonisms. Fontane made of the same disgusting qualities the most refreshing ingredients of his breathable atmosphere. He saw, or wanted to see, the possibilities of a progressive synthesis between the different idealisms. The simplest test of the cultural sentiments of these two men is perhaps their opinion of the proletariat, the newest, lowest class. Nietzsche saw in it only the rebellion of the masses and the advent of the sub-human; Fontane (letter to James Morris, Feb. 22, 1896) the opposite: ' All interest is with the fourth estate. The bourgeois is atrocious, nobility and clergy are antiquated. The new, the better world begins only with the fourth estate . . . What the workers think, speak, write has simply overtaken the thinking, speaking and writing of the former governing classes. There everything is more genuine, true, full of life.'

At the very end of *Ecce Homo* Nietzsche claims the title of ' Immoralist,' exposer of the vanities of ' moral order.' He feels Christian morality beneath him, himself ' beyond.' An observer like Fontane would with one glance *compare* the massive efforts, and achievements, of Christian morality, and find nothing to choose between that infinite sum of quiet heroism and Nietzsche's lonely balloons of grandiloquent postulates. Of course they soar higher; because their vacuum seeks the thinner air. Fontane described the decent compromises of which his generation was capable; Nietzsche inspired only the fancies of individual egoists, mostly artists, of the next generation. His heroics were all over-compensations of his ungallant mishaps. As a warrior he was wounded not in action, but in training; as a male nurse he was sicker than his charges; as a meek professor he was losing his students; his life was that of a roaming invalid; he could not hurt a flea. And so he preached the cruel hardness of the Immoralist.

Nietzsche had an irresistible way of sublimating his basic envies into glittering apostasies. Thus he raised his envy of Wagner into the suspicion of all art, he raised his envy of Schopenhauer into a conquest of German idealism, he raised his envy of Bismarck into a contempt of everything German. But the subsistence of envy in all these resentful relationships makes him a sublime specimen of the *bourgeois enragé*. One has to hear him without his bewitching speech rhythms, one has to read some of his last works in English, to find that he sounds almost Bolshevik. And then again, he is a resplendent specimen of nihilism, nihilism without its lethargy or apathy, nihilism in shining armor, so to speak, or nihilism in dress uniform.

Perhaps it may be said that two therapies were tried on ailing and senescent Victorianism. The Fontane treatment tried sedatives, the Nietzsche treatment tried stimulants. Although neither succeeded in saving the old patient, Nietzsche was by far the more gifted, not the more beneficent, surgeon. He simply had the higher viewpoint and the wider range. He had by nature almost a command of the whole field. He could understand his opponents perfectly. His relationship to old Gottfried Keller is an example, little documented as it is. When Nietzsche in a letter to Taine (April 4, 1887) insists that for him Keller is ' the only German poet alive,' it is an opinion that has not only the acumen of unerring discrimination but also the weight and warmth of something like a lifelong conviction. And if he counts Keller among his few dependable readers, there is nothing in the known facts and correspondence that would contradict the claim. It is apparent that on the side of Nietzsche there was a steady and regularly manifested devotion, on that of Keller a more occasional courtesy or tolerance. But the mere coexistence, the mere fact that these two demanding minds had that much room for each other, gives us an inkling of the true range of Victorianism. The patriarch of the age of Keller died in 1890, seventy years old. The *enfant terrible* of the age of Keller disappeared into the night of insanity in 1889, at the age of forty-four.

IV

The Age of Wagner?

German Mythology

Richard Wagner first gave concerts in England in 1855 (not of his own works, to be sure), and one of the few early articles that contain first-hand information happens to include a recollection of that season. ' In 1855 . . . the Philharmonic Society invited him over to London, and whilst here he conducted eight concerts. He was not popular: he was surprised to find that the band thought it unnecessary to rehearse, and the band was surprised that he should require so much rehearsal. But he drove the band in spite of itself, and the band hated him. They said he murdered Beethoven with his baton, because of the freedom and inspiration of his reading . . . He did not care for the press, and he was not much surprised that the press did not care for him . . . But the power of the man could not be hid even from his enemies; his culture astonished the half-educated musicians by whom he was surrounded, his brilliant originality impressed even his own friends . . . Thus Wagner passed through England . . . leaving behind him a vague impression of power and eccentricity, the first of which the musical press did its best to kill, whilst fanning the second into a devouring flame, which swallowed up Wagner's reputation.' (H. R. Harweis, *The Contemporary Review,* 1877).

That gives an idea of the difficulty which Wagner had to be accepted. It was the same in Germany, in France, and in England. The vast silences which covered up entire stretches of his career are felt in the next paragraph of Harweis, where he simply says, ' Twenty-one years flitted by, and little enough was heard of R. Wagner in this country.' One prevailing argument against Wagner had been formulated a few years earlier by F. Hueffer: ' Among the numerous accusations which Wagner's innumerable adversaries have raised against his creative power one is grounded on the fact of his having investigated the metaphysical and historical side of his art. The two faculties of speculation and execution — these wise men assert — are never found combined in the same individuality ' (*Fortnightly Review,* 1872). This theoretical objection contained a good rule. That R. Wagner was an exception from that rule was proved, in a way, by his reception in America. There people did not bother about his theories and allowed themselves to be conquered by his music. An investigation into 'The Early Influence of R. Wagner in America' (by Viola Knock, in *Deutsch-Amerikanische Geschichtsblätter,* 1914) shows that in the very years when the well-developed musical agencies of England resisted him, the very new musical life of America made a place for him. 'To admire a man who reaches the pinnacle of his greatest aspiration in spite of insuperable opposition seems to be a special asset of the American people.' The Philharmonic Society of New York (founded in 1842) and the Germania Orchestra of Boston (founded in 1849) played Wagner from 1853 on. 'It was in 1855 that C. Bergmann, who had been a member of the Germania Orchestra, was suddenly called to conduct the last Philharmonic concert of that season. At this concert, he brought out the Tannhäuser Overture and made what was probably the greatest success of his life.' 'Their dissemination [of Wagner excerpts] through the length and breadth of the land was due primarily to the superior work of Th. Thomas . . ." By 1872 he could give an exclusively-Wagner program. 'That same night the New York Wagner Verein was organized with great enthusiasm.' This was only one year after the first Wagner Verein had been organized (in Mannheim), marking the final breakthrough of Wagner's ideas.

Even entire Wagner operas were performed at that early stage. 'Bergmann in 1859 had conducted Tannhäuser at the Stadttheater on the Bowery,' had repeated it in 1861. 'Tannhäuser and Lohengrin were given in the same theatre in 1870 under the direction of O. Neuendorf.' In 1884 Leopold Damrosch ventured to introduce German opera to the Metropolitan Opera House. 'And of the thirty-three performances of the season Wagner led with thirteen.' To the great relief of the stockholders, the venture proved a complete success. In the next season 'out of sixty-one performances Wagner opera received thirty-two.' The *North American Review* (June 1887) explains this stark preference simply by the immense superiority of the Wagnerian *texts.* 'Wagner chose his subjects from myths. His characters are ideal, inasmuch as their actions are never motivated by conventionalities, as they would be in modern life. Their passions are the very opposite of what we find in the plays of contemporary French dramatists. Instead of being involved, mixed and conflicting, they are simple, direct and unalloyed as is the fear and anger of a child.'

The same *North American Review* (1879) had received a last manifesto from Wagner. 'The "old" world, and especially that part of it included in our new Germany, will hear no more from me directly on this subject' (namely on the aims of his art). This article of the old Wagner, 'The Work and Mission of My Life,' attests the revolutionary in him. 'The wretched conditions of our national art . . . had led me to look most seriously into the influences that controlled our whole civilization, to begin a most thorough discussion of the possibility of changing the existing order of things.' He still felt as a man ' set apart from the body of the nation,' which could never satisfy his urges for a cultural reformation. He even expressed a sweeping preference for those ' Germanic ' elements that *left* the old soil and founded other states, France and the Anglo-Saxon nations. Whereas, as he drastically pointed out, ' That part of the race which has remained in Germany — that part which bore the special, distinctive name of Germans, and even in the old days stayed quietly at home — has always represented the peculiar type of German " Philistine." He lets himself be hampered and hemmed in on every side.' The most personal statement of the long article is that of his instinctive attraction toward the revolutionary spirit: ' The only element in history which had always attracted and inspired me had been this effort of the race to mutiny against the tyranny of a traditional and legalized formalism.' This again leads him to the very thing which the *North American Review,* eight years later, singled out as the reason for his popularity. He advocates it in words which show how well the later American critic understood the core of his *literary* method. ' It is only in the pure *Mythos* that this true human element presents itself to the man of every age alike — in the simplest ,clearest, most typical forms, and in an atmosphere of thoroughly natural feelings and sympathies, divested of every abstraction and conventionality.'

That ' mutiny against the tyranny of traditional formalism ' had manifested itself practically in the revolution of 1848 and had made the main incision in his life and career. In 1848, although conductor of the Royal Opera House in Dresden, he was an enthusiastic supporter of the revolutionary movements. In 1849, he was one of the leaders in the fight against the victorious counter-revolution. In disguise he fled through Germany and took refuge in Switzerland. He was thirty-five years old and had a career as conductor and composer behind him. Since the age of twenty, he had filled successfully various conductor posts in northeastern cities. Since he was thirty, he had scored local though hotly contested successes with operas of his own (*Rienzi* 1842, *Flying Dutchman* 1843, *Tannhäuser* 1845, *Lohengrin* finished in 1848). The most promising career in the whole field of the German arts was terminated in 1849, when his part in the revolution outlawed him, presumably for life.

He was a genuine revolutionary, but more so as an artist than as a politician. Thus the best formulations of his ideas are not in his Dresden speeches of 1848 and not in his essay *Art and Revolution* of 1849 ,but in his sketch of ' The Nibelungen Myth ' and in his drama *Siegfried's Death* of the same years. Into that myth and into this drama he packed all his ideas of a regeneration of human society.

The years of his exile in Switzerland were to be filled with the ever-expanding work on this Nibelungen theme. The setting to music took till 1874, although the literary work was completed in 1852.

The writing of the *Ring of the Nibelung* was extraordinary: Wagner wrote the whole cycle backwards. After *Siegried's Death* was completed, the poet felt the need to develop *Siegfried's Youth* in equal detail. When that was done, he felt he needed the prehistory of Siegfried's parents. And after that, he needed to present the whole state of the world into which these heroes were born. As he worked his way backwards, he moved from the Siegfried legends popular in Germany into the lore of the Germanic gods found in the Scandinavian Eddas. A bewildering diversity of mythological themes is worked into the four dramas of the *Ring*. But working it backward helped to give the tetralogy that cyclic consistency, that presence of the leading themes, that resurgence of dominant feelings, which has made it the most successful cyclical composition in the world.

The Rhinegold introduces us to three classes of mythological divinities; the dwarfs or Nibelungs of the inner earth, the giants of the mountains, and the gods of the air. The first represent cunning, the second force, the third honor. The power of the world is symbolized by the ' gold,' the treasure of nature, which is useless beauty to the loving soul, but means of power to the loveless. The inventiveness of Wagner puts the gold in the keeping of the beautiful nymphs of the Rhine, from whom the ugly dwarf king steals it, forswearing all love. The upper gods, however, need the gold to keep the giants in line (=the world in order). And as they can get it in no other way, they get it by trickery. They satisfy the giants, and so the world is in order — but the order is based on wrong ,especially on wrong in high places. ' Goodness and truth are only down here,' the Rhine nymphs end their song.

What is most amazing in this last conceived of the dramas is that it surpasses the others in visual imagination. The underwater scene in the Rhine, the scene in the mines of the dwarfs, the scenes before Valhall (mountain castle plus heavenly city) are of a splendor of conception and contrast which strained all resources of nineteenth century theatre. But bolder and wilder were the ideas of mythic cosmology which Wagner forced into the elementary gestures and elementary drives of his assorted sprites. And unmistakable is the revolutionary message that wrong rules the world, that even the world's splendor holds the germs of sickness and decay.

The Valkyrie contains more mystery than the other plays. Gradually it unravels, backwards and forwards. With the first scene we enter the world of human beings. Wotan, in his perplexity over the 'legal' wrong in the world, has created *free* agents, who by sheer freedom of action might restore innocence again. But Wagner's imagination endows the individual carriers of this critique with such an overflow of life that they always threaten to exceed their functions in the drama. The love story between Siegmund and Sieglinde, brother and sister, is too powerful for the purpose and for the god. The quarrel and leave-taking between Wotan and Brunnhild, father and daughter, has such accents of tenderness and discord, fortitude and resignation, that we forget how the fate of the unborn Siegfried and the fate of the Ring are cunningly interwoven with every phase of their argument. It is perhaps the very tension between this function and this vitality which makes the *Valkyrie* such good drama. Wagner is always too massive, he does not know the virtues of economy, neither in his expression nor in the ideas expressed, neither in his themes nor in their elaboration. But in the *Valkyrie* the very length to which he drives the Siegmund-Sieglinde act, the very thoroughness with which he exhausts the Wotan-Brunnhild relationship, turn into revelations by means of his inventiveness, which refuses to add fortuitous detail, but insists on discovering profound links that lay buried in the sagas of the centuries.

In *Siegfried*, the different worlds of the Ring-cosmos meet in a series of clashes. Mime, the dwarf-king's brother, educates Siegfried to be the killer of the last giant (dragon). Brunnhild, the Valkyrie, becomes Siegfried's bride. And Wotan, the wisdom of the world, and the power and the glory, resigns before the ascent of the innocent doer. The oldest and most hackneyed motifs have been absorbed in their new meaning. The gay story of the ascending hero is set off by the sombre crossings of the descending god. The psychology of the venomously selfish Mime is translated into waggish mimicry. The elementary brutality is overgrown with a luxuriant nostalgia for nature and the natural things. And the mystery of all-engulfing sex is celebrated in the superhuman puberty rites between Brunnhild and Siegfried.

Wagner still counted so little on posterity that he retold in every drama the essential links of the other dramas. How could he assume that most of us who see one drama remember the action of the others? But could we really say that we mostly understand? As the leitmotifs glide by us, sometimes in flashes of recognition, sometimes dimly associated, and sometimes wrongly connected and mistaken for related ones, they keep us in a daze of musical wondering, reminiscing and guessing. Similarly the logical, psychological, and mythological ideas glide by us, in half-understood or not understood words. We catch them on the wing; or we do not catch them. And the result is that delicious suspension between knowing and feeling which makes even the (accompanying) literary experience a musical mode.

The musical impact is foremost in everybody's mind. The literary message is almost absorbed in it, but it was there, independently, from the beginning. A third element contributed to the robustness of the Wagner structures. If we believe his own testimony, it was neither the music nor the words which were the source of his dramas, but that third thing: the vision. At the origin of every drama he had visions of simple actions, gestures, scenes, which symbolized elementary states of soul. This visible, scenic, theatric element he pursued with the utmost tenacity all his life. Thence his endeavors to gain personal influence on the way the dramas were performed (in Paris, in Vienna, in Munich); the utopian demands to have a theatre of his own; and the models of mimic action which the old man at Bayreuth gave to *all* his actors, from his incomparable modelling of Mime to his incredible acting of the goddesses. From all the accounts we have (and mostly by vain artists), Wagner was more unquestionably a great actor than he was an original musician and a creative writer.

The stupendous tetralogy cracks at its many seams, but nowhere more so than in *The Twilight of the Gods,* where the too well known legend of Siegfried's death had to be incorporated into the doom of the gods. It could all be averted if Brunnhild gave up Siegfried's ring (the Rhinegold). But Siegfried has to be drawn (by a cup of oblivion) into the world of men, who send him to win Brunnhild for another. The agent of mischief however is Hagen, the dwarf-king's son. So we have again three orders representing the world: the dwarfs (Hagen), the gods (Brunnhild), and instead of the giants the heroes (Siegfried). In the entanglement, the revolution of man is not triumphant; Brunnhild and Siegfried do not sacrifice one order to another. They finally see redemption only in sacrificing themselves. And thus Schopenhauer-Wotan's wish is fulfilled, 'Das Ende! das Ende!' But the end has several implications. One is said in music: that love knows no death. The other is said in words: that the power of gold returns to the innocent waters. And the third one is said in the burning scenery: that the old order falls, the tyranny of traditional formalism is over.

We have not dwelled enough on the representative ideology of the *Ring,* sociological and political. We can simply quote what is still the best of commentaries on the *Ring,* Bernard Shaw's *Perfect Wagnerite* (1898, 1909). 'The Ring, with all its gods and giants and dwarfs, its water-maidens and Valkyries . . . is a drama of today . . . It could not have been written before the second half of the nineteenth century, because it deals with events which were only then consummating themselves.' (p. 1) 'Really the dwarfs, giants, and gods are dramatizations of the three main orders of men: to wit, the instinctive, predatory, lustful, greedy people; the patient, toiling, stupid, respectful, money-worshipping people; and the intellectual, moral, talented people who devise and administer States and Churches. History shows us only one order higher than the highest of these: namely, the order of heroes' (p. 32).

'... And this dilemma will persist until Wotan's inspiration comes to our governors, and they see that their business is not the devising of laws and institutions to prop up the weaknesses of mobs and secure the survival of the unfittest, but the breeding of men whose wills and intelligences may be depended on to produce spontaneously the social wellbeing our clumsy laws now aim at and miss... The most inevitable dramatic conception, then, of the nineteenth century, is that of a perfectly naive hero upsetting religion, law and order in all directions, and establishing in their place the unfettered action of Humanity doing exactly what it likes, and producing order instead of confusion thereby because it likes to do what is necessary for the good of the race' (p. 69).

A man not susceptible to music like Shaw is witness that this huge poem was capable of conquering the most sturdy literary mind of the age. When Gottfried Keller came back to Zürich in 1856, he found himself much attracted by Richard Wagner, and his letters repeatedly refer to Wagner's *poetry*: 'He is certainly a poet, for the text of his Nibelungen trilogy contains a treasure of original national poetry.' (To Hettner, Feb. 21, 1856) 'Richard Wagner is a genius and very entertaining; he has the finest all-around education and is really profound. The text of his Nibelungen trilogy is a work of fiery and luxuriant poetry and has made on me a much deeper impression than all other poetical works which I have read in a long time.' (To L. Assing, April 21, 1856).

The Communist Manifesto

It is hard to believe how little Karl Marx was known in England and America during his lifetime. Although he lived in England after the revolution of 1849, although he contributed to the *New York Tribune* regularly from 1852 to 1862, he had significance for so few people that he was not discussed in the periodicals destined for the general public. The first extensive article in England seems to have been in the *Fortnightly Review* of 1875, the first in America in the *Quarterly Journal of Economics* of 1895, and that was when the posthumous third volume of *Das Kapital* had appeared at last. The English article was by the young but prominent barrister, economist, and statistician John Macdonnell and is distinguished by an evident grasp both of the merits of Marx and of his alienness to English mentality. After contrasting him with more flamboyant socialists of the time, Macdonnell continues: 'I have good reason to doubt whether his publications are much known here, or whether most educated Englishmen are aware of their influence abroad . . . Though Marx has lived much in England, and though he has written voluminously and forcibly in our language — though the illustrations and the many proofs of his chief work are drawn from English experience — he is here almost a shadow of a name. People may do him the honor of abusing him; read him they do not.'

The article then devotes six pages to Marx's economic theories, in the end warning the English not to dismiss them for surface reasons. ' I only fear that English economists will too readily pass by the truths concealed by uncouth phraseology and wild words. In the nondescript deposit left by this turbid and vehement stream that disdains to keep within the banks of a sober reasoning there are some jewels.' All the English articles in the nineteenth century (there were few) keep to this tone of sober discrimination. What we miss in them is a realization of the immense potential in the work of Marx and of the very dynamite in his style. His gigantic pretense to be a scientist was contradicted by mere scientists. His devastatingly arbitrary logic was argued against by mere philosophers. His violently effective journalism was counteracted by mere journalists. The authoritative orders which he issued to history were countermanded by mere students of history. The man was so treacherously inconspicuous that nobody succeeded in seeing all of him at the same time. In Macdonnell's article (in all the early English articles) there is no mention of the *Communist Manifesto*.

The *Communist Manifesto* of January 1848 was anonymous, published in the name of the newly reorganized ' Committee ' of German Communists living in London. K. Marx and F. Engels, after preaching to the first ' congress ' of these men, were commissioned to write their platform, and in response wrote the most brilliant piece of rhetoric of the nineteenth century. Rhetoric not covering the lack of substance, but making the fullest use of it : a wide and accurate knowledge, years of bold pamphleteering experience, an identification with a humanity-wide cause, a whole arsenal of collective thought, a concentration of collective aggressiveness.

Although the German *Manifesto* was soon translated into four other languages, its echoes were so well drowned out by the immediately following revolutions in all parts of Europe that we cannot trace them. Even had the times been more quiet, the echo might have been weak, because the *Manifesto* corresponded remarkably little with existing reality. It was useless as an assessment of the past, powerless as a weapon for the present, but priceless as a future mythology. Indeed, the fifty-page pamphlet was destined to be *the* mythology of the future.

In the middle of the booklet Marx tucked away his own miniature — the founder of the mythology of the proletariat: 'Now a portion of the bourgeoisie goes over to the proletariat, and in particular, a portion of the bourgeois ideologists, who have raised themselves to the level of comprehending theoretically the historical movement as a whole.' He was the best equipped of those bourgeois ideologists. Son of a well-to-do bourgeois, from the western border of Germany, married to a Prussian noblewoman, prevented from a university career by his affiliation with the theologically most subversive group of young scholars, he had in the journalistic career of a few years repudiated all affiliations, and broken injuriously with all fellow socialists except his own adherents. Although at that time it was only an impudent claim, for posterity it was a simple fact, that he alone was at 'the level of comprehending the historical movement as a whole.' He had a clearer eye than anybody before him for the germs of the future in the present, and a more ruthless determination to extend the barely visible lines of the present into a past where, with irresistible assurance, he decrees, 'The history of all hitherto existing society is the history of class struggles.' That is an enormity; but the compact corroborations of the next pages make it hard to withstand. The whole description of the bourgeoisie, seen through the eyes of lucid hatred, brittles with generalisations overpowering for the unprejudiced and especially the uneducated mind. But the swiftness of stroke is catching even to the exacting: 'Of all the classes that stand face to face with the bourgeoisie today the proletariat alone is a really revolutionary class. The other classes decay and finally disappear in the face of modern industry; the proletariat is its special and essential product.' Everywhere one is amazed how Marx saw conditions which hardly existed as yet, especially in Germany. But any barely existing proletariat, how could it help materializing quickly, impetuously, consciously, after having been so definitely ordained by its prophet: 'What the bourgeoisie therefore produces, above all, are its own gravediggers. Its fall and the victory of the proletariat are equally inevitable.'

It was not inevitable at all, as history; nothing happened the way Marx predicted. But there is in this language the inevitableness of a myth, which has taken hold of millions of people who now actually believe that its predictions have been accomplished. It is all in the power of thought and language. If one wants to see how great a writer Marx is here, one may compare him with Wagner. To be sure, Wagner has this much of the poet, that his words lose considerably in translation, whereas one may confidently quote the *Manifesto* in English, and it has practically the same force as the original. We soon realize that there is little to compare. Wagner's prose is made of an endless gush of noble sentiments. In Marx's prose there is no sentiment, it consists of an unheard-of amalgamation of fact and volition.

There is always the whirr of an arrow on the way to its mark. The array of facts is so overpowering, not because they are incontrovertible, but because they are so vehemently tendentious, defiant, challenging. Wagner's prose is so boring because it wants so little of us, it tries ineffectually to persuade us to agree to some reform of the arts in which we can't quite get interested. Marx is so exciting because he is so activating, because every one of his small paragraphs demands a complete subjection of our intelligence, of our hopes and fears, of our basic interests. In every one of his aphorisms the whole of civilization is at stake. Wagner's is a subjective voice, in the long run only bearable because behind it there was a great personality. Marx's personality does not matter; this is not the voice of a person, but the uncannily transparent medium for the aggregate voice of history and ideology, human conditions and social aspirations. It is not only the voices of Marx plus Engels, indistinguishable, plus the motives of the workmen with whom they liked to discuss, plus the formulations of all their ideological predecessors. The solidarity in that voice is still larger. It is, sometimes, the massive voice of a class of millions, whole generations, which for once found a single trenchant articulation, because it was focussed in one comprehensive brain.

Wagner's *Art and Revolution* and Marx-Engels' *Communist Manifesto* are of the same year, 1848. Both are utopias based on historical reasoning, materialistic or idealistic. If we take the text in Wagner's *Sämtliche Schriften* (1911) and the *Manifesto* in the 'Crofts Classics,' they have almost the same number of pages. Even though the same words do not have the same effect, some entire sentences sound alike. Marx's anticipation (p. 18), 'the proletariat is recruited from all classes of the population' is, however, outdistanced by Wagner's apprehension (p. 27) that in the modern world 'the slaves have not become free; but all men have become slaves.' The most knowing paragraph in *Art and Revolution*, the only one to which Marx might have granted a nod of approval, is one about the *laws* of history (p. 32): 'the historical development of social mankind is independent of our prescriptions. Nothing is man-made in history, every thing makes itself according to inner necessities. But the conditions at which all this movement aims must be the opposite of the present one.' Thus Wagner arrives at the certainty of 'the inevitably imminent social revolutions' (p. 40). And on his last page there is even — not the word *communistic*, but its equivalent *gemeinsam*: he hopes that the theatres 'will be the first community-owned institutions, in which the concepts of money and money-making will be extinct'; 'art and its institutions will be the precursors and models of all the community institutions of the future.'

The emotional affinity of Wagner with the socialist-revolutionary cause can not therefore be very doubtful. Still, the pamphlet *Art* and *Revolution* and the pamphlet *Communist Manifesto* are, so to speak, trajectories which intercross only once, after which their lines proceed in eternally different directions. The one led to the mythology of the Nibelungen world with its symbols of — largely ethical — differentiation between human aspirations. The other led to the mythology of historical materialism and the class-less society of the future. Wagner's world of *differentiation* is characterized by a *cumulation* of means, from different arts, almost from different cultures, and by a painful qualitative unevenness. Marx's ideal of *indifferentiation* is couched in a very unified medium, it is a construction of language of purely intellectual claims.

There is in the later sections of the *Manifesto,* when the description of the bourgeoisie is succeeded by the delineation of the aims of the proletariat, a supreme disdain for actual conditions in favor of those prescribed, arranged, ordained by the mind. The identification of mind with matter, of the desired event with the 'law' of history, is so complete that the terms can be reversed: 'The theoretical conclusions of the Communists are in no way based on ideas or principles that have been invented . . . They merely express, in general terms, actual relations springing from an existing class struggle, from a historical movement going on under our very eyes' (p. 23). In the following pages the features of the bourgeois age are, under our very eyes, dissolved intellectually: property, freedom, culture, family, country. One after the other they are neatly decomposed in the all-dissolving acid of a superior mind. All the (idealist) ways of philosophy, that have ruled mankind for thousands of years, are swept aside with a stroke: 'Does it require deep intuition to comprehend that man's ideas, views, and conceptions, in one word, man's consciousness, change with every change in the conditions of his material existence, in his social relations and in his social life?' 'What else does the history of ideas prove, than that intellectual production changes its character in proportion as material production has changed?' In this form, in the form of two rhetorical questions, did the boldest and most far-reaching idea of the nineteenth century enter world literature. The 'does it require?' camouflaged the deepest historical theory (Hegel) and its inversion. The 'what else' stipulated in one sentence what might have taken volumes to deduce and what may take centuries to prove.

The whole *Manifesto* is like that. It proclaims historical materialism and establishes it. The consequences are there, logical, compelling, and imperative as they will never be in reality. Every 'truth' is so overdrawn that there is no room for doubt. The *Manifesto* refuses or misuses any opposing views so effectively that they cease to exist. All the good conscience is on its side, because moral values are only to be tolerated as long as they work in its favor. Just as, on the last page, the watchword is to fight *with* the bourgeoisie wherever you cannot yet fight against it, so Marx's little group of Communists in the 1848 revolution supported the most promising group (liberal reformers) by a consistent run of stabs in the back. Yet although his was the most outrageous subversiveness among the many vociferous journalists of the Revolution, when he was finally arrested for incitement to sedition, he defended himself with such determination and cleverness that the jury acquitted him and 'thanked him for an unusually instructive lecture'! But in the end, like Wagner, though not quite as desperately, he had to flee from the country.

The German Symbolists

Although Switzerland was the main refuge of Wagner during his exile, his main artistic hope was in Paris. He had lived there from 1839 to 1842; he was there again 1849 and in 1850, hoping for some chance for his art-work of the future in revolutionized France. Eventually he got more help from the imperial government of Napoleon III in 1859-61, so that *Tannhäuser* was even performed at the Opéra. But that was a youthful work, while Wagner was now occupied with more advanced dreams.

Meanwhile he was (like Marx) among the many revolutionaries of 1849 that were amnestied in 1861, and he turned his hopes to Vienna. There he heard for the first time another 'youthful' work, *Lohengrin,* which was thirteen years old by now. But he was unable to get *Tristan* produced. Being financially over-optimistic, improvident, generous, extravagant, he got deep into debt. Being journalistically over-articulate and voluminous, in private intercourse cocksure and demanding, and professionally so largely unsuccessful, he became the favorite butt of satire in the art world. It was a strange thing. He could look back to signal achievements as conductor, as organizer, as composer. Everything which people had let him do, he had done with an extraordinary combination of vision and practical sense, enthusiasm and hard work. But the other combination, of political *and* artistic progressiveness, had made him impossible all over Germany. His notoriety was in no proportion to his visible and audible achievements. His 'music of the future' seemed destined to remain forever in the future.

He was perhaps the most laughed-at man in Germany when, in 1864, the new king of Bavaria, Ludwig II, took it into his head to rescue him. Wagner elicited extraordinary responses, both as a man and as an artist. This time it was exclusively his art (his 'youthful' music dramas) which caused a young king to safeguard this artist from future want. The first artistic result was the production of *Tristan and Isolde* in Munich in 1865. The incredible advance over his last work (*Lohengrin*) caused much more dismay than admiration. The gap of these fifteen years remained for most contemporaries unbridgeable.

Tristan ushers in a new period not only in German music but also in German poetry. One might call the new poetry by the name which became popular in France twenty years later, Symbolism. *Tristan* is its prototype in several respects. It has absolutely no entertainment value; it is the impudently egocentric expression of the artist's soul, or rather of a state of his soul; at the same time it claims to be a metaphysics, a philosophical explanation of the world; above all, it uses all the most personally perfected means at the disposal of the artist, regardless of their being liked or even understood. It demands subjection, not being pleased. It demands that the hearer or reader transcend himself while hearing or reading, transform himself into a new hearer or reader.

The demand for a new art had been raised by Wagner in the bulkiest of his interminable treatises, *Opera and Drama* (1851), especially in the part 'The Character of Dramatic Poetry.' The claims which he raises there in behalf of the art work of the future are appallingly inclusive; they comprehend a radical re-orientation of society. 'The overthrow of the state means a healthy organic society. The overthrow of the state cannot mean anything but the realisation of the religious consciousness which society has of its humanistic character.' Here everything runs into everything else, and nothing is excluded. 'Common human nature is felt by the individual as the instinct of life and love. Only in society can he satisfy this instinct. His consciousness is religious, that is common [gemeinsam] and vindicates his nature. In the free self-determination of the individual lies the religion of the future.' As he moves from the immeasurably broad basis of art towards its apex, he moves within concepts familiar to every symbolist: 'For the poet, who must compress the multiplicity of life into a compact pattern, the available image is just this: the miracle. The miracle in poetry differs from the miracle in religion in that the poetic reason is not at all interested in belief, only in intuitive understanding.' This is soon followed by another characteristic of Symbolism, the frowning upon realism: 'The condensed image of actual life *has* to appear magnified, fortified, rendered unusual.' The climax of this section is perhaps this definition of 'the highest potential of poetry':

> 'a myth — made most transparent by drama
> — re-invented in the face of everpresent life
> — justified before a lucid consciousness.'

All this reminds one that Wagner was completely absorbed in the Nibelungen myths at the time. Two things had to happen to him before he was ready for *Tristan*: the revelation of Schopenhauer's philosophy, and the love of Mrs. Wesendonck. Out of Schopenhauer's drama between blind will and selfless imagination, out of his personal drama between powerful attraction and triumphant sublimation, he made the first and simplest Symbolist poem.

The symbolism drenches and almost drowns the story. Does anything happen? For a long act, Tristan refuses to talk to Isolde, then they talk. For another long act, Tristan and Isolde psychoanalyse their love. For the third long act, Tristan alone recapitulates his philosophy, and Isolde confirms it, alone. The 2400 half-verses would offer endless opportunity for story-telling; but we have more to guess, than we are told, that Tristan is the perfect knight, and therefore must get his childless uncle the perfect bride, *in order* not to become his heir. And because he is the perfect knight, he must not realize that he and the perfect bride have for ever been in love. Only when they resolve to die are they liberated for their love: the death potion turns into the love potion.

The intrigue is short-circuited, because the emotional state of consciousness is everything. If one looks at the text only, the Wagnerian massiveness is overpoweringly there. The poet poured himself forth with an unheard-of freedom. Wagner himself remembered above all this sense of freedom: 'Here at last I moved with fullest freedom, with complete disregard of any theoretical consideration; while I worked I became aware how I left my own system behind.' Even without the music the text is unbearably eloquent. What monotony of situation! what absence of incident! what paucity of ideas! what richness of expression! The rhymes of his earlier period, the alliteration of his Nibelungen-period, and all the tritest tricks of late Romantic rhetorics are used cumulatively. The sound-image of waves is never absent, neither in the short breath of the individual (half-) verse, nor in the immense aggregate mass of this whole grey ocean of anti-sense sound. In this watery waste of words, in this ocean of tautology, every short wave beats on the same shore line of meaning: the day-world (of social conventions) is the world of appearances; the night-world (of individual-universe intuition) is the deeper reality, And why? Tag=Wahn, because it is affirmation of the will; Nacht=Wahrheit, because it is negation of the will. Or perhaps thus: lust is the unconscious wish to be extinguished in procreation and progeny:

Nie-wieder-Erwachens
Wahnlos
Hold bewusster Wunsch. (1291)

In the climactic duet of act II the six times iterated key word is

' ohne ' (without), stressing the negative essense of Nirvana.

The third act is only philosophy. It contains nothing but the confirmation that the message of act II was not merely sensual delirium, but a valid generalization from all vital experience. The shepherd's tune which haunts the act has a plain interpretation: everything in life sings the will — and its death:

. . . Mich sehnen — und sterben. (1933)

But although he now curses his surrender to sex, he never knows what is stronger, the will to live (sehnen) or the will to die (sterben); and combining, cumulating the two, he dies in Isolde's arms.

In this first German Symbolist poem, one striking difference from French Symbolism is already marked. While the latter almost cultivates obscurity, glows in an infra-red light only, the works of German Symbolism suffer from a glaring light, from over-exposure, from over-obviousness. Apart from that, an essential affinity there was from the start. The first man to say the right things about Wagner, after Wagner himself but even before Nietzsche, was Baudelaire.

In a private letter to Wagner (1860) he said that from the first hearing he found that this ' was *his* music ' for reasons that had nothing to do with music. ' It represents greatness and it drives to greatness . . . everywhere it has something exalted and exalting.' A long article of Baudelaire's was the most notable defense Wagner received in the Paris of 1861. It not only approves of Wagner the dramatist by ' finding in those texts that were translated an excellent construction, a sense of order and proportion which recalls the architecture of the tragedies of antiquity.' It insists on artistic aims dear to his own aesthetic. ' I underwent a spiritual operation, a revelation.' ' No musician equals Wagner in painting space and depth both natural and spiritual . . . to translate, by subtle gradations, all the excessiveness ,immensity, ambition found in the spiritual and natural man.' One is constantly reminded of the last words of his sonnet ' Correspondences ' : ' Qui chantent les transports de l'esprit et des sens.' Indeed, he was reminded of it himself and quotes half of this sonnet on the ' forêts de symboles.' Thus the founder of French Symbolism was the first to recognize the founder of German Symbolism.

The best student of Wagner, however, was Nietzsche. At the time he was preparing *The Birth of Tragedy* he wrote; ' The condition for great art is understanding the world by means of symbols. For us it is music which has become the mythology, the world of symbols. Music is for us what their symbolic myths were for the Greeks.' *The Birth of Tragedy* itself is the attempt to understand the Greek world in the way he understood Wagner's world, ' by means of symbols.' But his own colossal attempt to write an entire book in the stipulated medium was *Zarathustra,* this dance-suite of symbols or similes or ' Gleichnisse ' (for here he prefers this more Lutheran word). At the end of *Zarathustra I* he gives away his newly-conquered medium playfully :

' Upward flies *our* inclination : thus it is a simile of our body, the simile of an uplifting. Similes of such upliftings are the names of virtues.

Similes are all the names of good and evil : they do not make statements, they only beckon. A fool is he who expects knowledge from them.

Heed o my brothers every hour in which your mind wants to speak in similes : there is the source of *your* virtue.'

Later too in *Zarathustra* he is fond of this ' speaking in parables.' ' Here all things come coaxing to your speech and fondle it : this is the back on which they would ride. On every simile you are riding to your truth ' (III,9, The Homecoming). ' How lovely that there are the words, and the sounds ! Are words and sounds not rainbows and light-bridges between the eternally different?' (III, 13, The Convalescent). When he speaks of ' Worte und Töne,' can he be *not* thinking of Wagner? At any rate, this is the disciple who learned from Wagner that there is no limit to symbolism. Every chapter of *Zarathustra* lives on it, each of its books climaxes in symbolic poetry, and the bracket, that is the Preface and the Fourth Book, is entirely in parables.

The only one among the early Symbolists who was simply a poet, did not appreciate being just a poet either. C. F. Meyer was more pre-occupied with his dramatic Novellen, in which he was deliberately and conscientiously symbolic, than with his casual lyrics. But it is just here that he is most intimately, most familiarly symbolic. In contrast to Wagner's and Nietzsche's obstreperous propounding of their intentions, Meyer's seemingly accidental efforts are easily overlooked and overheard. Take one of his most unassuming poems, the three quatrains of ' Zwei Segel.'

Zwei Segel erhellend / Die tiefblaue Bucht !
Zwei Segel sich schwellend / Zu ruhiger Flucht.

It is at first only a series of momentary glimpses, distinguished by the parsimony of the method. No Japanese sketch could be more skimpy than the first double line which contains nothing but the contrast of bright and dark, the whiteness of the sails against the blue bay. The verb ' erhellen ' is so economical that it becomes invaluable. In the second double line, the wind fills the sails and sets them in quiet motion. The quiet u-sounds of lines 2 and 4 form the dark background to the bright e-sounds of lines 1 and 3, so that we get the blue-white picture also through the ear. And the quietly rocking rhythm . ′ . . ′ . . ′ . . ′ imposes first of all a hesitating and meditating reeding, and then it imposes the gentle rocking of the boats on the ripples of the lake.

Wie eins in den Winden / Sich wölbt und bewegt,
Wird auch das Empfinden / Des andern erregt.

Lines 5-8 focus on the notion of ' stirring ' in the elemental (' bewegt ') and in the slightly more mental sense (' erregt '). Whereas in 5-6 the movement is securely material, made of ' wind ' and ' swelling ' and neutral ' moving,' a suspicion of anthropomorphism steals into 7-8: the ' feeling ' of the other sail is ' roused.'

Thus we read lines 9-12 with a subconscious expectation of double meaning. On the surface, they are the natural observation that the two matched boats behave equally under equal conditions, are accelerated by the same breath of wind, and are arrested by the same lulls.

Begehrt eins zu hasten, / Das andre geht schnell,
Verlangt eins zu rasten, / Ruht auch sein Gesell.

Naturally. But some gusts of wind have come between the lines, have moved, then arrested our thought. We have become suspicious what naturally mated boats are these, what symbols sail there? In Meyer's arrangement of his poems the symbolism is quite obvious. The poem is not among his glimpses of nature or pictures of travel, it is at the head of the section ' Liebe.' Then we see, at a glance, the trifle in an entirely new light. It remains a delicate view of his Lake of Zürich. But it has also become a blissful glimpse into the kind of love he knew, matrimonial love, the perfectly matched couple. And since his happiness came so precariously late, we now understand ' erhellend ' as a more active participle than we thought: it *was* darker for them before; they have just come out into the sunlight of happiness.

But the impact of the poem owes little to the private story. The impact is already in the complete parallelism of the six double lines: the uneven lines of each quatrain (the feminine rhymes) are slight variations of each other; the same is less true of the even lines (masculine rhymes); but enough so to give each quatrain two halves which fairly mirror each other. The grammatical construction is of a similar doubling in the first and third quatrain, while the central quatrain is unified by the construction ' as one . . . so the other.' In the third the conditional clauses, latent so far, come to the surface. The whole is a picture of being conditioned in common, and mutually. Yet the initial picture of nothing but two sail boats in good weather is not lost. Even if we think of nothing but boats, the three quatrains have something intimating, intimate, almost ' innig ' — up to the choice of the arch-discreet old word ' Gesell.'

It is a virtue of Meyer's poems that one can read them either way — as simple or as symbolic — and find them satisfying either way. But they do possess that secret polyphony of meaning. R. Faesi neatly formulated the plastic (bildlich) and symbolic (sinnbildlich) potentiality of this poet: 'Meyer is *bildlich* as few other lyricists are; where he is most himself he is *sinnbildlich;* among German poets the first Symbolist.'

A fourth among these early German Symbolists (two Swiss and two Germans in Switzerland!) was not of Meyer's but of Nietzsche's generation, Carl Spitteler (1845-1924). In 1880, years before *Zarathustra,* appeared his prose epic *Prometheus and Epimetheus, A Parable,* the most labored treatment of a basic symbolist theme, the estrangement between poet and people. The conception dated back to 1863. Years of theological study, seven years as private tutor in St. Petersburg, lay between conception and hasty execution. The publication found absolutely no echo; a silence greeted it compared with which the reception even of *Zarathustra* was a murmur of responsiveness. And *Prometheus* almost deserved the icy silence, because it was the glorification of unpopularity. Prometheus chooses to worship only one god, his Soul, although she promises him nothing but suffering and solitude. Epimetheus trades his soul for a 'Conscience' of the rules of the world. Epimetheus is made ruler of the world by Jehovah. Prometheus lives first as a hermit, then as an outcast. As a story, the book lives on overexalting what is simply excellent and on debasing what is quite normally base. As poem, it lives on the contrast between the dazzling splendor of the world and the unfathomable gloom of the grand soul.

Pagan and Christian mythology is treated with such a high hand that the difference ceases to matter. All these walking and talking symbols become obvious in their extensive speeches, in their plastic gestures, in their consistent actions. The imagination which keeps all this march in motion is not forced, it is exuberant. One cannot help feeling it now as gorgeous barbaric poetry, now as saturated Swiss pictorialness, now as hypothetical psychology. (Spitteler's first epic influenced Jung's archeypes, his last novel baptized Freud's *Imago.*)

Spitteler practically denounced his major works as *pseudo-* epics in the explicit contrasting of 'Mythus und Epos.' 'Mythic poetry is basically religious poetry. It deals with the eternal riddles and has therefore a thoughtful, serious, melancholy character. Its genuine appropriate form is the short symbolic tale; symbolic because everything metaphysical cannot be handled poetically except by means of the symbol. Without the symbol, the metaphysical would remain abstruse. Epic poetry, on the other hand, is altogether worldly . . . One who is both a mythic and an epic poet must practice two essentially opposed poetic processes: first he must imagine a profound myth; and then he must murder it again.'

Emphatic symbolism, that is the earmark of these Germans. In the French, symbolism is often more a suspicion than a system — so that hosts of scholars have found satisfaction in explaining and complicating them. With the German Symbolists one has less fun; they are so systematic as to be coarse-grained. That is why in contrast to the delicate fragments of the French Symbolists their German contemporaries offer us sturdy and massive books (even Meyer, if we think of his Symbolist Novellen). The quantitative, however, is only the most superficial characteristic. It is matched by another, more intrinsic, the elementary. Each of these four men was equipped with an education, a culture, and a worldly experience compared with which their Parisian colleagues were provincial. Yet their highest yearning seems to be for the elementary in every form. One might qualify as ' elementary ' their psychology, their philosophy, their religion, because their whole imagination was steeped in the elementary. That is why three of the four put their best effort into creating or recreating a mythology. In each case their mythologies spanned the most advanced ideas and the most elementary symbols. There is never a question of the subtleties of *suggestion* as in the Poe-Baudelaire-Mallarmé canon. But there is a vaster synthesis in any one of the Germans than in a Mallarmé or Rimbaud. French Symbolism is suspended, so to speak, between the music of Wagner and the music of Debussy; German Symbolism between the music of Wagner and the painting of Böcklin. Among other things, that points to its greater concreteness, substantiality, density; also to a more primitive and popular stamp. To all of their symbolism one might apply what Wagner claimed for all human consciousness: it is religious, that is, ' common.'

Marx's Kapital

' I must now leave the subject with the confession that I never took up a book that proved better worth reading than *Capital,*' said Shaw in an early article on Marx (*National Reformer,* Aug. 1, 1887). Yet these articles, starting in 1884 were (like most things written in England at the time) directed against Marx. The communist philosopher was unwelcome everywhere. After the revolutions of 1849 he was banned from most countries. He chose England as a refuge and made the best of it. Small socialist groups continued to exist in Germany, and Marx from London and Engels from Manchester kept up their influence through correspondence, hoping every few years for new outbreaks, for tokens of their kind of revolution. But as there were fewer and fewer signs of that, the other side of Marx claimed its right, the scholar in him. While the journalist was trying to keep his family from starvation by articles for the New York *Tribune* — many of them refused and discarded — the real work of the remaining three decades of Marx's life was *Capital.* A preliminary section was published in 1859 as *Critique of Political Economy.* That was also the subtitle of the main work, of which Marx finished and published only the first volume, in 1867.

After 1861, when Marx was free to return home, he found that no German state was eager to give back to him a citizenship which he had renounced in 1844. So he stayed in dismal London. Later, when he felt tempted by Switzerland, it was still the reading room of the British Museum which held him. That was the arsenal where he forged the big gun of the Marxist system, *Das Kapital.*

Das Kapital begins and ends in boredom. Its first chapter and its last volume are next to impossible to read for the non-specialist. And Marx himself lost interest long before the end. There are few books which have such a slow start; as if the great journalist he was wanted to leave no doubt of the methodicalness of his foundations. At the end of the first chapter the layman is still surprised to learn that merchandise or commodity 'is, in reality, a very queer thing, abounding in metaphysical subtleties and theological niceties . . . As soon as it steps forth as a commodity, it is changed into something transcendent [sinnlichübersinnlich].' The first chapters, dealing with the transformation of merchandise into money and money into capital, fail to convert the non-professional, who believes that all merchandise is by nature a compromise, that is, the opposite of the metaphysical. But Marx's doctrine of the surplus-value has something of an inverted theology.

There is scant attention given to the bourgeois attempts at improving the workers' condition.The most impressive pages are documentation of inhuman exploitation, which rouses the reader's anger the more as humanitarian rhetorics is entirely absent. Marx's favorite documentation is from English sources (the parliamentary records called Blue Books) and from English conditions. He studied at close range the industrialization where it had advanced farthest. He could give the rest of Europe a gripping preview of some horrors in store. And the picture, in spite of the gradual reforms, did not seem to be luridly colored. Said G. B. Shaw in 1887 : 'I am strongly tempted to launch into a description of the extraordinary picture of modern industrialization which gives the book its main force and fascination.'

Not only the content, the style too bristles with antagonism. 'The adversaries . . . are attacked with a savage concentration which has inaugurated a new epoch in the technique of public vituperation' (I. Berlin, *K. Marx,* 1959, p. 233). 'It is curious that Marx should have required the other side to be always corrupt' (J. Barzun, *Darwin,*

Marx, Wagner, 1958, p. 181). It is more curious when the attacks are directed at fellow socialists of different opinion. He is never tempted to compromise; he doubts the criminality plus stupidity of the opponent as little as his own impeccability plus infallibility. ' The extraordinary impression he makes does not depend on the soundness of his views but . . . on his own imperturbable conviction of their validity ' (G. B. Shaw).

It is difficult to give an idea of the crabbed structure, overwhelming documentation, and tenacious theorizing of the book. The superficial reader only sees hundreds of tales of woe, a thousand reports on wretched working conditions, unspeakable living conditions, and large-scale unemployment. But these are all arrayed to prove the main point, that half the worker's time goes unpaid, is pocketed by the employer, is the primary source of capital. That is first and last a theory. But Marx treats it more and more as a fact, and he claims that every case of social injustice proves this fact, that his accumulation of grievous circumstances is an accumulation of proof. Of course he proves many things, but not his theory. His mythical plus-value is better explained by the interplay of industry and commerce, and by the mass of people exerting *two* economic functions, one as workers and one as customers, and by the rising standard of living. But Marx forces his reader to think only of the fundamental injustice of capitalism. And Marx is a powerful reasoner, keen and relentless, whether we believe him or not.

In practically everything, he was the antipole of Victorianism. His contemporaries were worriedly conservative: he grimly dedicated all their concerns to extinction. They endeavored to trace something ineradicably good in all men: he was satisfied that there was nothing but depravity in all classes, except the class of the future. Their realism consisted in accepting the world as it is, in making it more liveable by adaptation, patience and understanding. Those were pseudo-virtues for him; while suspicion, resentment, discontent, and revolt gave truer promise of a better future. Victorian literature prolonged the idyll of a half agrarian society, its man was reluctant to turn his back on nature. In Marx's writing the real proletarian of his time, the peasant, had hardly any place; he could not transform him into an industrialized workhand fast enough, to make him ripe for the final harvest. But the main point is more difficult to seize; it lies at the intersection of two lines. One line goes from Marx's revilement of everything in existence to his strange optimism for the future. The other line goes from the Victorian praise of the present to its urge for resignation, self-sacrifice and often self-extinction. The optimism there and the sense of tragedy here are both hard to motivate, unless one simplifies them into, on the one hand, the ascending direction of a greener and greedier type, and on the other, the descending direction of a finer and wearier culture.

The very capitalist among artists, the one who was least a man of nature, most a product of city society, the one who spent all his life imagining how to get a plus-value out of the accumulation of divergent art values, Richard Wagner, who was politically not very far from Marx, was miles apart by that sense of the tragic. His heroes interested him in the degree in which they failed. This is most remarkable in the *Ring,* where the powerful gods, Wotan and Brunnhild, are the greatest sufferers and resigners. They ought to be, by superior wisdom, the ones in whose keeping the power of the ring belongs. But the two times they have it they cannot get rid of it fast enough. It is the giants and the dwarfs who have it during all the ages of the tetralogy. Is it the capitalists and the proletarians? Whatever they stand for, Marx is sinister Hagen, who wants the race of Alberich to spread the serfdom of the dwarfs over all the other creatures. Wotan and Brunnhild want to bring freedom to all creatures, including the dwarfs, by surrendering, extinguishing themselves.

Marx was too ample a mind not to wonder about the brave new world which the revolt of the masses and the dictatorship of the proletariat must bring about. But it was not his job to utter misgivings. At the end of *Capital I* are the famous pages where he predicts the simple changeover from monopolism to communism as a dialectical process *within* capitalism: 'One capitalist always kills many. Hand in hand with this centralization develop . . . socialized labor, the entanglement of all peoples in the net of the world-market, and with this, the international character of the capitalistic régime . . . But with this too grows the revolt of the working-class, a class always increasing in numbers, and disciplined, united, organised by the very mechanism of the process of capitalist production itself . . . The knell of capitalist private property sounds. The expropriators are expropriated.'

It is no accident that at this very place Marx appends a footnote quoting (for the first time?) from the *Communist Manifesto,* for here Capital is taken over by Communism. 'The other classes perish and disappear in the face of modern industry, the proletariat is its special and essential product.' Then the dwarfs will inherit the earth, and we will all be proletarians, one class. Victorian literature had the opposite dream. It looked everywhere for the man outside his class and outside all classes. Its sanest authors craved for the cranks and for eccentric ideas. Even when they were spokesmen of a traditional class as Gotthelf was of the Swiss farmers, or of a political solidarity as Keller was of Swiss liberalism, they fancied a man or woman between the parties, the one alone, against the others or without. They saw that there were classes, but that they were just good enough for the background or the choruses of their work. And more often than not, the background was that *against* which the hero moved. They tried to perpetuate the classless man, they desired the *free* man to abide.

Probably these writers saw the wave of the future; but they cultivated a considerable island which that wave had not reached yet. Marx only saw the wave more clearly than anybody; he described it with a clairvoyance as if it were already present. To the English he always seemed singularly precipitate. And when events allowed a little sample of proletarian rule, in the Paris Commune of 1871, Marx was consistent enough to defend what the rest of the world abhorred. It cost him what little sympathy there was for him in England. In his own circles too he was a lonely man. Among the German emigrants he always had more enemies than friends. 'I have never seen a man,' wrote Carl Schurz, 'whose bearing was so intolerably arrogant. To no opinion different from his own did he accord the honor of even condescending consideration; every argument that he did not like he answered either with biting scorn at the unfathomable ignorance that prompted it, or opprobrious aspersions upon the motives of him who had advanced it.' When he had made himself master of the first International, he purged it one by one of all personalities who might balance his influence. The result was a weakening of effectiveness, and eventually the secession of the English. Rather than let the reins of the International slip from his hands, he moved the seat of its council to the United States, so that the organization could 'die peacefully.'

In most of his short-range political predictions he had proved wrong. Russia, autocratic and agrarian, had been the butt of his ill-wishes in countless instances. It proved to be the country where his following grew almost as quickly as in Germany. From England and its advanced industry he had expected the ripening of the proletarian revolution. He found the conditions there not worsening according to prediction but moving towards *de*proletarization. Practically the whole European proletariat chose that route. But in England the feeling for Marx was most tepid. It took seventeen years until, after his death, an English translation of *Das Kapital* appeared.

Wagner's Germany

In spite of the most favorable circumstances Wagner could not establish himself in the Germany of 1865. Different causes brought about his removal from Munich: his excessive influence upon the young king, his aristocratic and ecclesiastic enemies among the political leaders, the passive resistance of the artistic leaders, the growing hostility of the press. One major complication was his unmistakable passion for his friend's wife, Cosima v. Bülow. He practiced sublimation no longer but, fifty years old, accepted the passionate devotion which offered itself in this superior woman. When he left for Switzerland again, it was not for the old exile; he was under the protection of a king for good. Wagner established himself on the Lake of Lucerne. There he wrote the music to the *Mastersingers* and the later parts of the *Ring*.

He was still a revolutionary, but only in art. His expectation of a renewal of public taste vaguely turned toward the German princes, several of whom he had got to know. But only the most romantic and noble-minded of them, Ludwig of Bavaria, remained his unshakable supporter. Between the dreams of that young idealist and Wagner's faith in the essentially human (das Volk) there seemed to be no friction. But Germany had other preoccupations. The north was expanding its industrialization, and Prussia was expanding its influence. Economic unification was a necessity, political unification was a dread for southern Germany and Austria. The peerless leadership of the universally hated Bismarck steered Prussia through a sequel of victories on the battlefield, and greater ones on the conference table and in general diplomacy. When France attacked Prussia in 1870, all the of Prussia. When the German armies were victorious, the surprise German states found themselves, somewhat surprised, on the side knew no bounds. The French had dominated Europe for centuries; how was it possible now, in a war of their own choosing, to be conquered? The feeling of German nationality, humiliated so long, suddenly changed into national complacency. It was even possible to unite the twenty-five sovereign German principalities into one Federation.

It was Wagner's king, the king of the largest state after Prussia, who cast the decisive vote for the unification, though with a heavy heart. The feelings of men like Wagner, Nietzsche, Marx, Engels were as strained as the public situation. Every one of them was a Bismarck-hater; but in the events of 1870 all felt, temporarily, German. Even the Swiss C. F. Meyer and G. Keller could not help seeing unified Germany as a step in the right direction. Wagner's temporary nationalism inspired his most ephemeral works. His ambitious plans for a theatre of his own forced him to cultivate the notion that the rise of Wagnerism and the rise of the new Germany were equally 'national' affairs. Privately he was as dissatisfied with the prevalent emphasis on military, political, and economic progress as the most articulate of the young Wagnerites, F. Nietzsche. Publicly, he tried to interest all classes of the new Germany in his idea of a Wagner theatre in Bayreuth. It barely succeeded and was only a semblance of his old dream of a new center of dramatic art. What was realized owed little to the noisy agitation for him in the cities of Germany, much to King Ludwig's generosity, which several times averted bankruptcy, but most of all to the aging Wagner's efforts on concert tours, and to his unexpected talents for organisation. Bayreuth was always on the brink of failure, in financial as well as in artistic respects. From the latter, Wagner saved it singlehanded.

The way to Bayreuth had been devious. Munich, the Bavarian capital, was so sporadically sympathetic to Wagner that he recommended to the King, as a possible nursery for their cultural schemes Nürnberg, a model of medieval city life, the town of A. Dürer and Hans Sachs. Instinct more than calculation drove Wagner still farther north from Nürnberg. In the farthest corner of his king's Bavaria, therefore closest to the geographical center of Germany, he found Bayreuth (then 20,000 inhabitants). There, under never-ending difficulties, he built his plain wooden theatre (1872-4). There he managed to realize *one* season of 'Festspiele' performing the Nibelungen tetralogy (in 1876) and one more festival season performing *Parsifal* (in 1882). After 1876 his disaffection with the new Germany was complete. There were times when he thought of taking his whole 'works' including the Bayreuth idea to America. And while the Wagnerians multiplied in Germany, Wagner lived as far away as possible during his last years. He found serenity in Naples and Palermo, and death in Venice (1883).

Marx died a month later; and the age of their triumph began. No, there is no comparison. The ascendancy of Marx was a slow one and became triumphal only after 1917. The sweep of Wagnerism was most general in the eighties and nineties; after 1917 he receded into the dimensions of a respectable classic. In spite of their contemporaneousness they were heralds of different ages, Marx the Moses of the promised inheritance of the proletariat, Wagner the high priest of the heritage of the middle class. It was not a mistake when that middle class fancied him more than any other artist. The deeper instincts of that class and the abysmal obsessions of this artist were made for each other. Nobody was fooled by the mythological disguise of most of his operas. And in one of them he treated his middle-class sympathies without any disguise, in *Die Meistersinger von Nürnberg.*

The Mastersingers is the most casual among his masterworks. He wrote the drama, rapidly, during his last stay in Paris, in 1862. After his bitterest disappointment he wrote this indulgent comedy about the compromise between art and public. The writing itself is a compromise; in the rhymed doggerel there is verse of all grades: sheer waste of words; poor imitation of the actual style of sixteenth century mastersingers; easy-flowing eloquence; funny, racy naturalness; packed statement and excellent epigrams. But the plot is the most felicitous Wagner has thrown together, an intrigue so simple that it serves all purposes. And the main purpose is to bring art to the people.

The old bourgeois (Pogner), ' whom God has made a rich man,' has found all over Germany ' that the bourgeois gets little praise ' for being the only one who still cultivates art. So he offers as a prize for the best original work at the next festival of the master-poets — his daughter and his fortune! He would not mind if the young nobleman Walter, who has shown such a sudden interest in Eva Pogner and in poetry, had a little chance. Alas, the strictest critic in the poets' guild, Beckmesser, is the champion among the eligible men. But the unpredictable element is (the widowed) Hans Sachs, the popular poet, who would even want to give the audience a voice and vote in the contest: Since we are mixing things of the heart and matters of art, ' let the people be the judge.' This seems too much of an innovation. Pogner and Sachs can barely get the others to admit the unknown nobleman to candidacy. Beckmesser calls him ' Neu-Junker-Unkraut ' in good Marxian fashion; his instinct tells him that the nobleman's natural gifts give him a headstart also in bourgeois society. But Walter is all-too original. His strong bid to be accepted as an equal is drowned in a pandemonium of class prejudice.

The second act is the idyll of the German town, rendered by the artist who ' belongs to Paris only ' (Nietzsche). During one evening twilight Hans Sachs grows to realize the unfairness of any Masters' Guild against any ' born master.' In friend Beckmesser he sees the weakest side of professional jealousy, and also the ridiculous side of an old man's wooing. He uses the old fool to prevent an elopement of the young lovers. He gets the best help from the easily roused rivalries between friends and neighbors. The scene of boisterous abuse and slapstick rumpus seems of questionable taste. But Wagner would not have lavished on it the whole battery of his literary and musical inventiveness if he had not wanted to emphasise the pettiness plus vehemence of German class conflict and provincial conflict. This meanest of all grand scenes is (reduced to a street brawl) the wrangle of provincial jealousies and grievances, ' die deutsche Frage.'

So many parts of Wagner are period pieces. The worst and the best of his time were powerfully combined in him. Primitivism and luxury, revolution and tradition, vitalism and ethics, paganism and Christianism, Schopenhauer and Nietzsche: he was powerful enough to incorporate them all. This comprehensiveness is perhaps at the root of his cumulation of arts. And the public responded so affirmatively because it seemed that here was ' something for everybody.' Nietzsche ends *The Wagner Case* with the accusation that what the

Wagner movement brought to the fore was 'the pretence of the layman, the art-idiot... And the confidence in genius, the impudent dilettantism (its model is in the *Mastersingers*)!' Indeed, this was art for the layman. Even if your literary or musical or scenic mind was underdeveloped, Wagner allowed you to add up your deficiencies, and you resulted as a genuine enthusiast, not as Nietzsche's complete idiot. The layman was grateful that something accessible from *many* sides existed. But Nietzsche (end of *Nietzsche Contra Wagner*) 'needs another art ... an art for artists, only for artists!' And Wagner stands convicted of having given us art for the average man.

The third act of the *Mastersingers* is the closest Wagner came to self-presentation. In the 'Wahn' monologue all the loose ends of the preceding evening's adventure are caught up. They are also blown up into 'the world's illusion.' It is Schopenhauer set to verse. Then Hans Sachs sets out to take charge of the illusions, 'without which good things rarely succeed.' He starts to work on the young nobleman, the young genius (or dilettante, as Nietzsche calls him) and admonishes him to try to *please* those 'honest men' from whom he has so much to gain. This view of reciprocity (within the bourgeoisie and between it and its outsiders) is the picture we get in Keller and Fontane; it is the opposite of the picture we get in Marx. Hans Sachs, however, acts only as the spokesman of the artists' union. He simply instructs his noble apprentice to combine a respect for the rules with a heed of inspiration. The results are so extremely satisfactory that four or five stories can be concluded in private: the artist can manage the affairs of the world, when he does not want anything for himself.

But art has to prove itself publicly too, and Wagner rises to the occasion with the climax on the festive fair grounds. Although Pogner is the 'master rich and generous' who today offers 'his highest good plus all his goods' as the prize, Hans Sach's, the popular poet, is the center and director of affairs. He is confident that the nature of man and the nature of things will prevent an untoward conclusion. Beckmesser tries to sing Walter's song; Walter has only to sing it in the right way to prove his superiority, and 'the people' are so swayed that they close the contest by acclaim. A last hesitation of the nobleman to be unionized motivates Sachs' paternal warning, 'Don't despise the masters — not to your noble ancestors, to your personal accomplishments and the good will of your fellow citizens you owe your (future) happiness... Even if art did not remain aristocratic, it remained genuine art... The German nation will disintegrate: true values will live only in your artists' works.'

From the first act on we have been prepared to see Eva = woman = 'the people' Now we see Walter (=the aristocracy) and Eva (=the people) lean affectionately on Sachs (=art), while Pogner

(=capitalism) does homage. That too-well-staged resolution of social disharmonies was the expression of a hope that all classes might find their center in a 'middle class,' and that the *middle* class would be the carrier of all that is best in material and spiritual life. This is Wagner's gloriously naive solution of 'die soziale Frage.'

The dream was not exclusively Wagnerian. We could easily put into that final tableau, among the mastersingers of Nürnberg, any other of the mastersingers of Victorianism, the figures of Keller, of Meyer, of Hebbel, of Fontane, all those poet-burghers in and around Germany. They would all lend themselves to similar sentiments, because this leaning on one another, this converging of tendencies, was *the* art in which all Victorianism excelled, the art of vital compromises. There was also the hope that Germany, that Cinderella among nations, would be especially fortunate in those compromises, would perhaps even enjoy some supernatural help. In 1870 Cinderella was invited to the ball of nations. And as she rose in splendor, the hopes of the noble compromisers fell. It made little impression on them that Germany not only led Europe politically, but that she was the international model of social progress, social welfare, and social legislation. After 1876 the arch-compromiser Wagner wrote, 'German decadence cannot be stopped' (1878). And in the end he emphasized the distance between his old ideals and the new reality: 'My hopelessness is complete as far as Germany and the German conditions are concerned.' (1880)

The Mastersingers, however, was a comedy, written by a friend of G. Keller — and Wagner always appreciated the humorous side, the Seldwyla-side of Keller most. The Seldwyla-side of Nürnberg is as extensively treated as the ideal side. The comedy in the *Mastersingers* is satire of professional and social narrow-mindedness. The petty bureaucrat Beckmesser is as German as the large-minded poet Sachs. Wagner's and Keller's pictures of Germany, both from the fringe or across the border, are not very unlike. Only Keller is bourgeois in the sense of 'kleinbürgerlich,' which is more provincial, and Wagner in the sense of 'grossbürgerlich,' which is more cosmopolitan.

The Mastersingers bears the date of 1862; it must not be read as a monument of the general complacency after 1870, but as a document of the general idealism before that. It is representative of the later time only insofar as that idealism never quite died, as there was in the increasing audience of Wagner a vague desire to follow his flights, to understand his complex meaning, and even a willingness to be educated and elevated by him. His art was not a mirror of reality, but its complement. Like every artist he felt, if everything was 'Wahn,' art was not only the highest but the most enduring. The best-known line he wrote during his first stay in Paris was: 'I believe in God, Beethoven, and Mozart.' And the best-known lines he wrote during his last stay in Paris are the last lines of *The Mastersingers:* 'Our Holy Empire may go up in smoke — But let us keep our Holy German Art.'

Postscript

The 'good old time' of the nineteenth century was characterized by social unity and provincial diversity. At least those two traits assert themselves in the present picture. There was a social coalescence, a flowing together of all achievements in a middle class. The middle class was not just the representative, it was the comprehensive class; it thought and felt and aspired for the whole. And the voices of the various German lands were never heard more clearly; the voices of Austria and Switzerland were so strong that they dominated this decentralized period.

There are names dear to the literary historian which threaten insistently to intervene; but wilful exclusion seems a lesser sin than a luxuriance of names and titles. Instead of the concert of a huge national literature we hear a chamber music of the most distinguished voices. But these voices must answer and deny, rival and support each other. Distance lets us hear a conversation even where at the time there seemed to be a mutual ignoring. One has only to select the unique voices, and they weave themselves into a loose counterpoint. From beginning to end, in structure and in texture, selection remains the main problem. For the sake of unity of tone, the Victorian (international) voices of criticism have been favored over twentieth century judgments.

The essays are meant for the average student of letters, with no special knowledge of nineteenth century German literature. Therefore the scholarly sources are indicated only where they need to be emphasized. But the links to general literature are emphasized wherever they can be found. German prose appears in translation, whereas German poetry is transposed in a line-for-line interpretation.

830.9
Fuerst, Norbert
c. 1
6.00
The Victorian age of German literature
3 1405 00773 0918
JAN 18 1988
DISCARD
The Emmet O'Neal Library
Mountain Brook, Alabama